Tennis
Confidential

Other Sports Titles from Brassey's

Tennis
Confidential

Today's Greatest Players,
Matches, and Controversies

Paul   Fein

Foreword by Bud Collins

BRASSEY'S, INC.
WASHINGTON, D.C.

Cataloging-in-Publication Data on File with the Library of Congress

ISBN 1-57488-427-1 (alk. paper)   *2878   7355   8/02*

Printed in the United States of America on acid-free paper that meets the American National Standards Institute Z39-48 Standard.

Brassey's, Inc.
22841 Quicksilver Drive
Dulles, Virginia 20166

First Edition

10 9 8 7 6 5 4 3 2 1

To my parents, whose love and devotion have meant everything to me.

Contents

List of Illustrations

Acknowledgments

I am very grateful for the generous help I have received towards producing this book.

This book is primarily about pro tennis players, and their kind cooperation made it possible for me to tell their compelling stories. I found them to be smart, fair-minded, funny, opinionated, and, most of all, earnest. Overall, they are a pleasure to work with.

I would like to thank all those hardworking members of the ATP, WTA, ITF, USTA, other national tennis federations, and client managers from management companies, who provided me with valuable information and expertise and arranged interviews with players, coaches, officials, and authorities for me.

Suzi Petkovski, my longtime colleague and friend, spent many hours critiquing the content and style of this book with the same rigorous analysis and broad knowledge that made her an excellent editor at *Australian Tennis Magazine*.

Donna Doherty, formerly the top-notch editor at *Tennis* magazine, also shared her expertise and made constructive suggestions.

Before her untimely passing in July 2000, Marcia Bauer, a wonderful Internet friend and grammarian from Palatine, Illinois, expertly edited many of the pieces in this book.

Matt Suher, of Stanmore, England, helped my cause considerably by providing me with valuable tennis information that I used, as did Bernie Bloome, another old and loyal friend from Springfield, Massachusetts.

Hans-Jürgen Dittmann and the International Tennis Hall of Fame provided beautiful and dramatic photos that nicely complement the written text.

Eddie Moylan, my cerebral and genial tennis coach at Cornell University (and before that a former world top-five amateur player and U.S. Davis Cup coach in the 1950s), deserves credit for igniting my passion for tennis and teaching me so much about it.

I also wish to thank all those friends of tennis, especially Bob Chandler, Bucky Adams, and Susie Altman, who discussed tennis issues with me over the years. Their points and counterpoints corrected my errors and helped crystalize my thinking.

I am much indebted to my mother, Lillian Stockser Fein, and my twin sisters, Elizabeth Amy Fein and Jane Cynthia Nielsen, for their unflagging encouragement to write this book.

Finally, the guidance of Brassey's editors Chris Kahrl and Don Jacobs brought the entire project to fruition.

Foreword

C*overing the Court* might be a good subtitle for *Tennis Confidential*—except that it's been taken. Al Laney, once a luminary of the since-vanished *New York Herald Tribune,* perhaps the best of us all who've tried to put the game into words, used it for his tennis memoir years ago. But just as readers were fortunate that Laney manned a typewriter in his day, so they are in this day that Paul Fein is on the job at his computer.

Covering the court completely is what Paul is about. Digging into every aspect—the personalities, the politics, the finances, the how-it's-done, and the times-it's-been-done-superlatively—he has assembled a compelling mosaic of the sport.

From Agassi to Zina, Australia to Zimbabwe, he chronicles the goings-on that set professional tennis apart from other games, its international and universal character. And its flavor, which he conveys with insight, as well as with a quality too rare: good humor. Also his opinions, never half-hearted, as displayed in "Overkill," where he's justifiably concerned about the power crisis.

In the United States, I'm sorry to say, tennis is the most undercovered of the leading pro sports. There aren't enough writers who follow it regularly and constantly—and with Paul's obvious love of the game, even as he detects its flaws. I'm pleased that Paul has succeeded in filling a portion of a huge gap. His attachment goes back quite a while.

Not that he was sitting next to Laney at Cannes in 1926 when Suzanne Lenglen turned back Helen Wills in a clash of goddesses that some still consider the "match of the century." (Certainly it was front-page stuff then across the planet.) But he writes about Suzanne and Helen's lone meeting (also Cochet's inexplicable comeback over Tilden at Wimbledon the following year) with authority and respect. Paul's a today guy, all right, yet one with knowledge of and regard for the game's entire panorama.

He is more than an aficionado. Paul's understanding of the game is that of someone who has been embroiled in it at a high level: as a player (Cornell varsity and top-class New England tournament competitor among his credits); professional coach; umpire and line judge; tournament organizer; and broadcaster. Like so many enamoured of the game, he had an early up-close relationship as a tournament ball boy.

He retains a boy's excitement at discovering the fascination of tennis, even as he looks at it now as a connoisseur and critic. Although Paul didn't attain the eminence on court of two of his Springfield, Massachusetts, townsmen, Alfred Chapin and Tim Mayotte (top-ten Americans of the 1920s and 1980s, respectively), he's well aware of the difficulties and means of such exceptional achievement.

Paul Fein lets you in on the whole tennis picture, and you see it better through his eyes and words. I'm sure you'll enjoy it as I have, and as I suspect Al Laney would have, too.

Bud Collins, *Boston Globe*/NBC
April 26, 2001

Introduction

What are Venus and Serena Williams, Pete Sampras, Anna Kournikova, and Andre Agassi *really* like? And what is it like to be up close to John McEnroe, Martina Navratilova, and Jimmy Connors?

Tennis fans often ask me about these legends when they aren't bending my ear with their unminced opinions about the latest burning issue.

Aficionados follow tennis so fervently because it's an individual sport—doubles notwithstanding—and its top players are supreme individualists who command our attention. Besides performing spectacularly, they express themselves through compelling, not-so-private lives. Anna's latest beau, Andre's new $23-million mansion where he and Steffi will live, the Williamses' many business, entertainment, and educational pursuits, and all their verbal volleys matter as much as their on-court volleys.

Tennis followers, in contrast to those in some other sports, nearly always play or have played the game themselves, and that makes them quite knowledgeable. They also care deeply about a sport they feel doesn't get a fair shake from the mainstream media.

This book is a collection of my best articles, which have appeared in magazines and newspapers around the world. It culminates my longtime effort to give tennis lovers what they relish: insights into the top players, a chance to relive the greatest matches in history, in-depth analyses of momentous controversies and fascinating trends, and juicy quotes and amusing factoids that add yet more flavor to our riveting sport.

I decided to include Q & A interviews, which almost never appear in sports books, because they best allow athletes to show their minds and speak from their hearts. I hope the interviews I've chosen will enlighten and entertain you. Some may enrage you. But tennis players, thank heaven, don't let their rackets do all the talking.

Before I share my twenty-five-year adventure as a freelance tennis writer with you, I would like to assure you that I have never been beholden to a magazine publisher nor to any of the professional and amateur organizations that administer tennis. I strived to write with neither fear nor favor both to inform my readers and to improve the sport that has given me and millions of others such great pleasure.

I hope you enjoy reading *Tennis Confidential* as thoroughly as I've enjoyed writing it. Feel free to e-mail me at lincjeff1@cs.com with your comments.

PART 1

Portraits of the Stars

Venus Williams:
The Ghetto Cinderella
1998

A girl's got to keep herself busy," Venus Williams was saying midway through her Australian Open debut. Especially if she's having an excellent adventure in a faraway land.

So Venus and younger sister Serena, the hottest sister act in sports, started trash talking, claiming they could beat any of the guys ranked two hundred or lower. A bespectacled, smoking German, number 203 Karsten Braasch, took up the challenge as the gender defender against the whiz kids from the States. "I just decided I wanted to join the ATP tour," quipped Serena. "This week, I can be on two tours."

The strange and startling saga of Venus, the "Party Crasher"—as *Sports Illustrated* provocatively headlined her smashing 1997 U.S. Open debut as an unseeded finalist—and Serena has already confirmed much of what the late Arthur Ashe predicted in 1988. "Given the same chance as others have had, blacks could dominate tennis in as little as ten to fifteen years just as they have dominated in other sports," he said.

Even more controversially, Ashe also forewarned that if blacks did take over, "it will create problems because their behavior, speech, and dress is just a completely different culture. Tennis is a very conservative game with deep roots grounded in Victorian English moral codes and traditions. Minorities—in particular, inner-city minorities—have cultural norms that are diametrically opposite those of upper-middle- and upper-class white American standards."

Larger-than-life black athletes have long roiled powerful emotions in race-sensitive America. When flamboyant Jack Johnson, who romanced white women, became the first black heavyweight boxing champion, whites rioted in several major cities. Muhammad Ali was vilified for opposing the Vietnam War and

Venus Williams. Hans-Jürgen Dittmann

refusing to be inducted into the U.S. Army, but "The Greatest," as he bombastically promoted himself, emerged as an irreverent hero to both blacks and whites and as the most famous sports figure of the century.

Courageous Althea Gibson confided that she made it as the first black champion in tennis partly "because I was game to take a wicked amount of punishment along the way." The American tennis establishment finally, and grudgingly, allowed the twenty-three-year-old from Harlem to break the "color barrier" and enter the 1950 U.S. Championships at Forest Hills, but only after they required her to be tested to confirm she was a woman. When Gibson played the then-amateur tour, nearly all the white girls shunned her; to make matters worse, the Negro press relentlessly criticized her because she was "not militant enough" as a civil rights crusader.

The legend of how young Venus escaped from the concrete jungle of crime-ridden Compton, California, to grace the stately lawns of staid Wimbledon has been cleverly orchestrated by her idiosyncratic father, Richard. With an Ali-like flair for sucking the media into his Venus flytrap, Williams engagingly relates how Venus and Serena ducked bullets during their practice sessions by hitting the ground and rolling toward the gate. "There were more AK-47s than school-books," says Williams, who claims in his newsletter that he was beaten up several times by gang members before gaining their respect. Fortunately, the local hood-lums in their notorious South Central Los Angeles neighborhood generally took pride in the tennis prodigies and protected them.

Born fatherless and poor in Shreveport, Louisiana, Richard Williams picked cotton as a teenager before moving to Chicago and then Los Angeles, where he set up a small security firm. (In the 2001 book *Venus Envy,* author L. Jon Wertheim investigated Williams's claim and wrote: "Those who knew Richard as a child say the story [of his being the son of a sharecropper and his picking cot-ton] is absurd.") He first took notice of tennis in 1978, two years before Venus was born, when he saw Virginia Ruzici receive thirty-five thousand dollars in prize money for winning a tournament, more than he earned in a year. So he said to his wife, Oracene, "Let's make two kids, put them in tennis, and they'll be superstars." They already had three girls, and Oracene thought he was crazy.

As the legend goes, when four-and-a-half-year-old Venus played for the first time, she hit 550 balls without missing in about forty-five minutes. By age six, she lived and breathed tennis so obsessively that Williams "took every one of them tennis rackets and broke 'em up" and wouldn't let her play for the next year and a half.

From age nine to eleven, Venus terrorized the southern California junior cir-cuit, racking up a perfect 63-0 record, while Serena, fifteen months younger, was almost as devastating. Williams dubbed Venus the "Ghetto Cinderella" and was convinced that she'd be his ticket to a better life.

"I really got into tennis so I could get a million dollars," candidly admits Mr. Williams. "I didn't have the right motives in the beginning at all. I was just like any other [tennis] parent then."

The junior circuit, according to Williams, showed him how parents, intoxi-cated by the lure of potential fortune and fame, damaged their children. "You see all the white doctors and the way they beat their kids," recalls Williams. "I've seen girls that were afraid to walk on the court with Venus and ten times as afraid to walk off the court afterwards. I've seen parents say, 'You let that little nigger kill you like that.' " Disenchanted, Williams pulled his talented daughters out of junior competition forever.

Since no tennis champion had ever bypassed the valuable experience of jun-ior tournaments, the move defied conventional wisdom and proved extremely controversial. It also heightened the legend or, as some cynics charged, the myth. The press, players, coaches, parents, and the tennis establishment couldn't figure out the Williamses. Was the father, who called all the shots, crazy, or was he crazy like a fox? And how good *were* his much-heralded daughters?

The mystery fascinated the tennis world for three and a half years after the family moved to Florida, where highly regarded Rick Macci coached them at his international academy. Macci described Venus, then a 6'1 1/2" woman-child, as "a unique combination of Monica Seles and Martina Navratilova," and Serena as "the best athlete I've ever coached, boy or girl."

Talk may be cheap, but it was always colorful and usually fun with the Williamses. And since both girls were told by their father for years that they were destined for greatness, they genuinely believed it, too. At fourteen, supremely confident Venus, sounding like the early Ali, crowed: "I could go *beyond* number one. With the way I play and my height and aggressiveness and courage and no fear, I could change the game. It's like Michael Jordan and the rest of the players in the NBA. He was a step ahead of everyone else."

FASCINATING FACTS:

- Venus Williams started receiving free tennis equipment from manufacturers at age six.
- Oracene Williams created a project called Education Reevaluation Diagnostics because "our country is turning out uneducated children." It aims "to re-evaluate students and help them fill in what they have missed."
- Oracene Williams notched a 4-0 record in fistfights against childhood bullies in her tough Saginaw, Michigan, neighborhood.

Richard Williams kept everyone off balance with his exaggerations, confusing comments, and contradictions. He often asserted that "any parent who allows his child to play pro tennis before she's sixteen is crazy and should be shot," but he did exactly that with fourteen-year-old Venus. He decried the pressure and great expectations heaped on tennis whiz kids even as he hyped his prodigy zealously and bragged, "Venus Williams gets more media attention than anyone in sports except Michael Jordan."

Cynics sneered that Williams was only trying to inflate potential endorsement contracts by refusing all bidders for several years. He also gave the tennis establishment fits by snubbing the many management companies that courted his family. Finally, in 1995, Williams had Venus sign a five-year endorsement contract with Reebok for a reported $12 million—more than world number one Martina Hingis's $10-million deal with Tacchini—after Venus had played only one pro tournament.

Venus's pro debut turned out to be as compelling and sensational as it was ballyhooed. After winning her first-round match at an Oakland tournament in November 1994, Venus proved she was for real when she exploded to a 6-3, 3-1 lead against world number two Arantxa Sanchez Vicario before bowing.

Not only hadn't fourteen-year-old Venus played a tournament in three and a half years, but she hadn't even practiced the week before her remarkable performance. A cunning iconoclast, Williams had instead taken his daughters that week to a Jehovah's Witnesses assembly, Busch Gardens, and Six Flags, an amusement park in Atlanta. He sensibly explained: "If you're happy and well-balanced and no one is pushing you to do something, then you can do your very best because you feel like you're doing it for yourself."

Venus and Serena would not burn out from "too much, too soon" as Jennifer Capriati sadly did. Venus played only three pro events in 1995, five in 1996, and ten in 1997. Ironically, she was faulted for playing *too few* tournaments and thus stifling her development. But Williams, now Venus's coach and manager, didn't at all care what the so-called experts thought. The fifty-five-year-old maverick told the TV program *60 Minutes*: "Anyone who is a professional tennis player, or anyone who has anything to do with professional tennis, I don't think very much of them, no way."

For years Williams had preached passionately about the importance of higher education, and his three oldest daughters were in college or graduates. "Ninety-nine percent of the junior stars are not educated, they don't speak well, they don't represent themselves well," he charged. "I doubt if any junior stars have ever come close to Venus and Serena when it comes to education and speaking. My girls today can match the Japanese and the Germans in their high levels of educational attainment."

The hyperbole notwithstanding, on today's pro tour—where college graduates are rare birds and a mere high school diploma is almost a badge of academic achievement—the Williams girls stand out. Venus takes courses at Palm Beach Community College, while Serena attends a private school and is also college-bound. Consistent honor students, they show their intellectual enthusiasm by taking textbooks with them to tournaments and reciting Shakespeare to each other during plane and car trips.

"I like *Macbeth* most of all because it's a really good play, and I've always wanted to see it live," says Serena. "The 'Tomorrow, and tomorrow and tomorrow, / Creeps in this petty pace from day to day' speech is wonderful. I never thought I'd be the one to say this, but it's just deep."

Venus showed her flair for the theatrical with an unforgettable debut at the 1997 U.S. Open. It coincided—or rather collided—with the debut of Arthur Ashe Stadium, the centerpiece of the National Tennis Center's $254-million renovation, and it eerily confirmed Ashe's prediction of racial-cultural clash.

The statuesque "Ghetto Cinderella," wearing eighteen hundred clanging red, white, and blue beads in her braided hair, was, as she noted, "different in every way from the mainstream player" as she overpowered smaller and less athletic white opponents with punishing ground strokes and explosive serves up to 119 miles an hour. Venus's take-no-prisoners attack was reminiscent of Gibson, who described herself as "aggressive, dynamic, and mean" when she won the U.S., Wimbledon, and French titles forty years ago.

The similarities extended to their off-court personas, too. Venus's penchant for boasting—such as defeating top-tenner Iva Majoli last March and afterwards claiming, "I could have beaten her three years ago"—turned off other players. Top-fivers Monica Seles and Lindsay Davenport, among others, were miffed when prima donna Venus dissed them by haughtily walking by and not even responding to a friendly "Hi." And several players complained that she hung out exclusively with her mother, Oracene, and Serena and snubbed the tour's social events.

Venus has said she would like to be the Tiger Woods of tennis. But, so far anyway, she lacks his gregarious, upbeat personality and admits, "I don't come to tournaments to make friends, to go to parties, to hold conversations. I come to be the best, and I'm not mean and cruel and dirty."

"They both obviously have a chip on their shoulders to a certain extent," says Angela Buxton, Gibson's longtime friend, confidante, and former doubles partner. "That causes them to speak out in a very confident, superior manner. They say: 'I will beat so-and-so' and 'I'm going to be the best' and 'You haven't got a chance.' Althea did exactly the same thing in the fifties. It doesn't lead to popularity. But this game isn't for popularity stakes. The other side of the coin is they both intimidate or at least get into the heads of the other players."

In the U.S. Open semifinals, Venus's past indiscretions and her father's seething racial hostility caught up with them and nearly overshadowed her heroic victory. A confrontation was inevitable. Irina Spirlea resented the tremendous media attention Venus, sexy Anna Kournikova, fifteen-year-old rookie sensation Mirjana Lucic, and teen queen Hingis received at the expense of tour veterans like herself.

Hot-tempered Spirlea, who was thrown out of an Italian tournament for cursing and giving the finger to an umpire, had ousted Kournikova, Amanda Coetzer, and number two Seles at Flushing Meadows before slugging it out with Venus in the most riveting match of 1997. Venus escaped the first of two match points with a brilliant running backhand passing shot and pulled out a 7-6, 4-6, 7-6 cliffhanger. After winning, Venus jumped up and down in jubilation and cried out, "Oh man, this is just like a dream. I'm gonna have to calm down. I'm *so* happy."

Venus would soon have to temper that happiness, though. Spirlea and Venus had collided during a second-set changeover, and it appeared that Spirlea also "intentionally" kneed her when they collided. While Venus downplayed the incident, Spirlea angrily blamed it on Venus's imperious attitude, telling the media: "She thinks she's the fucking Venus Williams, and she's not going to turn. That's it. I'm sorry she feels that way."

Williams joined the Bad Dads Club of tennis by pouring gasoline on the fire. The roguish coach, who infrequently attends his daughters' matches, phoned the Associated Press from Florida and termed the bumping episode "a racial thing" and called Spirlea "a big, ugly, tall, white turkey." Without citing evidence or naming anyone, Williams also charged that several women on the circuit had made racist remarks about Venus. The unproved accusations outraged many in the sporting public and the media and prompted flat denials from several tour players.

Venus was eventually forced to respond to reporters' persistent questions about her father's allegations. With a wisdom her father lacks, seventeen-year-old Venus said: "I think with this moment in the first year in Arthur Ashe Stadium, it all represents everyone being together, everyone having a chance to play. So I think this is definitely ruining the mood, these questions about racism."

Williams had played "the race card" and lost. His tawdry sideshow poisoned the atmosphere, but Venus still stole the show with her spectacular tennis, courage, and electric smile. Racism? Not at Flushing Meadows during that tumultuous fortnight when the overwhelming majority of spectators rooted for the black phenom. Racism? Venus played six of her seven matches on the Arthur Ashe Stadium court, and only beloved teen queen Chrissie Evert had ever before received such royal treatment. Racism? United States Tennis Association president Harry Marmion proclaimed, "Venus Williams is the best thing that has happened to American tennis for the last twenty years."

Bringing up Daddy isn't easy for the Williams girls. Venus may have been the goddess of love, but this Venus must summon the patience of Job to defend her way-ward father against the barrage of media criticism. Annoyed by a question she refused to answer, Venus glared suspiciously at a veteran American sportswriter last year and engaged in this testy exchange before terminating the *TennisMatch* interview.

"Aren't you going to ask me the hated question?"

"What's that?"

"Why do I get along so well with my dad?"

"Actually, I wasn't."

"Well, I don't answer that anymore!"

While Venus has pulled no punches and taken some heavy hits, sixteen-year-old Serena, a blithe spirit, has stayed serenely above the fray. "Venus isn't very friendly or outgoing with the other players," says Davenport. "But I think Serena's hysterical—a really funny girl and very outgoing."

Serena has plenty to smile and laugh about. With the best athletic talent and physique since Martina Navratilova, muscular 5'10", 155-pound Serena started tearing up the circuit last November when she knocked off number four Monica Seles and number seven Mary Pierce in Chicago. "I've always believed Serena would ultimately be better," predicts Williams.

The "Ghetto Girls," as Williams calls them, thrived—sans Daddy—in the sunny, relaxed Down Under atmosphere, which they likened to southern California. At the Sydney International in January, Serena took out Lucic 7-5, 6-3, and despite visibly limping, bravely overcame a 6-1, 5-2 deficit to upset Davenport 1-6, 7-5, 7-5 in torrid thirty-three-degree (Celsius) heat. Meanwhile, Venus, cramping but never quitting, beat top-ranked Hingis 3-6, 6-4, 7-5 for the first time.

Davenport said Serena was better than Venus already, and an unlucky draw at the Oz Open gave Serena the chance to prove it. Serena whacked another seed, number six Spirlea, 6-7, 6-3, 6-1 to set up a second-round duel on Center Court against her best friend—Venus. "What's love got to do with it?" joked Serena. "I don't have time to come along slowly; we both want to be number one."

Serena read some *Hamlet* to prepare for the intrafamily intrigue. But Venus handled the pressure of the sibling rivalry better and won 7-6, 6-1 in a match about which Oracene rightly said, "We couldn't lose. The family wins." Afterwards Venus gave Serena a sisterly hug, and they reinforced the "We Are Family" theme by locking hands and bowing in unison. If the "Ghetto Girls" keep improving at this meteoric pace—Serena, amazingly, has knocked off five top-tenners in only a tour-record sixteen matches—expect to see that trademark bow after plenty of Grand Slam finals.

The Lipton Championships nearly showcased the first all-Williams semifinal. Top-ranked Hingis escaped two match points against equally clever Serena in the quarters before Venus pulverized the no-longer-smirking Swiss Miss 6-2, 5-7, 6-2 in the semis and then stopped Kournikova for her biggest title. In the understatement of the year, Hingis afterwards conceded: "It's difficult to play the Williams family two matches in a row."

In Australia, both sisters smarted from losing "Battle of the Sexes" sets to Braasch. Serena, a 6-1 victim, vowed revenge: "This time next year I'll beat him. I have to pump some weights.... I have to work hard to be on the men's tour." Although Venus fell 6-2 to Braasch and lost to Davenport in the singles quarters, she captured the mixed doubles title with Justin Gimelstob for her first Slam trophy.

If all the world's a stage, Venus is plotting many more brilliant performances. "I've learned a lot in Australia," she said. "No matter how badly I am playing, I can still win. I'm winning and everything is wonderful. Serena and I are dominating the game, and we're not leaving."

FASCINATING FACTS:

- Reebok's $40-million agreement with Venus Williams is the most lucrative deal for a female athlete in history.
- An 8"x11", autographed photo of Venus Williams sold for eighty dollars at the Sydney Olympics and outranked all other Olympics athletes' photos in value, according to a chart published in *USA Today*.
- When President Bill Clinton phoned Venus Williams to congratulate her for winning the 2000 U.S. Open, she dictated the direction of the conversation and requested, "Can you lower my taxes, please?" When President Clinton suggested he'd like to have a special exemption for athletes, Venus wisecracked, "Should I read your lips?"
- When Venus and Serena Williams played in the 2001 U.S. Open final on Saturday evening, September 8, it marked the first prime-time Grand Slam final, the first meeting between African-Americans in a Grand Slam final, and the first final between sisters at a major tournament in 117 years.

The Wild and Wacky World of the Williamses

Richard:

"We will not step back and be the nice people they think we are. They have to realize we're from Compton, California. In Compton, you don't take no bull."

Venus:

"I've actually never played in an audience that wasn't for me. The day will come when they are going to be for the other player. I'll be prepared for that."

Richard:

"Venus is not really interested in socializing. I have never seen a boxer say, 'Let's have a doughnut and coffee [before a fight].... The Lakers never did it in basketball. Football players don't do it."

Richard, on why he doesn't attend his daughters' tournaments:

"You sit there, with your head going this way, and this way, clappin' like a seal at the zoo, and I'm tired of that."

Serena, on her father's forbidding his daughters from dating until they are eighteen:

"I'm not really thinking about that right now. There are things far more important now, like my tennis career, like my education, like Jehovah. And all that could explode if I got too involved with boys."

Richard, on his daughters' doubles prowess:

"It'll be very difficult for anyone to beat 'Double Trouble.' They move too fast, they volley too well, they serve too hard for players to return consistently. They'll become number one in doubles before they become number one in singles."

Venus, just before losing to the number two seed, American Lindsay Davenport, at the 1998 Australian Open:

"I am the best player in the U.S. Actually, I'm the best player in general."

Richard, on his calling Irina Spirlea "a big, ugly, tall, white turkey":

"I love Irina Spirlea. I don't see any prejudice at all. I met with her and apologized for making a stupid statement. She's a professional, and I shouldn't have talked about her that way."

Venus, on becoming number one:

"There has never been [any doubt in my mind] because I was always told I'd be number one in the world, and I always believed it. And that's what I've worked toward."

Richard:

"Tennis kids are the worst socially developed people you'll ever see. No school. Can't spell well, can't think well, their lives are all screwed up."

Serena, on being a Jehovah's Witness:

"It's number one in my life. If it weren't for God, I wouldn't have anything. Religion has helped me realize who I am. It's helped me not to get ahead of myself and not to get bombastic. It keeps me humble."

Richard:

"If I had to do it over, I wouldn't put them into tennis."

Zina Garrison-Jackson, the black 1990 Wimbledon finalist:

"People don't understand what it's like for Venus because she has a whole race pulling for her. She's carrying a lot of weight."

Richard:

"The only thing that can keep Venus from becoming number one by the age of eighteen would be an accident."

Oracene:

"Nobody has ever walked up to my daughters and said hello. They look the other way. They want them to be their Stepin Fetchit."

Katrina Adams, a veteran black tour player:

"Everything said about Tiger [Woods] has been positive. And everything said about Venus has been negative."

Richard:

"There's so much racism in America that Americans don't care about black people."

Richard, on making people angry with his inflammatory remarks:

"I'm not trying to please people who want to be angry. Let them be angry. If anyone should be angry, it should be me." *

Billie Jean King:

"Venus is awesome, that's all. Awesome. She reminds me of Althea Gibson—tall, black, fast, powerful, ambitious, confident. Venus will be the Althea Gibson of the twenty-first century."

Richard:

"Venus should go straight to the Hall of Fame. She's going to be there anyway, so why waste time?"

Serena, after being asked about how she rallied so successfully from the baseline against Hingis in the Lipton quarterfinals:

"A lot of people think that black people can't rally and just think they're athletes and can't think. As you can see, that's not true. I can rally. Venus can rally."

Venus:

"People talk about all this pressure on young tennis players, but the only thing stressing me out right now is all these chemistry formulas I've got to learn. I would say that, basically, I'm a laugher. I like to have fun. Sometimes, when I think about this whole thing, it just makes me burst out laughing."

This story received a 1st Honorable Mention award in the Nonfiction Division of the 1999 CNW/FFWA Florida State Writing Competition.

2

That's Life—on the Agassi Roller Coaster
1999

That's life, that's what people say.
You're riding high in April,
Shot down in May.
But I know I'm gonna change that tune,
When I'm back on top in June.

From the *enfant terrible* of tennis to the charismatic heartthrob to the aging star, Andre Agassi has lived the poignant lyrics Frank Sinatra sang in "That's Life." And what an unpredictable roller-coaster ride the Las Vegas showman has taken for thirteen years!

Just when Agassi was written off as an underachieving has-been at twenty-nine, he stunningly won the French Open for a career Grand Slam and a slice of tennis immortality. Only Rod Laver, Don Budge, Fred Perry, and Roy Emerson had previously captured all four major men's singles titles, and versatile Agassi became the first to do it on three surfaces, grass, clay, and hardcourts. And then, after gaining the Wimbledon final, he climaxed his summer-to-remember by dramatically winning his second U.S. Open title and ascending to number one in the world.

Agassi attributed his *tour de force* in Paris to "sheer destiny," but in May he seemed more down and out than destiny's darling. Back then he and actress Brooke Shields announced their highly publicized divorce after a two-year marriage.

On the court, Agassi floundered, too. After crashing out in the Australian Open fourth round and Lipton first round, he stumbled in his European clay opener. An error-filled 6-1, 7-6 Italian Open loss to Pat Rafter so deflated him that ever-colorful Agassi confided, "If I play like a schmuck, then I am a schmuck." Even more ominous, a lingering shoulder injury caused him such pain that he was on the verge of withdrawing from Roland Garros until the day before it started.

Andre Agassi. Hans-Jürgen Dittmann

Agassi found himself flat on his face in 1997, his worst time since critics labeled him a loser and the "Great White Hype" before he belatedly won his first Grand Slam crown, the 1992 Wimbledon.

So when Agassi said, "My only good result in 1997 was marrying Brooke Shields," he wasn't just joking. Agassi got fat, injured, and lazy, and was beaten so regularly that he nosedived to number 141. For the first time since Boy Andre turned pro in 1986 (remember the bleached-blond heartthrob/rebel wearing pink thigh-hugging cycle shorts, earrings, and painted fingernails?) he finished out of the top 100 in the rankings and failed to reach a tournament final.

Agassi fell so low that he took a wild card to play a fifty-thousand-dollar challenger event in his hometown of Las Vegas in November 1997. And he couldn't even win that! The local paper described the disappointed capacity crowd for the final as "a community that worships him." They, like Andre's Army of loyal admirers worldwide, had to wonder: Had they just witnessed the beginning of the end of their hero's starry but roller-coaster career?

Agassi downplayed the humbling if not humiliating Las Vegas experience that a USTA official said was "like Springsteen playing the corner bar." The low-light came when the former king of tennis flipped the manual scorecard during changeovers like a commoner.

Shields knew best how badly her man's fragile self-esteem had to be suffering. "The times [Agassi] doesn't feel good about himself outweigh the times he does," Shields had revealed in a 1995 TV interview on *60 Minutes*. Not even having a gorgeous, celebrity girlfriend, the number one ranking, his own private jet, and a reported $100-million Nike contract then was enough to make the complicated Agassi feel consistently good about himself. But why not?

Theories abounded. Shields explained, "Unless you have a real sense of belief in yourself deserving those things, then they become very relative." Agassi reinforced that theory when he confessed that his famous "Image Is Everything" Canon camera commercial "brought [him] a lot more grief than anything else."

Other theories about Agassi's lingering angst blamed his obsessed father, Mike, for relentlessly pressuring him to become a champion since he was a toddler, his teenage years at the Nick Bollettieri Tennis Academy that "took away my love for the game," and his fears that he had tragically wasted much of his prodigious talent. Agassi tellingly confided to the *New York Times:* "I've played this game for a lot of reasons, and none of them have ever quite been mine."

FASCINATING FACTS:

- Andre Agassi signed his first autograph at age six.
- Mike Agassi estimates his son Andre hit a million tennis balls a year between the ages of five and thirteen.
- When teenaged Andre Agassi was once asked where his father came from, he answered, "From hell."

To make matters worse, newlyweds Agassi and Shields were having "teething problems"—which would eventually prove fatal—because he wanted to live in Las Vegas, while she preferred Hollywood, reported the *Evening Standard* (UK). "She has stopped enjoying coming to Las Vegas and living in my bachelor pad. She smiles and has no idea what she is requesting me to do," said Agassi. "I just look at her and think I would rather live with that smile than my bachelor pad."

While Shields smoothly adjusted to married life without compromising her high-profile career—she starred in the successful sitcom *Suddenly Susan*—Agassi didn't. He started living the good life at their $6-million estate in the Pacific Palisades area of Los Angeles with his alluring wife, often attended Hollywood gatherings, played few tournaments (twelve and only one Slam in 1997), trained little, ate a lot, and put on twenty-two pounds. As Agassi simply put it, "I enjoy tennis when I'm intense about it. I enjoy my life when it's intense. And you can't have both."

At least not Agassi. And at least not in many odd-numbered years of his up-and-down career. He even considered retiring from competitive tennis.

Not everyone criticized Agassi, though. All-time great Chris Evert recalled that she took three months off from the tour when she got married because she didn't know where to put her emotions. "For the first time in his life, he has to give, and he does that," pointed out Evert admiringly last year. "He's supported her, helped her, and took a step back and let her shine. That tells me something about the man. That tells me something about Andre."

By the late fall of 1997, unpredictable Agassi had regained his zest for playing tennis, and, equally importantly, had learned to balance the two passions in his life. Shields, who ironically had been blamed by some observers for his career collapse—which Agassi confided was "as tough a place as I have ever been in with my tennis"—enthusiastically supported his decision to redirect his priorities.

The rest of Agassi's inspiration came from near and far and even above. The indomitable spirit that Kacey Reyes, his trainer's teenaged daughter, showed after undergoing two operations for a broken neck touched him deeply. Agassi also drew strength from visiting then-President Nelson Mandela and the children of South Africa in December. And from reading the works of Pope John Paul II. The last source should not be underestimated, because Agassi has said that "my relationship with God is number one in my life."

Brad Gilbert, Agassi's coach since 1994, fearlessly predicted, "He should be able to win another three to five Slams." Rededicated, Agassi trained as if he believed it. Last year he recalled the months of daily sprints up sharp inclines and other grueling conditioning drills "that had me going so hard, I thought I was going to throw up."

Winning more major titles—he had captured them all except the French Open—was clearly on Agassi's mind, too. "When I play my level of tennis, nobody can beat me," he crowed in 1998. "If I can establish that before the Grand Slams, then I'm in a position to win a Grand Slam. That's ultimately what I want to do this year."

Agassi never came close, though, reaching only the 1998 Australian and U.S. Open fourth rounds in his best efforts. Still, he skyrocketed to number four in the rankings, led the tour with ten finals (5-5), including the Lipton, and tied Bill Tilden's seventy-two-year-old record of sixteen straight Davis Cup victories.

The Comeback Kid was on his way. Even so, 1999 French Open predictors doubted he could overcome hot, much-younger favorites such as defending

FASCINATING FACTS:

- Early in his pro career, Andre Agassi sometimes received in the mail photos of naked women with their telephone numbers written on the back.
- Andre Agassi underwent eight months of psychotherapy in 1994.
- Andre Agassi, who weighs 172 pounds, can bench press three hundred pounds, according to his physical trainer, Gil Reyes.

champ Carlos Moya, 1997 surprise titlist Gustavo Kuerten, and ultra-talented Marcelo Rios; the ghosts of traumatic upset defeats in the 1990 and 1991 finals; and his miserable five-set record—14-16 in his career and 0-5 at Roland Garros.

Agassi's oft-questioned physical and mental toughness passed its first test when, trailing two sets to one and being just two points from defeat in the second round, he dug deep to outlast France's Arnaud Clement 6-2, 4-6, 2-6, 7-5, 6-0. Two rounds later, Agassi, now suffering from a pulled muscle in his right thigh, fell behind Moya 6-4, 4-1 and rallied with his trademark devastating ground strokes to prevail 4-6, 7-5, 7-5, 6-1 for his first win this year over a top-ten player.

In what would be the most riveting French men's final since the 1984 Ivan Lendl–John McEnroe duel, thirteenth-seeded Agassi faced once number four but now number 100 Andrei Medvedev. The strapping Ukrainian came out inspired, whacking aces and big groundies, while Agassi appeared tight and as flat as a Las Vegas blackjack table. The A Train was getting derailed and quickly trailed 6-1, 6-2. "I was embarrassed, in shock," Agassi revealed afterwards. "It was gonna be a blowout, and Andrei was playing very well. I had flashbacks of losing the finals in 1990 and 1991, and the feeling I've long held that I'd never get another chance." Did Agassi lack the right stuff—at this defining moment in his career—as his legion of critics always charged?

As fired-up Court Central fans chanted "Ag-as-si!" and exhorted him with the wave, he finally loosened up enough to surge ahead 4-2 in the pivotal third set with a beautiful forehand, only to give the service break right back at love in the next game. He then escaped a scary break-point crisis at 4-all. Maintaining his resolve and momentum even when Medvedev brilliantly fought off three championship points at 5-3 in the final set, Agassi finally closed out the two hour, fifty-five minute battle with an unreturnable serve.

Shocked, Agassi dropped his racket and covered his face with his hands and then started weeping in joy. "The king is back!" shouted a French fan amidst the frenzied cheers of the sellout crowd.

"I never dreamed I would see this day. This was the greatest thing I could ever do," said the ecstatic Agassi after his historic 1-6, 2-6, 6-4, 6-3, 6-4 triumph.

Back on top in June and energized as never before, Agassi thanked "the people who have never stopped believing in me" and talked about his new dreams. "I certainly have a lot more belief that if I can do it here, I can do it again in a few other places."

Just four weeks later, the streaking Agassi almost did it again at Wimbledon, the birthplace of lawn tennis that he had snubbed three straight years as a brash kid and then stunningly won in 1992. He took out clay-court star Gustavo Kuerten in the quarters and then served big and returned even bigger to shred Patrick Rafter's vaunted serve-and-volley game in the semis.

The Wimbledon final was fraught with significance. Agassi was hoping to become the first male player since Bjorn Borg in 1980 to sweep Roland Garros and Wimbledon in the same year. Pete Sampras was gunning for his sixth Big W crown and twelfth career Slam to tie Roy Emerson's record. And everyone eagerly anticipated this revival of the 1990s' long-dormant but most riveting rivalry.

Ruthlessly efficient Sampras was "on fire" and "playing in the zone," as he later characterized his 6-3, 6-4, 7-5 virtuoso performance. "He walked on water today," agreed Agassi, who nonetheless briefly took over the number-one ranking.

Sampras beat Agassi twice more in summer hardcourt events, but had to withdraw from the U.S. Open with a back injury. The field further weakened when defending champion Patrick Rafter dropped out with a rotator cuff tear in the first round, but neither misfortune affected Agassi's intensity and focus. "I'll be disappointed if I don't win here because I want it so bad," he revealed after an easy second round win.

Shedding his shirt to show off his sculpted physique and shaved chest in practice and blowing kisses to the crowd after victories, Agassi connected to Flushing Meadows fans more than any favorite since Jimmy Connors. "I feel my tennis reflects who it is I am," confided Agassi. "And that feels good because you don't have to know me to have a sense for me. And that's important to me."

After Agassi disposed of third-seeded Yevgeny Kafelnikov in a 1-6, 6-3, 6-3, 6-3 semifinal, he faced another comebacker in Todd Martin, who overcame career-threatening injuries to regain his erstwhile top-ten form. Martin had to overcome qualifier Stephane Huet in a fifth-set tiebreaker and 1997 finalist Greg Rusedski, after trailing by two sets and then 4-1 in the fifth set.

The aging twenty-nine-year-old warriors, one bald and the other graying, staged what spectator Steffi Graf called an "incredible" final. Agassi's underrated but powerful serve helped him stave off all eight break points, and the relentless pressure of his pounding ground strokes eventually wore down the gallant Martin 6-4, 6-7, 6-7, 6-3, 6-2 for his second U.S. Open and fifth career Slam title.

Afterwards the ever-smiling champion pronounced, "This is the greatest time of my life," and mused about his roller-coaster career, saying, "If it wasn't for the valleys, the peaks wouldn't be as high."

Agassi, finally the consummate pro after wasting some prime-time years, predicted his best is yet to come: "I definitely feel I have more titles in me."

As another old swinger would sing, "That's life, that's what people say."

FASCINATING FACTS:

- The largest single fund-raising event ever held in Las Vegas was Andre Agassi's Grand Slam for Children, which raised $3.9 million in 1999.
- In 2001, William Hills, a London bookmaker, set 500-1 odds that the unborn child of Andre Agassi and Steffi Graf will win the singles or doubles title at Wimbledon.

This story received a 1st Honorable Mention award in the Nonfiction Division of the 2000 CNW/FFWA Florida State Writing Competition.

3

Anna Kournikova:
The Ego Has Landed
1997

Thank heaven for little girls—as Maurice Chevalier sang in *Gigi*—especially those with an attitude. Tennis' new baby brigade is bold, brash, and beautiful. Sugar and spice and everything nice, they're not. Their credo: Why let your racket do all the talking when a tart tongue can deliver much more delicious devastation?

Cheeky Martina Hingis, the Can't-Miss Swiss, is number one in the rankings but not among some of her peers who resent her arrogance and narcissism. When asked what becoming the youngest winner of a Grand Slam tournament, the Australian Open, meant to her, sixteen-year-old Hingis replied, "It's just another record for me. I mean, I have so many records already." When Hingis was compared with golf's new superstar, she shot back, "I think I'm even better than Tiger Woods."

Cocksure black American Venus Ebone Starr Williams, the surprise U.S. Open finalist, insists she'll dethrone Hingis and then face her toughest competition from her super-athletic sister Serena. She even crows, "I could go beyond number one because there are times when an athlete is just ahead of the rest of the league. That could be me. It's like Michael Jordan and the rest of the players in the NBA. He was a step ahead of everyone else. With the way I play and my height and aggressiveness and courage and no fear, I could change the game."

But the undisputed queen of the brat pack is Anna Kournikova. After the older and more advanced Hingis embarrassed Kournikova 6-0, 6-0 at the 1994 Junior U.S. Open, the Russian reportedly told her: "You won, but I'm prettier and more marketable than you." Round one in post-match repartee to Special K!

Bad as she wants to be, "Anna is a goddamm Dennis Rodman all over again," says her noted coach, Nick Bollettieri. "She's a very individualistic girl who is accountable only to herself. Like Rodman, she isn't outwardly concerned

Anna Kournikova. Hans-Jürgen Dittmann

about the world and does whatever she wants to do." Not since teen rebel Andre Agassi has Bollettieri faced the challenge of molding such talent without stifling a headstrong spirit. The former tough-guy army paratrooper, who once ran his famous Florida tennis academy like a boot camp, has finally met his match in the sassy, blonde bombshell. "I've never been able to control her," he admits.

The odd couple hooked up six years ago when Bollettieri was floored by the rambunctious mighty mite from Moscow. "From the moment I met Anna, she was very bold, very aggressive," recalls Bollettieri. "She takes over everything. And she wants it *now*. She doesn't want to share with other people. She wants her time. She wants the feature court. It's got to be for Anna Kournikova. If it rains, she doesn't care about the whole academy. She wants her court inside. She's on a mission. And nothing is going to stop her."

The prima-donna-with-a-plan took on and nearly took over the 1990 Kremlin Cup as a pushy nine-year-old. As part of the preliminary event before the nightly men's matches, Anna was the most talented of a dozen Russian youngsters who were supposed to rotate so everyone would get a chance to strut their stuff before thousands of fans in the huge Olympic Stadium.

"I got advance notice of Anna's attitude when she insisted on headlining every session's exhibition," recalls Gene Scott, who helped organize the pro tournament, in his *Tennis Week* column. "She was already not only the group's most gifted but best showgirl, if not show-off, and it was easy to be lured into giving Anna her way. I wasn't the only one beguiled."

FASCINATING FACTS:

- Anna Kournikova signed a long-term contract with IMG when she was ten.
- Ninety-six percent of the estimated $20 million that Anna Kournikova earned in 1999 came from endorsements.
- Anna Kournikova ranked number one among the most-searched-for athletes in the world in 2000, according to leading Internet search engines Lycos 50 and Yahoo!.

Shoving herself into the spotlight paid off. Poppi Vinti, the representative for Ellesse, the Kremlin Cup's official sportswear, rewarded Anna with dresses and shirts, all the better for the preen queen to show off her pretty but pouting face and precocious shot-making. Soon after, she was one of the youngest ever to sign a sports endorsement contract with Ellesse. By age ten she was a client of IMG, the world's biggest sports management company.

Anna didn't have to pass out business cards the way Monica Seles, another Bollettieri protégée, did as a hustling thirteen-year-old at the Orange Bowl International Junior Championships in Miami Beach. Tennis people knew Anna—for better or for worse. And she showed little respect for some of the game's biggest names. Asked if she would like to meet superstar Boris Becker at the Lipton tournament, twelve-year-old Anna replied: "I wouldn't." What about Steffi Graf? It turned out that she had no desire to meet her either. In contrast, 1970s whiz kid Tracy Austin did a term paper on her idols, Billie Jean King and Rod Laver, when she was in elementary school.

Like her or loathe her, Special K can really play, as she showed by reaching the semifinals in her Wimbledon debut. "The wonderful thing about this generation is that when you look at Martina and Anna and Venus, they are all complete players, and I don't think we've ever seen this in any other generation," marvels all-time great Chris Evert, who won Wimbledon and the French Open at nineteen, an almost ancient age for teen conquests nowadays. "Before, Margaret Court and Billie Jean King were serve and volleyers, then I helped the generation of baseliners. Now you have it all in players so young."

Anna, lean and fit at 5'6" and 112 pounds, brags, "I can mix it up and do everything." Indeed, she's a splendid athlete (her mother was a Polish tennis champion and her father a soccer star) blessed with great hands and reflexes that produce ground-stroke winners, feathery drop shots, and dynamic volleys in doubles net duels. But unlike Hingis, who hugs the baseline, hits the ball on the rise, and opportunistically attacks, Anna often rallies from five or six feet behind the baseline and hits much flatter shots with less margin for error.

After Hingis decisively whipped Anna 6-1, 6-3 at the recent French Open, Evert, a TV analyst for NBC, was disappointed with Anna's performance but said, "We do see a lot of raw talent, untamed talent in Anna. And a little bit of inexperience. She certainly has all the goods, and in time, she'll be playing better and better and becoming more confident."

Bollettieri boasted in his autobiography, *My Aces, My Faults,* "I know I am the best tennis coach in the world," adding, "That's my talent. I help young men and women live up to their ability."

However, lately he's questioned whether he, or anyone, can provide the discipline and direction Anna needs to fulfill her potential. "I've never had the authority to take drastic action to curb Anna," Bollettieri complains. "If the mother [Alla] would say, 'Nick, she's your student totally,' then I would do a lot of things 180 degrees differently. The direction she's going in is already mapped out by her and her mother. The same goes for the way she acts on the court. I didn't have anything to do with it. I just told her that when you act that way, be prepared to prove who you are because you're going to get opponents disliking you to the point that they're going to try harder to beat you. I gave her the facts of life."

One fact of life that rankles Anna is the age eligibility rule that was designed to protect her. The Women's Tennis Association, fearing more of the premature burnout that ruined the careers of Austin and Andrea Jaeger and saw Jennifer Capriati self-destruct with drug problems, decided to limit the tournament play of its wonder-girls. The rules do not apply to Hingis or Williams because they joined the tour before the restrictions were introduced on January 1, 1995.

But Anna, who turned sixteen on June 7, is limited to ten tour events (plus the season-ending Chase Championships) in the year up to her seventeenth birthday. "Venus is just coming out, and Martina is already there," says impatient Anna, ranked number forty-seven. "If I could have a little more chance to play, maybe I could be there also. I have to get experience. I have to learn how to win and to lose. How can I learn? All I can do is practice." (Recently, the WTA tour liberalized the age eligibility rule, and Kournikova will be allowed to play up to seventeen tournaments.)

The WTA's wrongheaded new ranking system—which paradoxically was created to *increase* tournament participation—further victimizes Anna. Dumping its point-average formula, which accurately measured the quality of each player's results, the WTA adopted a "Best 18" system that rewards quantity play. "Now it's all down to your points total, and some of the other girls are planning to play about thirty tournaments, which means they'll be better than me on the ranking list even if I was to win all of my ten events," rightly complains Anna.

To her credit, Anna has always taken on all comers and disdained those who didn't, such as the much-hyped Williams sisters. In one of her memorable put-downs a couple years ago, Anna said: "I watched Serena and Venus Williams play, and they're not that good. They've been given more attention than me, and they haven't even played tournaments. They don't know how to play points or how to win. I've put myself on the line. I play everybody. I'm not worried about them."

Indeed, Anna is a throwback to the young Jimmy Connors, a tough, smart-ass kid from the wrong side of the tracks who, ready for a fight, brought brass knuckles to junior tournaments. As a fearless, pint-sized kid, Anna used to venture into the mean streets of Moscow to find a wall to hit against. Then she'd come back and challenge boys to a match and often beat them.

Now teenaged boys swarm around the court during Anna's practice sessions, eager to eye her sexy, suntanned body only scantily covered in two-piece Lycra outfits. In tournament matches, her brief Adidas skirts reveal the best legs in women's tennis, and her abbreviated tops often fly up to expose yet more skin. Not since gorgeous Gabriela Sabatini arrived a decade ago has such a seductive pubescent quickened male pulses. Evert recently said Kournikova was "as sexy as a sixteen-year-old can be." And she *knows* it. Pam Shriver quipped at Wimbledon that Kournikova threatened to "wear out the mirror" in the women's locker room. Kournikova even predicts that in ten years women pros will "play half-naked."

Off the court, her provocatively tight and/or see-through clothes, adorable face, and haughty demeanor turn heads wherever she goes. But few guys have worked up enough nerve to ask Anna for a date, and one who did in a player's lounge was smugly rebuffed with "You can't afford me!" She's probably right, having signed several endorsement contracts that have made her a millionaire.

Tennis' femme fatale prefers older men. At the Indian Wells tourney in early 1996, Anna regularly visited the hotel bar and apparently had no trouble passing for someone much older. Her relationship with twenty-eight-year-old Russian hockey star and international playboy Sergei Fedorov also has raised eyebrows. Her mother reportedly chaperones them on dates. But with Anna, who knows? When recently asked if she was dating Fedorov, she broadly smiled and coyly answered, "Good question. I don't know. No."

FASCINATING FACTS:

- Hockey superstar Pavel Bure reportedly gave Anna Kournikova a diamond engagement ring valued at nearly $1 million in March 2000 before breaking off the engagement because of her domineering mother, Alla.
- Hockey superstar Sergei Fedorov gave Anna Kournikova 240 roses at the Franklin Templeton Tennis Classic in Scottsdale, Arizona, in March 2000.

Her fast-growing popularity is reflected on the Internet, where she has attracted legions of admirers from all over the world, but especially young Australians. One of the several Web sites devoted exclusively to alluring Anna has recorded fifteen hundred visitors in the past eight months. Romeo from the Philippines wrote: "Anna's a chick, and she stole my heart the very first time I saw her." Edson suggested: "If you want to go out with me, come to BRASIL." Homer, a passionate lad from Australia, said: "Go Anna! Go you babe you! You thrash that Hingis girl. Get your revenge. Hugs and kisses (I wish), Homer."

Telegenic Anna has said that if she weren't playing pro tennis she'd like to be an actress. She got the attention she craves in her first Grand Slam at the U.S. Open last year when she and fourteenth-seeded Barbara Paulus were the first featured match—televised on prime time—at night on the Stadium Court. With a flair for the dramatic that the 19,709 fans loved, the kid qualifier, behind 4-3 and 0-40 on her own serve in the third set, battled back to upset Paulus 3-6, 6-2, 6-4.

After Steffi Graf whipped her 6-2, 6-1 in the next match, Anna showed why Bollettieri says that "she's a little girl who doesn't know how to speak with the press yet." Asked what it was like playing the great Graf on such an important occasion, Anna brusquely replied, "It was what it looked like." At the 1997 Lipton, after beating Amanda Coetzer for the second time and then losing 6-3, 6-4 to Jana Novotna, her curt sarcasm again turned off the media. Anna answered the first post-match interview question of "What happened today?" with "I played a match."

Special K has somewhat toned down her act as a pro, but during her junior days she earned a reputation as a hellion on the court for angrily protesting line calls a la John McEnroe and pointing to the wrong ball marks on the clay. Disgusted with her constant arguing with the umpire and linespeople at the Continental Cup, a spectator in the stands quipped, "She'd even argue over position in bed."

The most publicized incident occurred when Anna was practicing on a court next to some British junior players. When an errant shot of hers flew onto their court, Anna loudly yelled: "British!" Having gotten their attention, she commanded: "Ball!" The incensed boys then whacked the ball over the opposite fence—commendable restraint considering some of the more violent options that must have crossed their minds.

Too often though, what Anna wants, Anna gets. And what if she doesn't?

"Anna is a smooth talker and has that smile," says Bollettieri. "She always says, 'You think it's okay if I do this?' Underneath, she's saying, 'I'm going to do it.' And she has to be in the bullseye all the time. The center of attention. If she isn't running the show, she's going to try to break it up."

Talking about young athletes who are pampered and live without rules, Martina Navratilova recently warned: "We're going to see more and more of these athletes falling on their faces, falling off their pedestals."

"A lot of them will fall flat on their asses," agrees Bollettieri, "but they probably will be quite secure financially because of their lucrative endorsement contracts." Bollettieri has predicted that Special K will earn $5–15 million a year before she's eighteen "because she's so marketable." Whether Special K will be distracted by fortune and fame—like Agassi—and fail to reach her potential remains the burning question.

At the 1997 Australian Open, Anna Dearest held court, explaining: "You cannot just be a great tennis player, or just be a beautiful person anymore to succeed in the game. You have to have it all, the talent, the looks, the brains, and the drive."

Who do you think she has in mind?

FASCINATING FACTS:

- Both Anna Kournikova and her mother, Alla, describe themselves as "a crazy Russian."
- Swiss player Patty Schnyder once asked Barbara Schett, Anna Kournikova's doubles partner that day, to give her a short ball so she could drill Kournikova.
- In 2001, Anna Kournikova, trying to contrast herself with the Williams sisters, remarked: "I'm not Venus Williams. I'm not Serena Williams. I'm feminine. I don't want to look like they do. I'm not masculine like they are."

4

Serena Williams: Not Just Venus's Little Sister
1998

After Martina Hingis outclassed her at the 1997 Lipton Championships, Venus Williams, sounding more like the winner, crowed: "My sister Serena and I will be fighting for the number-one spot as soon as she joins the tour."

People thought Venus was crazy or arrogant or both. Only eight months later, though—and two months after Venus reached the U.S. Open final—sixteen-year-old Serena lived up to her sister's hype at the Ameritech Cup in Chicago. She merely wiped out number twenty-seven Elena Likhovtseva 6-3, 7-5, number seven Mary Pierce 6-3, 7-6 and number four Monica Seles 4-6, 6-1, 6-1 before number five Lindsay Davenport stopped her rampage 6-4, 6-4.

Against Seles, 304-ranked Serena slammed thirteen aces with her 110-mile-an-hour serves and outslugged the nine-time Grand Slam champion from the baseline. She also displayed more speed, versatile shot-making, and athleticism than Venus did during her sensational U.S. Open.

Serena, fifteen months younger and nearly four inches shorter than Venus, self-deprecatingly says, "I'll always be Venus's little sister." But Richard Williams, the highly controversial father-manager-coach of the "Ghetto Girls," as he calls them, predicts, "I've always believed Serena would ultimately be better."

"When Venus said her biggest rivalry would come from her sister, a lot of TV announcers said Venus shouldn't disrespect Martina Hingis," recalls Williams. "But only Venus knew that Serena had more talent than the girls out there, more power, and a great deal of knowledge of the game. How Serena played in Chicago is nothing compared to what she'll be doing next year."

Serena's maiden trip to Australia in January quickly proved outspoken Williams right. At the Sydney International, Serena drew first blood against fifteen-year-old Croat whiz kid Mirjana Lucic 7-5, 6-3, and despite visibly limping,

Serena Williams. Hans-Jürgen Dittmann

bravely overcame a 6-1, 5-2 deficit to upset Davenport 1-6, 7-5, 7-5 in torrid thirty-three degree (Celsius) heat. Only a super-tough draw at the Australian Open—namely, a second-round showdown against her sister—prevented Serena from endangering more seeds after she bumped off sixth-seeded Irina Spirlea 6-7, 6-3, 6-1. Venus took their heavy-hitting battle 7-6, 6-1 in what promises to be one of sport's greatest sibling rivalries.

The Lipton Championships in March further showcased Serena's precocious all-court game and strategy. After disposing of seeds Spirlea, Barbara Paulus, and Patty Schnyder, Serena cleverly jerked Hingis all over the court and earned two match points before falling to the teen queen 6-3, 1-6, 7-6. That scare took its toll on Hingis, who, after losing to Venus in the semis, confessed: "It's difficult to play the Williams family two matches in a row." Surely the understatement of the year, if not the next five or ten years.

Serena is clearly destined for the superstardom that would give America its first homegrown female Grand Slam champion—if Venus doesn't do it first—since aging Chris Evert won the French Open in 1986. But how did the newest prodigy in tennis pull off her *tour de force* in Chicago after only eleven professional match-es—and after not playing any junior tournaments for nearly four years before that?

Abundant self-belief partly explains it. For years Serena and Venus have been told by their father that they'll be number one in the world in both singles and doubles. Serena's huge upset over Seles didn't surprise Rick Macci, who coached the girls from September 1991 to July 1995: "Other players see Seles as a superstar with great ground strokes and a bunch of Grand Slam titles. Serena plays Seles and sees an overweight, slow opponent not as athletic as her, and she expects to win."

Serena denies thinking that and calls Seles "a great athlete" but stresses, "I want to be the best. Whatever it takes to get there is what I'm going to do."

FASCINATING FACTS:

- In 2000 Serena Williams said her favorite place to visit was "the mirror in my house."
- Serena Williams's tennis idols are Billie Jean King, Maureen Connolly, and Althea Gibson.
- Serena Williams's motto is: "I seek romance."

Macci's top-notch coaching and the subsequent guidance by their father—defying the conventional wisdom that the girls need an established world-class coach—have adequately prepared the prodigies for the pro game. "I've always been practicing hard and playing a lot of matches, but not necessarily tournament matches," says Serena. "I figure if I can do pretty well against men, I can handle the women."

Williams, always the canny control freak while being a loving father, doesn't allow the girls to play sets against each other in practice, although they do hit regularly. Serena insists she doesn't feel any sibling rivalry toward Venus, "my best friend," but adds: "We both have tremendous competitiveness against each other in practice because then no one will stand a chance against us in tournaments."

Like Hingis, Seles, Steffi Graf, Tracy Austin, and earlier teen queens, giggling Serena is as tough as nails when she competes. "When Serena was ten, she was the only girl at the academy who played tag with a closed fist," recalls Macci. When reminded of that, Serena laughs and exclaims, "Wow! I wasn't aware that I did that. [But] yes, I agree that I don't really take much crap from anyone."

That remark prompted me to ask Serena about the famous "bumping" inci-dent at the 1997 U.S. Open. You may remember that after nasty Romanian Spirlea intentionally collided with and kneed Venus during a changeover in their tense semifinal, Richard Williams said Spirlea was lucky she bumped into Venus and not Serena because "she would have been decked [by Serena]."

"He was exaggerating," says the muscular, 5'10", 155-pound Serena, who owns the most powerful physique in tennis since Martina Navratilova. "Because if I did that, I would have been [kicked] out of the tournament and probably out for the rest of the year. It was meant as a joke."

Williams nicknamed Serena "Blackenroe" because her terrific athleticism and quick hands reminded him of John McEnroe. Her all-around game differs somewhat from McEnroe's, but Serena admits, "I used to want to be like John McEnroe. My dad went so far as to give me the racket McEnroe used. I haven't patterned my game after his because I don't serve and volley as much as him. I wanted to be like him as a person. He got into a lot of arguments. That controversy was very exciting for me back then."

More mature now, Serena has learned how to downplay or even defuse controversy. When I asked her if she had heard any racist remarks or seen any racial incidents on the women's tour, as her father had alleged, she replied: "If I had, I wouldn't want to discuss them."

During her travels with Venus and her mother, Oracene, to England, France, and Russia—where "the threesome thoroughly charmed Mayor Luzhkov at a private reception at Moscow's City Hall," according to *Tennis Week*—Serena picked up valuable on-court and off-court experience. "Venus had a little problem closing out matches, which she's mastered now," says Serena. "She'd win the first set, lose the second, and barely pull it out in the third. And I was able to learn how to close it out without struggling. I think the secret is keeping up your aggressive game and not letting your concentration go."

Serena hasn't had a problem closing out matches and is especially proud of a personal achievement: "Every match I play, if I win the first set, I never lose the second set. I'm trying to keep that reputation, even though I'm sure it [the streak] will have to end one day."

Serena attributes her ability to handle the pressure of big-time tennis mostly to her naturally calm temperament, but also to her first ten years, when ducking bullets in crime-ridden Compton, California, became an unwanted adventure.

FASCINATING FACTS:

- During the 1999 Newsweek Champions Cup, Serena Williams posted a flyer on the door of the men's locker room. The flyer displayed a color shot of her whacking a forehand and the challenge, "ANYONE. ANYTIME. ANYWHERE."

- In 2002 Serena Williams will appear in a comedy called *Black Knight*.

Her mother once described Compton's black ghetto as "the most deplorable place to live." Serena agrees but says, "I think, though, it was good so we would understand [how] to be a little tougher and stronger and more independent. If you're tough, you don't find it as dangerous as some say it is."

Serena's father ran a small security-guard service until 1990, when the girls' promising tennis talent and income potential enabled the family to escape to Florida. In 1994 they purchased an eleven-acre estate with a mansion, three tennis courts, and a pond in a secluded area of Palm Beach Gardens. While a Rolls Royce is parked in the garage, a broken-down car sits incongruously in the front yard, presumably as a stark symbol of where the Williamses came from.

Almost embarrassed by their recent wealth—propelled by the reported $12-million contract Venus signed with Reebok and her own five-year, multi-million-dollar endorsement deal with Puma International—Serena insists her home "is not luxurious. It's just our place of residence. And one day it will all be gone. Actually, I keep things in perspective. I never forget where I came from, and yesterday I went back to the rougher areas [of Compton] to visit. I know that I could end up back there if things go the wrong way."

Williams preaches the importance of education at every opportunity and often decides whether Venus and Serena can play a given tournament based on their current school grades. "With technology nowadays, if you don't have education, you're lost," insists Williams. "You can be number one in tennis, but that doesn't mean you're going to be number one in life. What amazes me is that people don't talk about how well they play tennis; they say, 'You have very intelligent girls. You have really wonderful kids.' That's what I feel good about."

Unlike some kids who simply go through the motions at school, the Williams sisters truly enjoy it. Serena, a senior at a small private school, and Venus, who takes courses at Palm Beach Community College, love Shakespeare's plays. When asked what her main goal for 1998 is, Serena tellingly replied, "To get an A in zoology."

But don't get the idea that she likes everything about school. While skipping classes to whip her court elders at the Lipton, Serena mildly complained, "I'm getting behind in algebra II. I mean, it's really ridiculous. Some things you never use in life. You use physics a lot every day in life, and I love physics. But you don't use algebra II."

All the Williamses (except Richard) are Jehovah's Witnesses and deeply religious. "It's number one in my life. If it weren't for God, I wouldn't have anything," says Serena. "Religion has helped me to realize who I am. It's helped me not to get ahead of myself and not to get bombastic. It keeps me humble."

Much like the well-balanced Hingis, Serena has plenty of other activities to keep her happy and relaxed. "I like to go surfing in the morning. And I like to rollerblade, skateboard, and play the guitar," she says. She and Venus also have fun with their dog, Princess.

The sky's the limit for the "Ghetto Girls," and one can only wonder what the late Arthur Ashe would have thought of the strange and startling saga of the

Williamses. In 1988 Ashe predicted: "Given the same chance as others have had, blacks would dominate our sport as they have done in other sports."

"I think Arthur Ashe's prediction will come true very shortly with the two girls," says Williams matter-of-factly. "Venus and Serena could be the most important symbols now in American tennis. When you see girls coming from the ghetto of Compton, where we came from, it lets everyone know you can do it. The most important thing is that just living in America you have a fighting chance to succeed—even if you don't have exactly the same chance—if you're willing to fight for it, regardless of your race or creed. That's what's so great about America."

Two other far-less-heralded but intriguing eighteen-year-old prospects from southern California form the new black power movement in women's tennis—mercurial Katrina Nimmers from Compton and 6'1" Alexandra Stevenson of San Diego. "I've watched Katrina for quite some time now," says Williams. "She's not quite as good as Venus, about two or three months behind. She's probably above the level Serena is. Alexandra's got unbelievable talent. Dr. Peter Fischer, Pete Sampras's first coach, helped bring her talent out a great deal. Alexandra's playing tennis on a level of about number thirty or thirty-five in the world now.

"In the year 2000, the top four players in the world could be African-American," predicts Williams. Ashe would have loved that.

FASCINATING FACTS:

- In 2001 Serena Williams admitted that she used to shop on the Internet for as many as six hours a day until she kicked her addiction.
- Serena Williams's favorite athlete is Los Angeles Lakers superstar Kobe Bryant, who says he stays "glued to the TV when Venus and Serena are playing."
- In 2001 Serena Williams was reportedly dating pro football star LaVar Arrington.

5

Gustavo Kuerten:
Going Ga-ga Over Guga
1997

He's just what tennis needs," raves hard-to-please John McEnroe. Indeed, Gustavo Kuerten is the proverbial "nice guy" without being bland or boring, and a colorful personality minus boorish antics. Throw in spectacular athleticism, and you can see why everyone is going ga-ga over "Guga."

Crowds loved Kuerten's smiling insouciance during his fairy-tale French Open. Chants of "Guga, Guga" reverberated in Stade Roland Garros and buoyed the unseeded, unheralded Brazilian to one of the Open Era's most shocking and exciting Grand Slam triumphs. The sixty-sixth-ranked Kuerten, who had never advanced past an ATP tour quarterfinal and was only 2-7 on clay this year, knocked off former French champions Thomas Muster, Yevgeny Kafelnikov, and Sergi Bruguera for the prestigious title.

The fact that twenty-year-old Guga looks like a cartoon caricature endears him to fans even more. His stringbean body, ingenuous face, unkempt curls, and eye-catching attire give him the most distinctive appearance of any top player since the young Agassi. Kuerten says his gaudy gold and electric blue soccer-style outfits—which prompted French Tennis Federation president Christian Bimes to advocate a stricter dress code—"show my personality." In Cincinnati, he promised his clothes would be flashier than Agassi's.

When the charismatic Kuerten made history as the first Brazilian man to capture a Grand Slam singles title, he became the new national hero and ignited a tennis boom in Brazil. Tennis racket sales jumped 40 percent in his hometown of Florianopolis during the French Open fortnight, and manufacturers sold $3 million of his trademark outfits in Brazil in the week following the tournament.

"Guga has brought so much happiness to the Brazilian people. You can't imagine," says Diana Gabanyi, his publicity director. "Everyone from the taxi

Gustavo Kuerten. Hans-Jürgen Dittmann

driver to the people at the bus station to the people in his hometown talks about him. Everyone loves him. His personality and smile captivate people. He's winning and he's taking Brazil's name throughout the world. Right now Guga is as big as soccer star Ronaldo. That's incredible!"

When I asked Guga what it's like being the hot new star in men's tennis, he laughed and modestly downplayed it. "My life has changed a little bit, but I don't see myself as a big star. I'm too young to be a star. I don't want to change. I just want to keep playing tennis and enjoy it."

Being a sports hero can be a mixed blessing in Brazil, where kidnappings of the rich and famous are rather common. "I'm not worried because I live in a small town where it's pretty quiet and not too dangerous," says Kuerten. "It happens most of the time in Rio de Janeiro and Sao Paulo. I just hope it doesn't happen to me."

Fame and fortune haven't spoiled Kuerten. He's spent very little of the $660,000 (roughly half a million dollars more than his previous career earnings) he pocketed for his French title, and he postponed making any endorsement deals until after the U.S. Open.

In his press conference following the French Open final, he confided: "My life is perfect, even before the tournament. I have everything I need. I have a good house, I have my mom's car that I use a little bit." That won't be necessary any more because a Brazilian bank that sponsors him recently gave him a small sports car.

Family and friends, not material goods, have always been paramount to Kuerten, and he misses them dearly during his extended trips on the pro tour. "I really enjoy being with them," he says. "Families in South America are very close, and they want to help each other." When Guilherme, his brain-damaged younger brother, became ill, Kuerten cancelled a date with the Brazilian president, a meeting that was to have celebrated his historic triumph in Paris.

The brothers have a poignant relationship. "Guilherme doesn't know what's going on, but he's happy," says Gabanyi. "And whenever he sees Guga, he smiles. In his eyes you can see caring." Guilherme gets all the credit for Kuerten's world-famous nickname. When he was little, he couldn't say "Gustavo," only "Guga," so it stuck. Now Guga gives his brother his trophies, which Guilherme treasures as if they were his own.

Their irrepressible grandmother, Olga Schlosser, has become Guga's secret weapon. She studies all the players and phones him at tournaments so "she [can] tell me how to play each guy," says Kuerten. Grandma Olga even showed up at Roland Garros, with Mama Kuerten and older brother Raphael, a teaching pro, for her grandson's history-making final.

On Father's Day, Kuerten gave a memorable interview to the Brazilian newspaper *Globo*. He talked about his beloved father, who suffered a fatal heart attack after umpiring a junior tennis match when Gustavo was a boy of nine. "Guga cried, and the whole country cried with him," says Gabanyi. "Brazilians are very emotional people."

Kuerten has dedicated his life to his father, Aldo. After he won the championship point against Bruguera in Paris, he recalled memories of him. "Every time I play, I think of my father because of his heavy influence not only in tennis and in sports but also in education and the rest of my life.

"He was a real sportsman," says Kuerten. "He played tennis, basketball, soccer—almost every sport. He really liked to try his best, and he always fought for what he wanted. So I think I got some of this from him. He just wanted his sons—me and my two brothers—to grow up and do well in their lives and have a good reputation. My father, for sure, would be very glad and happy if he knew I won a Grand Slam and got this [number nine] ranking."

Aldo would also have been especially proud of his son's humility. Before stepping onto the victory platform at Roland Garros, Kuerten brushed the red clay off his shoes. Then he modestly bowed to six-time French Open king Bjorn Borg—"a big idol for me"—before accepting his congratulations and the silver bowl.

A week after Kuerten dealt world number two Michael Chang his worst hardcourt loss since 1991—a 6-3, 6-1 thrashing in Montreal—Chang turned the tables and crushed Kuerten 6-1, 6-2 in Cincinnati. Instead of making excuses, the Brazilian graciously said, "I hope maybe to one day play like Chang."

Meanwhile, he's trying to incorporate some aspects of Marcelo Rios's game. He "really likes" to watch the talented Chilean play at tournaments and occasionally practices with him. "You can learn a lot from the way he hits the ball early and returns serve, and he moves very well," says Kuerten. "Rios is a great player."

McEnroe, now an incisive TV tennis analyst, praises Kuerten's studious approach to the game. "What I like about Kuerten is that he lost two matches [to Jim Courier and MaliVai Washington] in Davis Cup earlier this year but claimed that was a great learning experience. And he's clearly learned from the losses."

Boris Becker, who never reached the French final in his fourteen-year career, is fascinated by Kuerten's coup in Paris and explains what makes him so effective: "He is not a one-dimensional player. He can serve and volley, he can stay back. Obviously his physique is excellent to be able to come through three five-set matches. He never seemed to get nervous; he always kind of knew what he was doing. The whole combination made him a champion."

Brazilian Thomaz Koch, world-ranked number twenty-four in the 1960s, pays Kuerten the highest compliment: "I never saw anyone come into a competition this important as an unknown and keep his emotional stability to the end. It's incredible."

Kuerten's mental game wasn't always so strong. In fact, the turning point in his career came only four months earlier at an indoor tournament in Memphis. "Gustavo used to say, 'This player is so good. I can't beat him,' " relates Larri Passos, who has coached Kuerten since December 1989. After Kuerten played terrific tennis to whip Byron Black in the first round, Passos sat down with his gifted *protégée* and preached the power of positive thinking. "I said, 'Look in my eyes and believe what I am going to say. You can beat every player that's out there if you really believe it.' And he looked into my eyes and shouted, 'I believe it. I can beat them. I can. I can.' "

In the next round Kuerten routed Agassi, and afterwards they repeated the same confidence-building ritual. "I put in his mind that he could beat all the players, and he could go to the top twenty," says Passos. At the French Open, Passos cajoled him again—"I kept telling him, 'You can win it because you are in great shape and everything is going well.' "

The thirty-nine-year-old Passos says, "Sometimes it's like a father-son relationship. I met him when he was nine years old. And his father told me: 'It's time for Gustavo to start practicing and working on his tennis.' That time I told his father that he was too young [for coaching]. So I waited until he was fourteen. Then I took him. I remembered his father's wishes. For Brazilian kids, it's not just the technical aspects of coaching because Brazilian kids are more emotional.

FASCINATING FACTS:

- Gustavo Kuerten often sings in the locker room after playing tournament matches.
- Gustavo Kuerten is the only player ever to defeat Pete Sampras and Andre Agassi in the semifinals and final of the same tournament, a feat he achieved at the 2000 Masters Cup.

Sometimes you have to be strict, but other times you have to show more warmth and be comforting. That's the best way for Latin people."

Like many young Brazilians, Kuerten has fun surfing and playing soccer. "When I get a week off, I relax and go with my friends in Brazil to surf [in the Atlantic Ocean surrounding his island city of Florianopolis]. There is no pressure there in the water," he says. "No problems." His other off-court passion is samba music. "In the morning I wake up every day and listen to it. I really enjoy it."

Religion also plays a key role in Kuerten's life, although he doesn't get a chance to go to [Catholic] church as much as he'd like when he's globe trotting on the tour. "I think God is someone who looks out for us and takes care of us," he says. "I'm healthy all my life, and I've had such wonderful opportunities to play tennis. So I believe someone is helping make life a little bit easier for me."

Kuerten's carefree nature belies his keen sense of right and wrong. He'll occasionally protest line calls, although he acknowledges, "It's a difficult job. The umpires try to do their best all the time. Everybody makes mistakes. If I see a mistake, sometimes I'll protest. Almost everybody does that."

What almost everybody *doesn't do,* however, is what Kuerten did during his three-set upset loss to Chris Woodruff in the Canadian Open final. When an obvious Woodruff ace was called out, Kuerten rectified the injustice by intentionally hitting the next shot out. "I think that's fair, and if I'm sure the ball is good, and it's a good play, that's it," he explained afterwards.

The only real grievance Kuerten harbors involves the Brazilian Tennis Federation's handling of his Davis Cup participation. "The federation says, 'We're going to pay you one hundred dollars (sic) to play the Davis Cup,' and it's an agreement," he says. "After that they say to you, 'We don't have any money. We're not going to pay you anything.' This is a big mistake. They don't keep their agreement. It's not the money, but it's a matter of honor and fairness."

Kuerten would like nothing more than to bring the Davis Cup title to Brazil, which has never advanced past the semifinal round in the fifty years that South America's most populous nation has participated. "In Brazil the Davis Cup is very big. They really care about it," he says. "This year we had a great match against the U.S. Now we play New Zealand to get back into the World Group. For us it would be a great pleasure to play in the semifinals or final in Brazil before the crowds."

That prospect seems unlikely unless Kuerten gets a stronger supporting cast than number 80 Fernando Meligeni and number 153 Jaime Oncins. "Meligeni is a great Davis Cup player, and Oncins is a good player," disagrees Kuerten. "You don't need to be a great ATP player in the rankings to play well in the Davis Cup. You just have to play emotionally and get hot. We were one of the big surprises last year, and we gave the U.S. a battle this year. We're young, and if we work hard, we can go far in the future."

Kuerten recently offered a controversial opinion: "I think tennis has been dead for a long time." What does he suggest to enliven the sport? "You don't have to change the rules of the game to make it more exciting," he says. "Each player has his own interesting style, but the players should enjoy it a little more and try to be more relaxed on the court. They should also be closer to the crowd in matches and to the people in practice. They should not go there [to tournaments] and just play and stay in the hotel and always try to avoid everyone. This will help tennis a lot."

Kuerten practices what he preaches by agreeably signing autographs for fifteen or twenty minutes after his matches and giving numerous candid interviews to the media in addition to required post-match press conferences.

"Personality is good in all sports. That's what the crowds like and they want to see," says Kuerten, who has become a favorite of fans wherever he goes. After the Canadian Open final, the crowd applauded him for nearly two minutes. The feelings were mutual. "For me it was a little bit emotional also, and it's great to have a time like that.

"I hope some day, if I have the results, the world will love me as much as Brazil loves me."

FASCINATING FACTS:

- Andre Agassi says that Gustavo Kuerten's one-handed backhand "is as good a shot as you'll see in the game."
- When his hometown of Florianopolis wanted to put a statue of Gustavo Kuerten on a main thoroughfare as a tribute to him in 1998, Kuerten politely declined.

6

Jennifer Capriati: How She Was Taught to Be the Best
1990

The touchy subject of who should get the credit and how much for a star's success isn't new.

Robert Lansdorp, Tracy Austin's coach for a decade, used to grow incensed when the more famous Vic Braden was mentioned as her first coach.

Lansdorp finally lashed back: "I don't like Braden getting credit for rolling a ball at Tracy in the crib, and [Roy] Emerson getting credit for her serve when it hasn't changed. I've done it and I've done it all.... It's like a work of art. An artist would feel robbed if somebody else put their name on his painting."

Lately, Rick Macci has felt similarly robbed. He coached whiz kid Jennifer Capriati for two and a half wonderful and important years, starting in January 1987, when she was ten. Now, Capriati-mania and the worldwide avalanche of publicity have largely ignored him and his crucial role in her spectacular development.

"To make the story more Cinderella-like for the public, the marketing line is that it went from Jimmy Evert [her first coach] to her dad [Stefano], and now where she's at today, at the USTA Training Center," says Macci. "It's like for the two and a half years at Rick Macci's [Tennis Academy] she disappeared and I didn't exist."

Macci reasonably acknowledges that before he began training her, Jennifer possessed champion qualities as evidenced by her Orange Bowl 12s crown.

"She was probably born a champion, and she fell into the great hands of Jimmy Evert, who instilled tremendous racket preparation and balance in her ground game."

Yet Macci knew that Chrissie clones with great ground strokes and little else can no longer attain the pinnacle of today's more athletic and diversified game.

Jennifer Capriati.
Hans-Jürgen Dittmann

"Jennifer had three-quarters of the package before she came to me, but the remaining one-quarter is the difference between being number ten, number five, or number one some day," says Macci.

FASCINATING FACTS:

- The first biography of Jennifer Capriati was published when she was fifteen.
- Jennifer Capriati said that if she weren't a professional tennis player, she would want to be a psychologist.
- Jennifer Capriati played twenty-four of her first twenty-eight professional matches on tournament center courts.

Their big "mission" was to develop the best serve in women's tennis. "The trap that a lot of women fall into in pro tennis is to just get the ball in play, instead of making the serve a weapon," he points out.

So the creative Macci devised a multifaceted approach that his enthusiastic prodigy thrived on. For both instruction and inspiration, they watched, on hundreds of occasions, videos of Martina Navratilova serving, "to try to imitate the fluidity and looseness of her service motion."

To perfect the classic throwing motion indispensable for an explosive serve, Capriati threw a football to Macci for fifteen minutes nearly every day for two and a half years. She also imitated a hula dancer to get her hips and shoulders to roll in sync during the serve.

Since Capriati was quite stiff and mechanical at the outset, Macci stressed wrist-snap to achieve maximum racket-head speed for greater power. So, standing with her feet locked up inside ball hoppers three feet from the fence, she tried, sometimes as many as five hundred times a day, to whack the ball downward and bounce it over the fence.

Even the minor detail of catching the ball Macci threw to her before each serve became purposeful. Capriati gently caught it on her outstretched racket.

"I wanted her to develop soft hands so eventually she could handle the racket like a magician when she's out of position, like a McEnroe," he explains.

All the effort and dedication have already paid off. Capriati, now 5'6" and a solid 125 pounds, has belted serves timed at ninety-seven miles per hour. Braden praised her serving technique as the best he'd ever seen in a girl her age when she was twelve.

What's more, Macci vastly improved her volley, gave her a topspin forehand, and positioned her more offensively nearer the baseline so her superb ground strokes could better attack the ball on the rise.

Macci's devotion and affection for her shined as brightly as his expertise. Besides an estimated two thousand hours of on-court coaching, Macci, thirty-five, baby-sat for her and her younger brother and took them out for dinner and the movies.

He also wrote her scores of motivational letters before the Capriatis moved to Grenelefe from Lauderhill, when her parents drove her two hundred miles each way every weekend for lessons.

Capriati appreciated all of it. In a touching note now framed in Macci's office, she wrote: "Do you know something, I really like my service, it's really gotten better. I can't wait to come here again. It's so fun. You're one cool dude, awesome and great. See ya soon! Love, Jen."

The love affair was mutual—and her departure last July traumatic. Macci would confide that it left him feeling "like I know what it's like to have a daughter who's died." Eight months later, the gratifying result of their fruitful relationship was her incredible professional debut at the $350,000 Virginia Slims of Florida. There, still only thirteen, she knocked off players world-ranked at numbers 110, 34, 19, 16, and 10 (Helena Sukova) and forced number 3 Gabriela Sabatini to play "my best tennis" before yielding only 6-4, 7-5 in the final.

Capriati has even bigger fish to fry, though—namely, the current queen of tennis. "Every time we played a match, the whole focus would be to prepare her to play Graf," recalls Macci. "I always hit the inside-out forehand and the heavy slice backhand crosscourt [like Graf].

"I had her competing with the best sixteen-and eighteen-year-old boys in the world all the time. I have no doubt I did all the right things to prepare her."

Macci is convinced that Capriati's style will match up quite effectively against the West German superstar. "Why? Because Jennifer's best shot is her backhand down the line, and Jennifer can keep the exchanges even or stay in control—whereas when Graf plays other people, she definitely is controlling the show."

Could amazing Jennifer beat Steffi this year?

"No doubt, in my mind. She has a very legitimate chance," predicts Macci. "One thing I've always liked about Jennifer is that she has respect for opponents, but she has no fear of anyone."

FASCINATING FACTS:

- The Jennifer Capriati–Martina Hingis final at the 2001 Australian Open ranked number three in the TV audience ratings for tennis matches in ESPN's history.

- Jennifer Capriati (2001 Australian Open) and Steffi Graf (1999 French Open) are the only players ever to beat Monica Seles, Lindsay Davenport, and Martina Hingis to win a Grand Slam singles title.

- After Jennifer Capriati's dream of a Grand Slam in 2001 was shattered when Justine Henin upset her in the Wimbledon semifinals, Capriati confided: "You know, it's funny. I was such an early starter, early prodigy, whatever, but really I feel like a late bloomer."

7

Bjorn Borg:
Bjorn without Tears
1982

The legend of Bjorn Borg will inevitably exceed the legacy. For the greater the hero, the more prevalent the fictions. But, whatever his faults, Bjorn was heroic. At a time when men's tennis cried out for it, he brought sportsmanship and quiet dignity. He won without boasting and lost without excuses.

As much as his grace under pressure and his fabulous achievements— five Wimbledon and six French Open championships by age twenty-five—I will remember his many trademarks. His emotionless face seemed incredible in a grueling individual sport filled with agonizing vicissitudes. His extraordinary stamina—did anyone *ever* see him out of breath?—became even more remarkable considering his counterpunching style and penchant for long rallies. While his fabled pulse rate of thirty-five turned out to be a myth Bjorn dispelled in his autobiography, his unheard-of stringing tension of eighty-two pounds stretched belief and gut so much that strings often broke while not in use.

Even casual followers of tennis could recognize his unique game. The almost violent thrust of his looping forehand with its Western grip and open stance seemed to contradict the tenets of classical technique. Yet few—perhaps only Tilden, Johnston, Kramer, and Lendl—hit forehands as effectively and consistently. His two-handed backhand, a rather wristy, flicking action, had a backboard steadiness and inspired a decade of copycat kids, especially in his now tennis-loving Sweden. And both wings produced heavy topspin. Borg would recall his early stroking: "It never bothered me that others were using different grips and strokes. I was stubborn." Who could argue with success either? Not even sneering purists.

*Bjorn Borg. International
Tennis Hall of Fame*

Wimbledon, where Bjorn reigned so majestically, figured crucially in the Borg legend from the time he was a blond heartthrob of seventeen. He was idolized and mobbed by hordes of squealing English schoolgirls, not to mention some of their mothers. Growing a beard—against the wishes of his fiancée and later his wife, Mariana Simionescu—and not shaving it off until he notched another title became his favorite Wimbledon superstition. Another Borg-Wimbledon tradition from 1976 to 1980 would be his annual victory gesture: the down-on-his-knees, arms-raised-skyward concession to emotion.

Other than his surprising first Wimbledon crown when Bjorn didn't lose a set, none came easily. Early-round escape jobs against dangerous sleepers in the draw like Mark Edmondson (1977), Victor Amaya (1978), and Vijay Amritraj (1979) displayed his resourcefulness and tenacity and added to his aura of invincibility.

The Big W fittingly showcased Bjorn's most magnificent and memorable matches. The 6-4, 3-6, 6-3, 3-6, 8-6 semifinal in 1977 involving close friend Vitas Gerulaitis contained such breathtaking shot-making that 1930s champion Don Budge called it the best match he'd ever seen. Millions of television viewers worldwide said the same thing about the 1980 Borg-McEnroe final. If the caliber of play didn't quite make it the greatest match in history, it would be hard to imagine a more thrilling, almost excruciatingly tense duel than the 1-6, 7-5, 6-3,

6-7, 8-6 epic. No one would forget their scintillating fourth set tiebreaker, a thirty-four-point ordeal that lasted twenty-two minutes, in which the champ had five championship points and the challenger seven set points.

Bjorn's pleasant but serious disposition made him a popular champion, and extraordinarily so throughout Europe. He proved the perfect foil for archrivals Jimmy Connors and John McEnroe. When pitted against the pugnacious and occasionally crude Connors or the argumentative and raging McEnroe, the contrasts could hardly be sharper. The good guy versus the bad guy ... the imperturbable, patient introvert against the intense, almost hysterical extrovert ... the bastion of Old World values and behavior staving off the Ugly American. The ferocity of the Borg-McEnroe confrontations seemed matched by passions aroused in the sporting masses for their favorite.

FASCINATING FACTS:

- Bjorn Borg wrote the book *The Bjorn Borg Story* when he was nineteen.
- At the 1973 Wimbledon Championships, three hundred teenaged girls dragged Bjorn Borg onto a road and pinned him down for more than fifteen minutes until police rescued him.
- Bjorn Borg received death threats at the U.S. Open for three consecutive years.

Years from now I'll also remember the little things. The odd couple formed by the wife and coach as they intently watched their man perform: Mariana, so nervous she chewed gum and smoked at the same time, beside the super-stoical Lennart Bergelin. The "for sure" expression Bjorn used so often for emphasis. The vertically striped Fila shirts that he habitually wore and everyone wanted— until they found out how much they cost. And, of course, that supreme tennis physique: lean, broad-shouldered, narrow-hipped, and capable of generating tremendous foot speed and unusual strength for a 5'11", 165-pounder.

The Borg legend would hardly be complete without a seminal experience that was to change a typically hyper-competitive young squirt into the one and only "Iceborg." At age twelve, Bjorn writes in his autobiography, "I was throwing my racquet all over the place and cheating all the time. I was a real nut case, hitting balls over the fence—everything." So the Swedish Tennis Association banned him from tournaments for *six* months and taught him a lesson he would never forget. He recalls: "I took it very much to heart; it was a devastating experience that I remember as if it were yesterday." Not surprisingly, he recommends the same drastic but simple solution to cure poor sportsmanship among today's *enfants terrible*.

But the "other" Bjorn Borg belied the popular image created and repeated by the uncritical media. On his road to the top, at the top, and even more so on the way down, Borg made money his god and showed little sense of responsibility to the game.

It was a sad irony indeed, and perhaps an ominous trend, that the guy who always insisted he wanted to win all the major titles he could, to be remembered ultimately as the greatest player of all time, became the king of the "one night stands" and the "special events" (the euphemism for exhibitions). He had the gall not only to flout the traditional Grand Prix tournament circuit and thus jeopardize its future, but to turn logic on its head by claiming, "Only Wimbledon, the U.S., and the French are important. All the other tournaments are not important."

The son of a middle-class clothing salesman had amassed $4 million in prize money and an estimated $70 million more in endorsements (he reputedly boasted fifty contracts), appearances, and exhibitions in a decade but needed a tennis history lesson badly. Even if he didn't think he was bigger than the sport, he clearly had forgotten his roots. Amateur associations, such as Sweden's, which gave him a start, are tennis' grass-roots lifeblood, and much of their revenue is derived from national tournaments on their soil. Not so for the hit-and-run exhibitions and even the now-contracting WCT circuit that pocket all the profits.

Borg made more money than any tennis player before him, but it was never enough. Worse, he claimed either ignorantly or hypocritically that "big money" exhibitions never hurt bona-fide tournaments. "Most of our exhibitions are in cities that can't have Grand Prix tournaments—or don't want them because they can't be guaranteed top players." Cities like, would you believe, Tokyo and Toronto, and countries like Australia, where he suddenly condescended to compete in four meaningless McEnroe matches for a $750,000 payoff, and South Africa, where a similar sum was in the exhibition offing until the apartheid heat finally made the moral price too high.

Time and again Jack Kramer, the creator of the Grand Prix concept and the first executive director of the ATP, blasted the greedy Swede. "It's like Willie Mays playing on Tuesday and Saturday and then going off to do home-run derbies on the other days," he would analogize. "The top players have found out that they can make more money *not playing* tournaments."

And Kramer warned of the growing complacency that the stunning success of Open Tennis had brought. "We need our champions to keep selling the game of tennis. When you are a champion and you don't feel like playing fifteen or twenty tournaments a year to keep the sport alive, then the sport has a problem."

Borg wasn't universally admired, as commonly thought. All tennis fans know that he never won the U.S. Open, but rarely (only once) did he even enter another Grand Slam tournament, the Australian Open.

What's more, Borg refused to compete at all (save some Davis Cup) in doubles like Tilden, Budge, Kramer, Gonzalez, Laver, McEnroe, and so many truly versatile champions. True, he never achieved much in doubles—although merely playing was bound to improve his volleying technique and reflexes—and it must be acknowledged that some of today's superstars don't bother with money-poor and energy-depleting doubles either. Yet the absence of *any* tournament doubles record has to tarnish his reputation and also deal the struggling event of doubles another setback.

As for the cherished Davis Cup competition, the verdict will be mixed. Bjorn's finest patriotic hours came when, at fifteen, he nervelessly rallied from two sets down to upset New Zealander Onny Parun, displaying what his countrymen call *is i magen*—ice in the stomach. Then, in 1975, at age nineteen, he led Sweden to its first possession of the Cup. However, during several other years he showed up missing (unlike a so-called villain named McEnroe) when his nation needed him, both in Cup action and important Swedish tournaments.

There were always reasons or excuses. He was exhausted. The unfair Swedish press were rapping him for moving to the tax haven of Monte Carlo. Tennis officials hadn't sufficiently appreciated all he'd done in the past. A scheduling conflict with an exhibition he was committed to. Perhaps bad advice from a vulture agent. Nonetheless, Bjorn was doing what he does so well: Be stubborn.

Stubbornness. He showed it with a mental strength that enabled him to hit a ball back one more time than any other clay-court player of his era, and, most likely, of any other era. He showed it with a remarkable determination to mold a game seemingly unsuited for grass courts into a five-time Wimbledon winner, a feat that still mystifies some experts.

But a stubborn pride also made this normally apolitical player buck the establishment's rules and lose and drop out in 1982. He rested and rusted and eventually returned. While his fellow players were divided on the merits of his case, some such as John Newcombe wondered: "If he's playing for history, why is he playing just exhibitions?" And Chris Evert aptly remarked: "I don't understand what Bjorn's doing. The only person he's hurting by staying away is himself."

Of such contradictions champions rise and fall. "Our virtues are most frequently but vices in disguise," La Rochefoucauld pithily put it three hundred years ago.

FASCINATING FACTS:

- Bjorn Borg won thirteen consecutive five-set matches from 1976 to 1980.
- One of Bjorn Borg's most expensive purchases was a fourteen-island archipelago off the coast of Sweden.
- At the Superstar Television sports competition staged in the late 1970s in Vichy, France, Bjorn Borg won six of the eight events.

8

Rod Laver: The Rocket Blazes into Tennis Immortality

1999

"From the very beginning the competition was always Laver," Pete Sampras once said. Sampras yearned to play like, behave like, and eventually surpass the feats of his boyhood idol, Rod Laver.

After practices, Sampras spent hours watching films of the Australian legend dueling archrival Ken Rosewall in dramatic finals at the 1971 and 1972 World Championship of Tennis Finals.

"I loved the way Laver played," recalled Sampras. "He had no holes in his game, had every shot, and could win on all the surfaces." Indeed, Laver exemplified the aggressive, all-court game that Dr. Pete Fischer, who coached Sampras from age nine to eighteen, wanted his immensely talented student to emulate. Equally important, Laver also represented the gold standard for gentlemanly conduct that Fischer was inculcating.

"I've always looked up to the older guys like Laver and Rosewall," nineteen-year-old Sampras said after his stunning 1990 U.S. Open triumph. "I really enjoyed that era. I think a lot of guys, especially my age, forget the Lavers and Rosewalls. All those were class individuals, and I would like to be in that category."

Until Sampras dominated the 1990s and put up dazzling numbers—like six Wimbledon and twelve overall Grand Slam titles and six straight year-end number-one rankings—Laver was recognized as "the greatest ever" by many experts. Laver *twice* won the Grand Slam—capturing the Australian, French, Wimbledon, and United States championships in a calendar year—something no one else has ever done.

As an amateur in 1962 Laver pulled off his Slam against fields diluted by the loss of several stars to the pro ranks. But no one questioned his supremacy when

Rod Laver. International Tennis Hall of Fame/Ed Fernberger

the lefty shot-maker, then thirty-one, repeated the record-breaking Slam in 1969 against an Open draw filled with all the world's premier players. To understand how prodigious this accomplishment is, consider that since then only Jimmy Connors in 1974 and Mats Wilander in 1988 have won three major titles in any given year.

And consider this intriguing question: How many more Slam crowns might Laver, who joined the pros in 1963, have amassed had he not been barred from those prestigious still-amateur tournaments from 1963 to 1967, during his prime?

Rodney George Laver was born August 9, 1938, into a tennis-loving family in the Queensland cow country. His father, Roy, built an ant-bed tennis court and a rough backboard and had ambitions for his three boys to excel as tournament players. Papa Roy's family joke was always, "We'll send one of the family to Wimbledon one day." He wasn't really joking. "But I thought it would be the oldest boy, Trevor. He was the one who looked good in those days."

"He didn't think much of my chances because I was so small, but soon after Charlie Hollis took over coaching us in Rocky (i.e., Rockhampton), Charlie told Dad that I'd be the best," Laver wrote in his 1971 autobiography, *The Education of a Tennis Player*.

Hollis believed Rod's two older brothers were too quick-tempered whereas Rod was more easygoing. "If we can build the killer instinct in him, then it'll be the perfect blend," said Hollis, who later presciently advised Roy, "Rodney's got the eye of a hawk. I believe we can make a champion out of him."

His semiretired father drove him to tournaments, sometimes as far as 450 dusty miles away over dirt roads, and Rod played tennis morning (getting up at five o'clock and bicycling five miles to the town courts), afternoon (following school), and night (with his father after finishing his homework).

Rod thrived on the hard training sessions with Hollis, who, like Fischer, required his protégé to cultivate a sense of tennis history and good manners. Hollis regaled the Laver boys with stories about the great players of yesteryear, such as Budge and "Gentleman Jack" Crawford, and quizzed them frequently. He also drilled Rod on dress and table etiquette when they ate together. "We want to be proud of you when you're becoming a champion," Hollis would often say. "You have to know how to act the part. You're representing the people of Rockhampton and Queensland and Australia."

Laver also felt a sense of responsibility to maintain another important Aussie tradition: winning. From Norman Brookes, Gerald Patterson, and J.O. Anderson early in the century to 1930s stars Crawford, John Bromwich, and Adrian Quist to 1950s and 1960s champions Frank Sedgman, Lew Hoad, and Rosewall, sparsely populated but sports-crazy Australia was second only to America in capturing Grand Slam titles and Davis Cups. "I didn't want to be the one to let the dynasty down," recalled Laver.

Hollis, much like Fischer a generation later, possessed the vision to mold a game for the ages. Fischer realized that no two-handed player had ever become a formidable serve-and-volleyer, so he revamped fourteen-year-old Sampras's backhand into a classical Eastern one-hander. Similarly, Laver recalls how Hollis made a crucial stroke change when he was twelve or thirteen. "Charlie Hollis told me lefthanders always had a little slice backhand and didn't do much other than keep it in play and were aggressive with the forehand. He said, 'You'll never win Wimbledon with a slice backhand. You've got to hit a topspin backhand.'"

Laver's game developed enough so that he won the state fourteen-and-under championship at age thirteen, and a year later he attended clinics in Brisbane directed by Harry Hopman, the renowned Davis Cup captain. Hopman, a physical fitness fanatic, saw the scrawny and then-slow and somewhat lethargic boy and, with irony, nicknamed him "The Rocket."

Although Laver would grow only to 5'8 1/2", he became remarkably strong thanks in part to squeezing a tennis ball every chance he could and perhaps even from going kangaroo hunting with his friends. His massive twelve-inch left forearm—which Arthur Ashe quipped was "a two-by-four with freckles"—equalled heavyweight boxing champion Rocky Marciano's, and his seven-inch wrist was an inch bigger than that of another heavyweight champion, Floyd Patterson.

At fifteen, Laver became really serious about a tennis career, so he quit school, moved to Brisbane, and started work for the Dunlop Sporting Goods Company. "Many times I regret my lack of education," he wrote, but, like high school dropout Sampras he knew a full-time commitment to tennis was "the best way" to reach the top. At seventeen, he gained valuable experience when Hopman took him and Bob Mark on a world tour.

In his breakthrough year of 1959, Laver reached his first Slam final at Wimbledon but lost decisively to Alex Olmedo. The Peruvian was allowed to play Davis Cup for the U.S. and later that year dealt Laver a four-set Davis Cup defeat, which Laver said "stands as the biggest disappointment of my career," even though Australia pulled out a 3-2 victory in the Challenge Round. It was the first of four straight Davis Cups Laver won with Roy Emerson and Neale Fraser.

FASCINATING FACTS:

- In 1969 Rod Laver became the first player to win more than one hundred thousand dollars in prize money in one year.
- To stay cool on hot days, Laver sometimes wore wet cabbage leaves on his head under an Australian floppy sun hat.

Fittingly, Laver grabbed his first Grand Slam singles title at the 1960 Australian Championships in Brisbane. After trailing Emerson 5-2 in the fifth set, "The Rocket" showed his incomparable talent for raising his game when it counted most by firing a fusillade of winners to take the last five games to reach the final. There, in another supreme test of skill and will in searing heat, Laver survived a match point and then outlasted a cramping Fraser on the seventh title point to prevail 8-6 in the fifth set. Hopman's brutal training methods had paid off, as they would for the rest of super-fit Laver's career.

Fraser turned the tables on Laver in the 1960 Wimbledon and U.S. finals, while Emerson, who matched Laver in athleticism if not spectacular shots, beat him in the 1961 Australian and U.S. finals. But sandwiched between those 1961 setbacks, Laver crushed American Chuck McKinley in an astounding fifty-seven minutes for his first Wimbledon title.

After taking the New South Wales Championships shortly before Christmas, Laver became a man with a plan for 1962. "I want to win the Australian, French, Wimbledon, and United States championships in one year," he declared. "Only one player has ever achieved the feat—America's Don Budge."

For the next ten months, the reserved Laver let his racket do the talking and history-making. Lady Luck inevitably plays a role in any Grand Slam, and Laver was fortunate to face a weary Emerson in the 1962 Australian final. Emmo had played sixteen sets and 184 games in the previous two days due to a backlog caused by inclement weather, and the fresher Laver prevailed in a close four-setter.

On Roland Garros clay, his weakest surface, Laver narrowly escaped defeat thrice. Unheralded countryman Marty Mulligan came within a match point of ending Laver's dream of a Slam; then Fraser served for the match at 5-4 in the fifth set; and in the French final, Laver rallied from two sets down to beat good friend

Emerson again. At Wimbledon—where Laver says, "It's what the atmosphere instills here.... You play your best tennis"—his booming serve-and-volley game overwhelmed Mulligan in the final to nail down the critical third leg of the Slam.

The gracious Budge practiced with Laver before the U.S. Championships at Forest Hills and predicted, "I am afraid that at long last my record is going to be toppled." He was right. Laver breezed through the outclassed field and outplayed Emerson in four sets to gain his coveted Slam.

But Laver knew he hadn't beaten the world's best players, namely pros Rosewall, Hoad, Pancho Gonzalez, Butch Buchholz, Barry MacKay, and Andres Gimeno. So he signed a $110,000 pro contract following the 1962 Davis Cup Challenge Round.

Laver found the pro tour more grueling than anticipated. He once played matches in 150 cities (including Khartoum, which had a revolution in progress!) in 250 days. The competition too was far more difficult. Hoad and Rosewall humbled the former amateur hotshot nineteen of the first twenty-one times they played. "I didn't find out who were the best [players] until I turned pro and had my brains beaten out for six months at the start of 1963," admitted Laver. By 1965, he regained his status as king of the hill but was tired of the barnstorming life and longed to compete again at the prestigious tournaments.

Laver, like nearly everyone in the tennis world except for a few reactionary national association leaders, was thrilled when Open Tennis finally arrived in 1968. Those who doubted that the aging pros were any good were promptly served notice when Rosewall, thirty-four, won the first French Open and Laver, thirty, won his third Wimbledon.

"I can remember in 1963 when I was asked to give my Wimbledon tie back because I had turned professional," said Laver, whose membership in the All England Club was revoked then. "So, playing Wimbledon and beating Tony Roche in the final of the first Open was really exciting for me. I could walk around, hold my head up, and have my Wimbledon tie back on."

Now that Laver was legitimized—even though being an honest pro was always better than being a sham amateur accepting under-the-table payments—he aspired to achieve the first "open" Grand Slam in 1969. "I was determined to do it again to prove to myself that I could make it against all the best."

At the 1969 Australian Open, Roche, a husky lefty with a similar game, battled him in one-hundred-degree heat in what Laver called "the longest match I ever played—ninety games—and by far the hardest" in a sensational 7-5, 22-20, 9-11, 1-6, 6-3 semifinal that Laver somehow won. He then knocked off Gimeno in the final.

After overcoming a two-set deficit against 6'6" slugger Dick Crealy in a second-rounder at Roland Garros, Laver faced Rosewall for the title. "The only way for me to beat Muscles is to have a really super day," acknowledged Laver. And he did, winning 6-4, 6-3, 6-4. India's Premjit Lall took the opening two sets at Wimbledon before Laver recovered; then he topped stellar grass-courter John Newcombe in a tough and dramatic four-set final.

Three down and one to go. "Rocket" exploded throughout the summer, winning every match going into Forest Hills. There he started the final slowly but then crushed Roche 7-9, 6-1, 6-2, 6-2 for the U.S. crown and his unprecedented second career Grand Slam.

Laver would win no more major titles. But he gained stature even in defeat after his memorable 1972 WCT Finals final in Dallas against old nemesis Rosewall. The match proved a spectacular advertisement for tennis. When the climactic fifth-set tiebreaker arrived, after three hours of live national coverage, NBC had pre-empted three regularly scheduled programs and the tennis had spilled into "prime time." A record tennis audience of 23 million people watched spellbound as two terrific, exhausted athletes displayed superb skills in a thrilling finish that Rosewall won after trailing 5-3 in the tiebreaker.

After his glory days Laver played World Team Tennis from 1976 to 1978 (hilariously copping "Rookie of the Year" honors at thirty-eight), entertained clients at his Laver-Emerson Tennis Holidays, served as a goodwill ambassador for five years on the Nabisco Grand Prix, and did clinics at corporate outings at hotels and resorts.

More recently, while doing promotional work for Mercedes and taping an interview for ESPN, Laver suffered a life-threatening stroke just before his sixtieth birthday. He says he still doesn't have full use of his right side, but you'd never know it from his busy schedule of tennis, golf, and fishing trips. "I've been pretty fortunate. I've done well," he says about his splendid recovery.

Laver still enjoys talking tennis and remains as modest and judicious as ever on the burning issues. While noting that records are made to be broken, he says, "I don't see anyone on the horizon who's going to win the Grand Slam, even once."

Should Sampras be accorded "greatest ever" status? "To be recognized as the best ever, he probably should be proficient on all surfaces," asserts Laver. "He's won the Italian Championships, so at least he can play on clay. But the French [Open] is an important event. To be recognized as number one in history, then I'd say that's a very big part of the record."

Where does Laver rank himself in the pantheon of greats? "Pride of performance is what matters. You don't worry about your place in history, but you're very happy with your career," he says. "I don't want to be recognized as the best player in the world. I just feel like I played as hard as I could, and I enjoyed playing."

Laver has "no regrets at all" that his heyday came at the dawn of the Open Era before he could become fabulously rich and famous like Sampras and Andre Agassi. But he is confounded by Mats Wilander's recent statement that John McEnroe, Ivan Lendl, and Jimmy Connors "weren't the nicest people in the world, they were the most selfish players, but they were great for the game. Tennis needs players who don't care about pleasing the sponsors, who don't care about being nice."

That's close to blasphemy for Laver, who learned right and wrong from his father, Charlie Hollis, and Harry Hopman. "That's not the right attitude," he says. "Tennis doesn't have to be [like] a wrestling match. Maybe that's where Mats is getting his idea—being spectacular and angry and throwing people out of the ring or something.

"Tennis isn't that type of sport," Laver says. "Members of a club would like to see their sons and daughters grow up and enjoy the sport and not be thrown to the wolves, so to speak. You're trying to get some etiquette into the game of tennis for youngsters. But at the same time Mats is saying the top players have to be angry. Those are conflicting signals.

"Nowadays when players question line calls and they have to call in the referee, they're calling that personality," says Laver. "I don't see that as being right."

FASCINATING FACTS:

- After losing to Rod Laver in the 1969 U.S. Open quarterfinals, Roy Emerson, who then held the men's record (twelve) for Grand Slam singles titles, helped train Laver, who trailed him by only two career Slam titles, for his semifinal match.

- Rod Laver and fellow Queenslander Frank Gorman used to bet milk shakes or an (imaginary) date with Marilyn Monroe so they would try harder when they played practice sets.

9

Lindsay Davenport:
The Nice Girl
Who Finished First
2000

Like the comedian Rodney Dangerfield who quips, "I get no respect," low-profile Lindsay Davenport gets dissed, too. She's had post-match press conferences cancelled because no journalists were interested. Until recently, the fan demand was so minimal that no Web sites paid homage to her. Even the prestigious *Sports Illustrated* misspelled Davenport's first name.

In her new and controversial book, *The Hidden Side of Women's Tennis*, Nathalie Tauziat writes about an Anna Kournikova–Davenport match where Davenport was "lynched" by a booing crowd who loved seeing a "beast" fall victim to a "beauty." According to tour veteran Tauziat, the Women's Tennis Association did nothing to intervene. "For completely anti-sporting reasons, no one at the WTA even batted an eyelid."

The ultimate indignity came last year. Unrecognized despite being 6'2 1/2" and the world number one, Davenport had to argue with airline staff to be allowed to take her rackets on a flight to Australia. When Davenport asked a Qantas airline employee why her closest rival was able to board her flight with rackets in hand, the employee replied, "Well, Martina Hingis needs her rackets." Eventually Davenport and world number three Alex Corretja smuggled their rackets on board, but not before, Davenport recalled, "We got into the biggest fight with the lady. We almost got like a fine or something."

Such a ruckus is almost unheard of for the self-described "normal" and "laid-back" Californian. On the other hand, Davenport has never minded the lack of attention that has made her a relatively unknown champion at age twenty-four. "I'd rather be the player who on the Monday after the tournament is getting all

Lindsay Davenport. Hans-Jürgen Dittmann

the press for winning the tournament rather than, 'She threw a tirade in the first week, went here to dinner,' anything like that."

Davenport was obviously contrasting herself with the tennis "Spice Girls"—Martina, Venus, Serena, and Anna—who dominate headlines with their romances (especially with handsome pro hockey stars), eye-catching attire, trash talking, and on-court antics. But her remarks also referred to highly publicized controversies caused by bad dads, premature burnout, lesbian issues, and exploitative coaches that have turned "the women's tour into an ugly, smoking battlefield of abuse, greed, and venality," according to a veteran tennis journalist.

Unlike the narcissistic Kournikova—whom Pam Shriver once quipped "wears out the mirrors" in the Wimbledon locker room—Davenport harbors a somewhat low self-image. "The other night I saw myself on TV and ran out of the room. Some people love being a star. I'm not one of those people," she confided a couple of years ago.

She recently reiterated that point, saying, "I'm not a big fan of watching me play ever." That's surprising considering she's trim and fit (after dropping thirty pounds from a hefty two-hundred-pound physique that had some players calling her "Dump Truck" behind her back) and boasts the best strokes in the business.

But what a difference those past two years have made in Davenport's late-blossoming career. She whipped Hingis to grab her first Grand Slam singles title at the 1998 U.S. Open, and just four weeks later bumped the imperious Swiss Miss from the top spot, which she had owned for eighty straight weeks.

Davenport disposed of all-time great Steffi Graf in the 1999 Wimbledon final and then won her third Slam crown at the 2000 Australian Open where she again conquered archrival Hingis.

Like fellow Californian Pete Sampras, she shines in high-pressure, high-stakes Slam finals, winning all three, plus her 1996 Olympics final, in straight sets. The parallel with Sampras extends to their down-to-earth demeanors. "I just really let the tennis—kind of like Pete Sampras—do the talking," she says.

A 15-1 underdog at the 1999 Wimbledon, Davenport was typically self-deprecating about her chances, revealing, "I honestly went in thinking, 'Oh, I'm so bad on grass, it doesn't matter.' "

After upsetting seven-time champion Graf at Wimbledon, Davenport talked about her growing confidence. "I told my coach [Robert Van't Hof], 'I want to play Steffi.' In past years, I would've said, 'Oh, Lucic, please win [the semifinal]!' But I wanted to play Graf; you lose to a legend, and if you win, it's more special."

Davenport put an exclamation point on her terrific 1999 by capturing her first Chase Championships with yet another demolition (6-4, 6-2) of Hingis. The assured young woman talked about how far she had come since five years earlier, when she was "so freaked out" by the barrage of media criticism saying she was "too fat and too slow" that she didn't want to play.

Now, says Davenport, "I wake up every day and go: 'God, I can't believe what I've done.' For some people when they hear that, it shocks them. Other players say: 'Oh, I knew I was going to win all these titles.' The truth is: I think I'm very lucky for accomplishing everything I did. I never thought I'd be at this point, to have won any titles, let alone a major."

FASCINATING FACT:

- When a well-known U.S. journalist opined that "America's role as a dominant force in women's tennis may be over for good" and sarcastically added "the *last* great American hope, Lindsay Davenport, has fallen to number twelve (at the end of 1995)," an infuriated Davenport fired off a letter to the offending magazine, asserting she certainly wasn't over the hill.

Her increased success, self-confidence, and more attractive appearance improved her public image. But how marketable can a media-shy, reluctant star be? "As a company you want someone with a lot of pizzaz," Davenport concedes, "and I'm not that type of player."

Once again, Davenport's achievements have exceeded her expectations. While not quite yet in the same endorsement league as the mega-rich "Spice Girls," she has quietly capitalized on her tennis success and all-American girl persona. Davenport now boasts endorsement deals with five heavyweight companies—Nike, Nabisco, Wilson, Rolex, and American Express—and "some are multi-million contracts," according to her IMG client manager, Tony Godsick.

Her five-year Nike contract for an estimated $12 million is believed to be one of the largest endorsements ever for a female athlete, reports *Street & Smith's SportsBusiness Journal*. Nabisco, America's largest cookie and cracker maker, signed Davenport to a two-year deal, and its sports marketing campaign will feature her with four hugely popular athletes, Mia Hamm, Ken Griffey Jr., Derek Jeter, and Dan Marino. Davenport will appear on Newtons boxes. Heady stuff for a star athlete who shuns TV talk shows and admits, "I don't like doing a lot with the media, and I don't like doing things on my day off."

During her off weeks, Davenport lives with her mother (her parents divorced four years ago) and closest friend, Ann, in a four-bedroom house in Newport Beach and drives a Tahoe SUV, both of which reflect her quiet, unostentatious lifestyle. When not hanging out with her old high school friends—she actually did graduate—she's playing with her two Rottweilers and visiting her nephews and nieces.

And yes, Davenport does have a boyfriend. He's Californian Jon Leach, a former top U.S. junior player. As for her ideal man, she confides: "I want a man who is secure on his own. Not somebody who follows me all around the place when I play."

That certitude carries over into the tumultuous world of tennis politics. Davenport, who has been elected to the WTA Tour Players' Council for four consecutive years, minces no words on the burning issues, especially the raging battle for equal prize money at all the Grand Slam tournaments.

"I want to know why the women are not getting what they deserve," Davenport declares. "How can Wimbledon not make any gesture to [acknowledge] our progress? I would sit out the event to make the point."

Let's hope she doesn't, though. With Graf long retired and playing doubles with Andre Agassi off the courts, Davenport rates as the favorite to repeat on the fast Big W grass. Her booming serves (which former star Tracy Austin rates "the best in women's tennis"), returns of serve, and groundies should again overpower Hingis, whom she's beaten five of the last six times. These weapons are also likely to be too much for the athletic but inconsistent Williams sisters and all other contenders.

Just as Chris Evert's sporting demeanor disguised her tough-mindedness, Davenport, who received the Prix Orange award, given by the French media to the most cooperative player at the 2000 French Open, admits her good-girl image can be overstated.

"Oh, I can be a total bitch some of the time," she told the *Boston Globe*. "I'm serious. You can't get to the top just by being so nice. I get into fights with my friends about little things."

The only time Davenport could be accused of being a bitch occurred when she became embroiled in a nasty battle of words at the 1999 Australian Open.

Following her loss to Amelie Mauresmo, a known lesbian, Davenport noted Mauresmo's powerful shoulders and shot-making by innocently saying, "A couple of times I thought I was playing a guy." Martina Hingis then poured gasoline on the fire by insulting the muscular, nineteen-year-old Frenchwoman: "She travels with her girlfriend, she is half a man."

To her credit, Davenport tried to undo the damage. After blasting reporters for taking her words out of context—"You have probably hurt a very nice girl"—she wrote a personal, heartfelt note to Mauresmo, saying how sad she was. Mauresmo graciously accepted the apology.

Sane and sensible she may be, but those who question Davenport's heart and ambition, such as Virginia Wade, had better think again. The former Wimbledon champ said less than two years ago: "The killer instinct is not very strong in her." Responds coach Van't Hof: "Lindsay might not show it as much as the other players, but she's very driven."

"Lindsay's gained a lot of confidence from winning last year," continues Van't Hof. "And she began enjoying the whole Wimbledon experience more than ever after seeing how much it means to everybody else and how much tradition there is and going to the Wimbledon Champions' Dinner. She could rack up a lot more Wimbledon titles in coming years."

Any other predictions, coach? "Yeah, if you gave me a thousand dollars, I'd bet that Lindsay ends up this year ranked number one in both singles and doubles."

Whatever destiny has in mind for her, levelheaded Lindsay will enjoy the ride and avoid disastrous crashes. As she once philosophized, "People can bring you so high up and put you on a pedestal, and so quickly they can push you off. And you can't be caught up in that."

FASCINATING FACTS:

- On April 17, 2000, Lindsay Davenport became only the fourth player since computer rankings began in 1975 to simultaneously hold the world number-one ranking in both singles and doubles, joining Martina Navratilova, Arantxa Sanchez-Vicario, and Martina Hingis.
- Lindsay Davenport is one of the few pro players who writes thank-you notes to tournament directors.
- In 1999 Lindsay Davenport was asked by a journalist: "Have you ever felt cursed by being normal?"
- Lindsay Davenport ranked number seventy-two on the Forbes Celebrity 100 list in 2001.

10

Martina Navratilova: She Served and Volleyed Her Way through Life

2000

In a letter that Martina Navratilova has framed, legendary actress Katharine Hepburn writes: "What a terrifying but thrilling life you have."

How right she is. All the dramatic wins, the traumatic woes, the controversial love life, and the courageous stands make Navratilova the most famous and compelling sportswoman of her era, if not the entire century.

Navratilova likes to say, "I played the game the way it ought to be played." She played the game of life with the same glorious adventurousness and conviction. She defected from her homeland, she skied uninsured, and she fought outspokenly for what she believed was right.

Her brave defection at the 1975 U.S. Open created worldwide headlines and made Navratilova a heroine to the Czechs "because I stuck it to the [Communist] system." She had gained the exhilarating freedom "to just play the tour, whenever and wherever I want"—which she needed to do to become a champion.

More than fifty years earlier, another dynamic, larger-than-life figure defied social and sartorial conventions to fly through the air with balletic ease on the courts of Europe. The incomparable Suzanne Lenglen, the game's first female superstar, lost only one singles match from 1919 to 1926. But her flamboyance fascinated the sporting public as much as her brilliance.

"Suzanne was an actress," says Navratilova. "She didn't have to do all that [airborne volleying], but she liked it. She was inventive, daring, and a total pioneer. She loved theatrics. So Suzanne was a combination of all that—and a great athlete. I would have given anything to have watched her play."

Martina Navratilova.
Hans-Jürgen Dittmann

Navratilova says she also would have relished sharing a long dinner with Lenglen and learning firsthand about the celebrated Frenchwoman's life and times. "It was really so amazing then for women to be athletic. [But] obviously, she didn't think being a woman and an athlete was a problem," says the admiring Navratilova. "I'd pick her mind about why she was playing and what she got out of it. And then I'd tell her about myself, and we'd compare notes."

Oh, what stories both could tell! This imaginary conversation between legends would inevitably cover Lenglen's acrobatic jumping and her then-shocking tennis costumes, like the white fur-trimmed cape she wore over a sleeveless silk dress with a pleated skirt and the trademark brightly colored bandeau around her hair. Even more scandalous and risque were the interviews she gave the press while in a bathtub.

But beneath all of her Gallic charm and animation lurked a sadness. Lenglen would likely have confided in the disarmingly honest and equally vulnerable Navratilova about her suffering: how she became the first tennis queen who was a prodigy driven by a well-meaning but fanatical father.

Nothing short of perfection satisfied the astutely analytical Charles Lenglen, an unfulfilled cyclist who got his vicarious thrills by molding his daughter into greatness. If Suzanne practiced poorly, he punished her by denying her jam on her bread. A stern taskmaster, Papa Lenglen sometimes scornfully scolded Suzanne on the court in front of others. She became so drained emotionally and physically that she looked older than she actually was. When she turned professional in 1926, she told a friend, "At last, after fifteen years of torture, I can enjoy my tennis."

Navratilova's oppression was different in nature but likewise heartrending. "I had to escape a regime; she had to escape a father," Navratilova points out. "She could be compared to a Mary Pierce or a Jennifer Capriati or a Mirjana Lucic. In that historical regard, some things never change. I guess my situation was a little tougher. Lenglen didn't have to leave her father. I had to leave my father, my mother, my sister, my grandmother, and my country."

Navratilova's journey from a suffocating, grim Communist regime— where her travel to foreign tournaments was sharply restricted—to the space and freedom of the New World actually began as a fantasy. "From the time I was little, I thought of America as a magical place," she wrote in her 1985 autobiography, *Martina*. Her girlhood impressions of this distant Shangri-La, formed by American films starring Hepburn, Spencer Tracy, and Fred Astaire and the pop music of Hank Williams and Ray Charles, belied the negative Communist propaganda.

When Soviet tanks rumbled into Prague in 1968 to crush the escalating reform movement, Navratilova, then eleven, sensed how resigned and depressed her society had become. "I saw my country lose its verve, lose its productivity, lose its soul. For someone with a skill, a career, an aspiration, there was only one thing to do: get out."

Navratilova's sudden defection involved intrigue worthy of a Hollywood action movie. With the FBI and Immigration Service secreting her in freight elevators in spooky Manhattan buildings, she applied for asylum and aid out of a friend's Greenwich Village apartment.

Shy, insecure, and lonely, Navratilova, only eighteen, immediately overdosed on the American Dream. She gained twenty-five pounds from fast-food binges in her first month and raided boutiques in Beverly Hills like a kid in a candy store. Overweight and overwrought from the stress of the defection, she admitted, "In that distempered summer of 1976 I was sure the entire world was against me. I have never felt so alone."

Navratilova hit rock bottom after a shocking, first-round upset loss to Janet Newberry at the 1976 U.S. Open. Crying hysterically afterwards, she was building an unfavorable public image that would haunt her and take years to erase.

After moving to Dallas and living with pro golfer Sandra Haynie, whose calming influence helped Navratilova mature, she met and fell in love with radical feminist author Rita Mae Brown. The unrelenting media began to label Navratilova an "acknowledged bisexual." Her stepfather, disgusted with her lifestyle, raged: "I'd rather you slept with a different man every night than sleep with a woman." When she fled from Brown after a raging, physical argument, she nearly got hit by a ricocheting bullet discharged from a pistol Brown claimed she threw but didn't know was loaded.

Concerned about improving her image, she became leaner, put on makeup, dyed her hair blond, and wore more feminine clothes. Navratilova, who used to cry at age twelve because people mistook her for a boy, recalled, "I started liking the way I looked in the summer of 1981."

So, increasingly, did the sporting public. After her terribly disappointing U.S. Open final loss to Tracy Austin, fans applauded and cheered her for more than a minute, and the new Navratilova cried tears of appreciation and joy. "I had never felt anything like it in my life: acceptance, respect, maybe even love."

But pressures on Navratilova still were undermining the brilliance of her game, and her friend and archrival Chris Evert perceptively said: "Her tennis isn't going to straighten out until she straightens out her life."

Navratilova's practice of serial monogamy continued with former basketball star Nancy Lieberman, a gung-ho motivator-trainer who jump-started Navratilova's floundering career. Transsexual strategy coach Renee Richards and nutrition expert Robert Haas joined the growing support system that turned Navratilova into a muscular, superfit athlete. The "bionic woman," as the media labeled her, began steamrolling opponents and, between 1983 and 1984, won six straight Grand Slam singles titles.

After the abrasive Lieberman clashed with Richards, the soap-opera plot thickened when Lieberman split and former touring pro Mike Estep replaced Richards. In 1984 Navratilova started a seven-year relationship with Judy Nelson, a poised, statuesque Texan and former wife of a dentist. "Life with Judy Nelson seemed to promise Martina fulfillment, at last, of the American Dream," wrote Adrianne Blue in her biography, *Martina Unauthorized*. "For what is that dream but fame, fortune, and a blonde on your arm?"

But this was no dumb blonde. Nelson had induced Navratilova to sign a notorious, video-taped, non-marital cohabitation agreement. By 1991, their relationship was deteriorating, and Nelson discovered that the great love of her life was seriously involved with another woman. So she threw Navratilova out of their house, and the "woman scorned" sued for half of what Navratilova had earned during their years together. After the painful and costly divorce case was settled out of court, Navratilova said, "All I know is that if I had done what she [Nelson] did, I couldn't look myself in the mirror."

Fame became as much of a mixed blessing as fortune to Navratilova when the Irish Republican Army threatened to kidnap her. "I used to carry a gun with me on tour because of the IRA threat," she told Britain's *Daily Mail* during Wimbledon in 1991. "I have several guns at home, and I would certainly use one if somebody entered my bedroom."

Navratilova has overcome life's slings and arrows without bitterness and achieved a host of records that will likely never be surpassed. She considers her seventy-four-match singles winning streak, the longest in the Open Era, and her 167 singles and 165 doubles tournament titles her "most unbreakable records." But who will ever smash her other incredible records, such as nine Wimbledon singles titles, thirty-one Grand Slam women's doubles titles, 109 consecutive doubles matches won (with Pam Shriver) and a perfect 28-0 combined singles-doubles Fed Cup record?

When Steffi Graf, who amassed more career Grand Slam singles crowns (twenty-two) than Navratilova, retired last August, she was asked who is the greatest player ever. Graf replied: "For me, she [Navratilova] is the uncontested number one; she has left a mark on the sport like no one else."

Navratilova won't be pinned down about who "the greatest ever" was, but she is typically opinionated about the question. "When I first started playing tennis, I wanted to be number one. Then I wanted to be the greatest of all time," she recalls. "And the closer I got to being called that, the more I realized that's bullshit because you can't compare [different] generations. And you can't compare Suzanne Lenglen to me. Because if I had been born then and played then, I would have been a different player.

"But you can take people from their generation and see how much they dominated it," explains Navratilova, who was named Female Athlete of the Decade for the 1980s by both the Associated Press and United Press International. "And perhaps you can say Lenglen was on a par with me. And I'm on a par with Steffi Graf."

Who makes Navratilova's all-time top five then? "I'm not going to give you the order because that's impossible. Without the [1993] stabbing, Monica Seles would definitely be up there," she says. "But Monica doesn't have the numbers, unfortunately. She had the talent for it, but it was taken away. That being said, I have to say Steffi, Billie Jean [King], Margaret Court, Chris Evert, and Suzanne Lenglen." And it goes without (her) saying it, Navratilova, too.

But the great ones are more than numbers and stats; they transform their sports. "I think I brought a new dimension to the game, and I'm most proud of that," says Navratilova, the most devastating and exciting serve-and-volleyer in history. "By that I mean the overall athleticism and professionalism and really picking every possible angle to make myself a better tennis player. Not just with nutrition and physical fitness, but also with coaching and tactics. I really didn't leave any stones unturned—once I got into it."

Navratilova likes to remind people that although she retired from the pro circuit in 1994, she is neither retired nor the retiring type. *Au contraire,* she's still firing on all cylinders. She has co-written (with Liz Nickles) three mystery novels and pens columns for *Conde Nast Sports for Women,* competes on the Legends Tour, captained the U.S. Fed Cup team in 1997, and does tennis commentary for HBO. Last November, ever-adventurous Navratilova secured her pilot's license.

FASCINATING FACTS:

- Conditioning coach and master motivator Nancy Lieberman fired up Martina Navratilova for the 1988 U.S. Open by putting clippings of quotes about Martina's being over the hill and ready for retirement on her bathroom mirror.
- Martina Navratilova had no corporate endorsements in 1992 other than for tennis rackets, shoes, and clothing.

Back home, Navratilova loves "being outside" in Aspen, Colorado, which she calls "a giant playground." She has learned to snowboard well and skis and plays golf and basketball. And here's a surprise: she's spent time in the shop learning basic carpentry and has built a couple of tables and boxes.

Navratilova's love of wild animals and the environment has taken her to Africa for several safaris. "People think of Africa as jungle, but it's wide open plains as big and beautiful as anything you've ever seen, and there are more stars than you ever thought existed," she enthuses. "Animals are roaming like they have for millions of years. So it's magical. The best part is that you can take the same drive every day, and every day you'll see something new."

Navratilova says she's also become "a better person, better friend, better family member. Tennis is a very selfish sport. To do it very well, you have to exclude everything else. And so it went with my family and friends. And I've been able to make up some of that in giving of myself to them, instead of just the other way around." Linked with London-based artist Danda Jaroljmek since the mid-1990s, Navratilova refuses to comment on any "significant other" in her life now.

At the end of her autobiography, Navratilova wrote: "I didn't know how I was going to make the world better, but I knew I was going to try." Retirement has enabled Navratilova to focus on various causes she's championed ever since she established the Martina Youth Foundation in 1983 to provide deserving but economically disadvantaged children with greater opportunities, new experiences, and inspirational contact with a champion.

Navratilova cares deeply about women's and animal rights and environmental issues and has been a member of the Sierra Club and PETA for many years and has given money to Greenpeace. She and actress Doris Day did ads denouncing steel-jaw animal traps. She's also served on Planned Parenthood's board of directors. "I've done all kinds of things for them. That's huge," she says. "Obviously, I wouldn't get pregnant by accident. But the whole issue is very, very dear to me and important for women worldwide."

As the world's most famous gay athlete, Navratilova has made the most impact on this front ever since she gave a moving speech before five hundred thousand people at the 1993 Gay and Lesbian March in Washington, D.C. "That was one of the most amazing experiences I've ever had," remembers Navratilova. "Hundreds of thousands of people were there, and they all *wanted* me to be there, which was a new experience for me—to be universally accepted by an audience. We've kept up with that cause by starting the Visa Rainbow Card which has raised seven hundred thousand dollars for gay and lesbian organizations."

Navratilova believes her biggest contribution to creating a better world has been as a role model. "Through me playing and being myself, more girls wanted to play the sport and thought it was okay to be athletes," she says. "And I've gotten numerous letters from people who said, 'You've saved my life because I was about to commit suicide. Then I realized you [as a successful homosexual] were there, and I'm not the only lesbian in the world.'

"Speaking my mind and speaking the truth and not altering my truth to accommodate others and not offend them is another contribution I've made," asserts Navratilova, a vocal opponent of Colorado's Amendment 2, which prohibits special rights for homosexuals. "If someone's offended because I'm gay, that's their problem, not mine.

"I don't want to be written up as a lesbian tennis player," she says. "In a better world where everyone tolerated everyone else, it wouldn't be an issue. I'm a woman. I'm an American. I'm a tennis player. And I'm a good person. Those are the essentials.

"They don't write about other people and say they are a heterosexual," argues Navratilova. "We have to make it an issue now in order for it not to be an issue later. That's what all revolutions are about."

FASCINATING FACTS:

- At the 1977 Wimbledon championships Martina Navratilova denied requests by photographers that she cover up her muscles.
- In 1993 Martina Navratilova said she regretted that "I will die not knowing everything I want to know."
- In 2001 Martina Navratilova, noting that only three years ago she appeared in her first major TV commercial, for Suburu vehicles, said, "Suburu was a big breakthrough for the gay community. I don't think being gay is going to stand in the way any more for athletes."

This story received 1st Prize in the United States Tennis Writers Association 2000 Writing Contest in the Feature category.

PART 2

Memorable Interviews

11

Pete Sampras: Pete Sampras Speaks from the Heart

2000

To be great is to be misunderstood," observed Ralph Waldo Emerson. Will Pete Sampras, a man of great simplicity and simple greatness, not receive his just historical due because he lacks charisma?

Will his spectacular career somehow suffer from a paradox: he was so dominating that he played few close and memorable finals and too seldom enjoyed a true rivalry?

Has he ruled tennis in an image-is-everything era where his classic virtues no longer found the appreciative following of yesteryear?

Sampras, now twenty-eight, has never been fully understood, and he knows it. "Enjoy what you see now, because I won't be around forever," he reminds people.

In this interview, Sampras speaks about his roots, his relationships, his reign, his records, and his rivals with the same honesty, intelligence, and passion that animate his championship performances.

Last June you said, "Taking the early part of the year off, I had time to reflect. I thought about [Michael] Jordan, [Wayne] Gretzky, and [John] Elway retiring after great careers, really helping their games get more popular. And I realized I want to do that." How do you plan to help tennis get more popular?

Playing Davis Cup will help. With the team that we've put together this year, that can only help the game in the U.S. People will follow it. I definitely want to be a part of Davis Cup more, obviously this year and for years to come. It's hard in an individual sport to carry the load and do everything. You can't be winning Slams and also be a spokesman for everything to do with tennis. But Davis Cup is a way to not only help myself and get motivated for some different situations but also to help make the game more popular in this country. I've also been appearing on some late-night TV shows. That helps people see me in a different light. I think seeing me in something other than tennis clothes is appealing to some people.

When you got sick and vomited in your memorable 1996 U.S. Open match against Alex Corretja, John McEnroe called you "a tremendous actor." After your hip-flexor injury in the 2000 Australian Open semis, U.S. Davis captain McEnroe insinuated you really weren't that injured and added, "I don't think Pete really wanted to make the trip [to play Zimbabwe] in the first place." What are your reactions to McEnroe's comments?

I'll talk about the more recent ones. To put it mildly, I was disappointed. I was a bit hurt that he questioned my integrity publicly. Obviously, he was panicking a little because of the [weakened] team he had [for the tie in Zimbabwe].

Frankly, I thought McEnroe's impugning your motives and integrity was outrageous.

It was. It was outrageous. And that's why I questioned whether I wanted to be part of the team this year. I rearranged my schedule to play Davis Cup, and here we are two months into it, and all of a sudden, we're not communicating. And that's not good. So I was hurt by it. But we finally spoke [to each other], and I'm happy to say I'm going to play. But there were times during that Davis Cup week that I really questioned if I wanted to do it.

You, in good faith, had made out your 2000 schedule for four potential Davis Cup weeks. What more commitment can a person ask for?

I agree. John has been known to say things off the cuff. I wasn't going to let the situation get out of hand. I wanted to talk about it and not let him question me like that.

Would you please tell me all about your new Pete Sampras Classic celebrity golf tournament in March and what inspired it.

We try to do something every year to help out the Tim & Tom Gullikson Foundation. Tim was a big golf fan, and I couldn't think of a better way to raise money for the foundation than to have a golf tournament. Now that I'm living back in L.A., we put it all together in a couple months. And we got a number of celebrities, such as Matt Damon, Andy Garcia, Wayne Gretzky, Evander Holyfield, Dennis Hopper, and Dennis Miller. We had a good turnout so it was fun. (The tournament raised ninety thousand dollars for the foundation, which funds support and care programs for brain-tumor patients and their families.)

Pete Sampras. Hans-Jürgen Dittmann

Andre Agassi said that what may ultimately end your domination is not age or injuries but the soft and easy Los Angeles lifestyle. Is he right?

(Laughter.) I kind of laugh about that, to be honest with you. No, because I know what it takes to do well, to practice and train to stay where I want to stay. I won't let anything get in the way of that. I live a very conservative life. Just because you live in L.A., everyone thinks you're going to go out and party. That's just not my personality and never will be. But, no, it won't make me soft by any means.

Five years ago some people wanted you to become more flamboyant like Agassi. But, instead, Agassi has become less flamboyant and more single-minded like you. Would you please comment on this interesting evolution.

Andre was more flamboyant in his earlier years. Now he's more into his tennis. Tennis has become more the priority. And he's definitely playing a lot better. Ever since he returned after the burnout [period of 1996 and 1997], he's playing at a level that will keep him at the top of the game for many, many years. It's been a transformation for him. He's seen the way I do it, my focus. He's always strived to have that. But before, it wasn't always the case.

Tennis magazine ranked you the tenth-most influential person in tennis, and wrote: "Sampras brought a classical style and temperament back to tennis." What are your reactions to your power rating and what Tennis wrote about you?

Those [ranking] things are purely opinion. It's flattering, but if I was five or ten or fifteen, it really doesn't do much for me. What they wrote is very telling, though. It's a great statement. There were years when the players who dominated the game were more emotional, to put it mildly. To say that I brought the classic temperament back may be a slight exaggeration. You've had the Borgs and the Edbergs. But, as far as being an American and being like that, it was probably very refreshing to see—for the media and possibly the fans.

You've noted that the biggest compliment you can ever get is for a parent to come up to you and say: " 'The way you are on the court is good for my kids. You're a great example.' " How important is being a great example or role model to you?

It's very important. As an older athlete—I'm not twenty-one anymore—I'm a little more aware of life. I'm aware of what I say and do on the court. How I act out there is going to influence kids. When a parent comes up to me and says you're a great example or a great role model and you're affecting others' lives in a positive way, it makes me feel great. And they've done that over the years. Fans say that to me all the time in addition to saying they like watching me play. Many times they see athletes who don't come across in the best of ways. So I've always found that a very big compliment.

Your career 31-8 record in five-set matches speaks for itself. But Agassi said: "I feel like I am stronger and fitter than I've ever been ... and this allows me the luxury of taking a three-out-of-five-set match and turning it into a sprint." Are you as fit as you have to be to stay ahead of Andre in your rivalry?

We are all fit [on the tour]. I feel I can go the distance against anybody if need be. In order to stay on top of this game, you need to be fit. Andre and I play close all the time. He's going to win his fair share, and I'm going to win mine. If it goes five sets, I'm fit and ready.

Of all your records, which ones are you most proud of?

Winning twelve Slams and being number one six years in a row. They go hand in hand. It's hard to understand how hard it was to be number one for six straight years unless you went through what I went through. That [record] may mean more to me than anything. Obviously, if you win Slams, you'll get a high ranking. But I was consistent throughout the years to stay at number one.

When you clinched your sixth straight number-one ranking in late 1998, the pressure had mounted so much that you suffered from exhaustion and lost hair.

Oh, yeah!

The record that impresses and amazes me the most is your 12-2 record in Grand Slam finals. And going further, the degree of your domination in those finals, losing a total of only five sets! How in the world have you done that?

(Laughter.) I can't explain it. When it comes to the big matches and big moments, I've seemed to shine over the years. Maybe it's experience, maybe it's confidence, or maybe it's both. Obviously, if you're in the final of a major [tournament], you're playing well and you're confident. And winning majors is what we play for. I guess playing well in those finals is a testament to handling the pressure. No matter how nervous you are going into a Grand Slam final, the guy you're playing is just as nervous and has just as big a fear of losing as I do. It's a one-on-one sport, and I've always prided myself on being able to handle the situation better than my opponent.

You confided that during the early 1990s your father doubted whether you had what it takes to become a champion. You clearly proved him wrong.

The reason he and a lot of people thought that was that here was this very good athlete with good hands and eyes who had the talent but ... in my junior years and when I turned pro, my mental state and my heart were in question. I wasn't even sure how much I wanted to be number one. I had the kind of personality that would have been happy ranked number five in the world and have an easier life. Just one loss changed my career and my whole outlook on the game. And that was that '92 U.S. Open final defeat to [Stefan] Edberg. That changed my career mentally.

On the best way for you to win the French Open, Roy Emerson, whose record of twelve Grand Slam titles you share, advised: "Pete is too good a player not to win the French. I think he just has to settle in Europe for the clay season, play 'em all." Does Emmo have a point about your simply getting more match-tough and proficient on European clay?

I've tried that. I've had schedules over the years playing Monte Carlo, Barcelona, Rome—the whole thing. And [as a result] I've gone to the French a little flat. And I've also tried not playing many clay tournaments. I've tried all the different possibilities. The year I did my best [reaching the semis in 1996] was the year I didn't play [clay] at all. But I was running on the emotion of losing Tim [Gullikson, his coach and close friend]. I've gotten different advice from different people. I've tried everything. This year I'll play a high level of tournaments going into the French. But I don't think I need to play on clay for two months to play well at the French. A lot of guys who play that much are tired by the time they get there. The best way is a combination of being fresh but also being in good match-shape from playing enough matches.

Strategically, Patrick McEnroe suggested you serve and volley more on clay. What about that?

I tried coming in a lot last year, probably too much, chipping and charging and serving and volleying on both serves. One area that I can explore is taking a little off my first serve and getting it in and using my volley. Instead of serving 125 [mph], I can serve 110 and get it in the court [more often]. I may experiment with that in the coming tournaments.

You said: "I don't look at myself as a historical icon, but the reality is, yeah, I am playing for history now." By that, do you mean that you want to be remembered as the greatest player in tennis history?

Well, I don't need it for my ego. I don't need it to feel good about myself. But ... it's something I'll never say. It's up to the people who follow tennis. It's so tough to compare this year to thirty years ago when Rod Laver won the Grand Slam. But I feel like I've got an opportunity over the next few years to break a few records. And results will always answer the critics about who is the best ever. It's not really for me to tell you that I am or am not. It's not important to hear [that] every day of my life. I want to be the best player I can be. If I can do that, that's good enough for me.

But would you like that reputation, that accolade?

Absolutely!

Do you believe your overall record now justifies "the greatest player in history" label? Or do you need more achievements on your résumé?

The tennis historians and the perfectionists won't consider me the best ever until I win the French Open. But I really think that's unfair. Not to take anything away from Laver or [1938 Grand Slammer Don] Budge, but the competition then wasn't what it is today, especially on clay. You can't compare thirty or sixty years ago with today. But I'm sure people will always say "Until Pete wins the French, I can't consider him the best ever."

I disagree with that opinion. I can conceive of scenarios where you win more Grand Slam titles and deserve "greatest ever" status without winning Roland Garros.

I know. But they're out there. Trust me. The old Aussies will always say Laver is the best ever. Laver worried about four clay court players [at the French]. I have to worry about fifty. It's just a different ball game now. That's why it's hard to compare the game today with thirty years ago. I seem to want to compare my tennis to [Bjorn] Borg-and-after kind of tennis. With the wood rackets thirty years ago, it's too hard to tell.

You have asserted that two of the most important criteria for measuring greatness are the total number of Grand Slam titles and the number of years ranked number one. You have a chance to break your and Emerson's twelve Slam titles this year, and you have already broken Connors's record of five straight years at number one. What other accomplishments and records are you now aiming for?

The Grand Slam record is the biggest priority of my tennis right now. And obviously the French Open. After those two, there is not much left in the game to do.

Talking about the paradox of fame, Patrick Rafter said: "When you haven't got it, you really want it; when you have it, you really don't want it." Do you agree with Patrick?

It's not quite so black and white. Fame has its benefits and its drawbacks. Your private life isn't quite as private, and you get recognized a lot. But it's part of what we do. We're making a lot of money, we're traveling around the world, and we're playing a great sport. We shouldn't be complaining about anything. Being famous takes its toll, but the older you get, the more you accept it. People are just trying to be nice and have some sort of connection with you. I wouldn't have said that when I was twenty. I was too naive to be aware of that then. Now I'm twenty-eight and appreciate the people more and appreciate what they say about me. So it's been good.

While watching the players at the 1996 French Open, French casting director Anita Benoist said: "I'd prefer to work with Pete Sampras, who makes me think of Antonio Banderas." Have you considered a movie career in Hollywood after tennis?

No. No movie career.

What do you think of the ATP's new "Mandatory 13–Best 5" ranking system and the ATP Champions (Points) Race?

The Points Race is a race, it's not a ranking. So far, it's been a little confusing. You have so many different number-one players. Now everybody starts at zero at the beginning of the year. You really can't consider this a ranking by any means. The new system is also confusing because you have the seeds [at tournaments] and the ATP rankings and the Points Race. You're never going to have a perfect system. A lot depends on what the media think of it because that's ultimately what gets out to the fans. If it's a confusing system, the fans are going to lose interest. I don't know if it's any better [than the old "Best 14" ranking system] now. Maybe you can tell me that.

The big problem is that the new system still counts only eighteen tournaments, which means roughly 25 percent of the tournaments everyone plays in good faith don't count. For example, you and Agassi have been victimized tremendously over the years by the "Best 14," and the new system is only slightly better in this key respect.

There are pros and cons to this system. This year I'm not planning on playing all the nine required [Tennis Masters Series] tournaments. So that's going to hurt my chances of being number one. I'm at a different stage of my career than I was five or six years ago. I'm not necessarily playing for a ranking. It would be nice to be number one, but I'm trying to give myself the best schedule and the best chance to do well at the majors. If you do well there, you're going to get a high ranking no matter how many tournaments you play.

You're twenty-eight and Agassi and Todd Martin are twenty-nine. The U.S. has no men players under age twenty-five ranked in the top fifty. It may be too soon to panic, but why aren't we producing any top-notch young male players? And do you have any recommendations?

It's definitely a concern for American tennis. Once the top group we have today—myself, Agassi, Martin, Chang, Courier—stop, it looks thin here. With the American mentality and the media, if you're not ranked one or two, you're just not good enough. I don't know what's going to happen. I haven't seen the young guys like [Andy] Roddick and [Levar] Harper-Griffith. So, if you look at Australia and the countries in Europe and South America, they're going to be dominating the game in five, six years. I don't have the answers. It goes in cycles. Maybe in fifteen, twenty years we'll have four young Americans who'll achieve what we just did.

There are only six serve-volleyers (Sampras, Rafter, Krajicek, Rusedski, Henman, Ivanisevic) now in the top fifty, and their average age is twenty-seven. How concerned are you about this trend? Isn't tennis more interesting and exciting with a diversity of playing styles?

It *is* more interesting when you have contrasts in games—the baseliners and the serve-and-volleyers. That's why Andre and I are a great matchup. That being said, the game has changed in the last ten years. Guys are staying back. The young Europeans and South Americans grow up on clay. They're not going to be serve-volleyers. It's a sign of the times. You don't have a lot of diversity today. The serve-and-volley playing style is pretty much gone.

But you've proven that you can have a big forehand with an Eastern grip and stroke. And you've proven that serving and volleying still wins.

Yeah, I appreciate that. But it's not an easy game to teach. It's not an easy game to play. It's a lot easier for a kid to be a baseliner—like it was for me before I changed to a one-handed backhand [at age fourteen] and changed my whole approach. It's much easier to stay back and grind it out. It's a lot simpler game to develop at a young age. The [court] surfaces where you come from have a lot to do with it.

Could we end up with two baseliners in the 2005 Wimbledon men's final?

Sure. It could very well happen.

How close are you to your parents and your brother, Gus, and sisters, Stella and Marion? And what role have they played in your personal and career development?

I'm very close to my family and siblings. Now that I'm living in L.A. and having all this time off because of these injuries, I connect with them and spend more time with them. They definitely gave me my foundation on and off the court. I've always been close to my siblings. What life is all about is being with your family. They have always been very supportive through the good times and the bad. They obviously support my tennis and want me to do well, but they know the big picture—that I'm not going to play this game until I'm eighty. I'll stop whenever I stop, and I'll have the rest of my life to look at other things. So they've kept me very grounded through this whole [1990s] decade.

What can you tell readers about Gus, Stella, and Marion because they are rarely written about?

They're like me. They're very shy. They're solid, good people. They're honest. They're the type of people that you'd want to bring home to your parents if you're going to marry one of them.

The late Bobby Riggs once said: "In my book a tennis player is a complete athlete. He has to have the speed of a sprinter, the endurance of a marathon runner, the agility of a boxer or fencer, and the gray matter of a good football quarterback." Is Bobby right? And if so, do pro tennis players get the respect they deserve?

Bobby is right. Tennis players don't get the respect like the NBA when they talk about the great athletes. In tennis, you need everything. You need durability, the hand-eye coordination, and the mental endurance because it's a one-on-one sport. There's no help from your coach or manager or anyone out there. Tennis players are tremendous athletes, some of the best in the world. You need every aspect of being an athlete that you can find. In some ways it's even more difficult to play [pro] tennis than to play in the NBA. There are no substitutions, no halftimes to recover. You definitely see someone's true character on the tennis court. So tennis does get overlooked.

A few years ago I read in a questionnaire that you said you were afraid of dogs. That obviously has changed because you have a pet Labrador named Samantha. What do you like most about Samantha?

(Laughter.) I don't have a dog. I don't know where that came from.

But are you afraid of dogs?

I had a bad experience with dogs when I stayed at [Ivan] Lendl's place when I was sixteen. I've never been a big fan of dogs. But I came back from a bike trip, and I walked into Lendl's place, and his five German shepherds were barking at me. I was in this area where they couldn't come near me. I've been a little petrified of dogs ever since then.

Tennis magazine rated Jeff Schwartz, the president of AMG Sports, as the fifteenth most influential person in tennis and wrote: "Pete Sampras is not only his best buddy, but he's also a client." Please tell me about your friendship with Jeff—and how he has helped you.

Oh, Jeff has been a good friend, one of my best friends. He's managed me for the last five years. It's a great relationship. He gives me good advice as far as my schedule and what to do. He's always been there off the court when I've gone through tough times and tough losses, and he's helped me through some personal things. He's been unbelievably supportive of my career. When you're at the level I'm at, it [what matters] is working with someone that you trust, that you like, and that you respect. It sure is nice making money, but you have to enjoy what you do and enjoy the people you work with.

Paul Annacone has coached you for the past five years, but he is extremely low-profile compared with some other coaches. What role has he played in your great success?

Well, he's low-profile because that's the way he is and that's the way I am. He's been overlooked in so many ways in what he's done for my tennis. Think about how we started working together. Here I am with Tim [Gullikson], and Tim gets diagnosed with brain tumors. I asked Paul to help me out. He was sensitive enough in the whole situation so that he basically started working and traveling with me. It's not easy for someone to handle that, if you think about it. We're not talking about tennis. We're talking about *life*. He was great through the whole experience. When Tim passed away, I asked Paul if he would continue to do it. Then he started to take more of a role. And through the years I've won majors and been number one. He's been very overlooked over the years. It's [because of] his personality. There aren't too many people bright enough to figure that out.

I believe your touring entourage also includes stringer Nate Ferguson, physical trainer Brett "The Moose" Stevens, and masseuse Walt Landers? Is that correct? Have I left anyone out?

You got it right.

What are your favorite sports teams, and who are your favorite players on them?

I'm a big Lakers fan. I'm a big fan of Kobe. He's going to be great. I'm a big fan of Shaq. And I'm a big fan of the coach [Phil Jackson] who has put it all together. Those three guys are the reason the Lakers are leading the league.

Your brother Gus said, "Pete will watch ESPN Sportscenter three times in a row even though he knows what's coming next." Given that you're a sports lover, who are your favorite athletes?

(Hearty laughter.) That's funny. I've enjoyed guys who are great at their sports, and when you listen to them and know a little about them, you wouldn't know that they're the best at their sports. They are very humble. They are great at what they do and committed to what they're doing and don't have a certain arrogance or cockiness about them. Their greatness is something left unsaid. You look at Jordan, [Wayne] Gretzky, [Joe] Montana. Those athletes are my role models—just for the way they carry themselves and act as people. Gretzky has nine MVPs, and he's the most modest of all.

You said that Michael Jordan "is the one person I would like to get some advice from." Specifically, what advice would you seek from him?

I'd ask him how his body has changed as he's gotten older and how he's maintained his fitness and conditioning for so many years. Another question I'd ask him is about motivation. I just felt for years I was playing against the same rivals—Agassi, Becker, Edberg. And now there is a new crop of players, and you need to find something deep down to get the same motivation to play against them. I was wondering how he got himself motivated after years of playing against Bird and Johnson, and now he's got these young rookies coming up.

What advice would you give to kids who want to be tennis champions?

As a kid growing up, I was more concerned about playing well than winning. I wanted to improve. Kids today are too consumed with just winning junior tournaments. As a junior I wasn't very good, but I was improving and playing guys who were much older than I was. That's the way my coach and family and I approached it. It obviously worked.

ESPN commentator Cliff Drysdale believes that what's best for TV is what's best for tennis. So he proposes reforms such as abolishing best-of-five-set matches, using no-ad scoring, allowing on-court coaching, and adopting round-robin formats to qualify for the semifinals. Do you see any merit in any of these proposed reforms?

No. People overreact when they hear negative things about the game. They claim we need to change the scoring system or change from three-out-of-five sets to two-out-of-three sets, or whatever. Great matches are what sell the sport. An exciting rivalry is the answer to everything. Andre and I had a rivalry a few years ago, and then I didn't hear any talk about changing the scoring system or any of this stuff I've been hearing. It's the players, it's the sport, it's the matches that matter. All this talk I hear about these changes is just a bunch of crap.

With your sports knowledge, integrity, courage of your convictions, and diplomacy, you would make a top-notch tennis politician. Have you considered contributing in that area, the way many past champions have?

At this stage, while I'm still playing, no. I just don't have the time or the interest at the moment.

The middle generation of top players—such as Moya, Kuerten, Kafelnikov, Rafter, Philippoussis, and Rios—while very talented, seem more like occasional Slam winners rather than champions. Who, among the younger generation—such as Hewitt, Haas, Federer, Ferrero, and Vinciguerra—impresses you the most as a potential champion? And why?

All those guys you mentioned have something about them that makes them capable of winning a Grand Slam. But I don't know if anyone has the whole package to win Slams year after year. That's very hard to do. [Mark] Philippoussis has the biggest game of anyone. That might win the U.S. Open or Wimbledon one year. But to do it year after year, it has to be an obsession, a passion. At times he's had that, but he doesn't have it enough. Someone like [Lleyton] Hewitt has the mental and the physical games to do well at majors. But to do it year after year, it takes a big game. To dominate, you need a game like Philippoussis.

So if Philippoussis had Hewitt's mentality, we'd have a champion.

Then you'd have me!

Since former number one Stefan Edberg called you the most complete player he's ever seen or played against, do you think you've changed tennis?

In some ways I feel I have a game that has some options that can do different things. I'm not just one-dimensional. Most guys you see are one-dimensional, if you look at the history of the game. I've always tried to be as complete as I can be. So, in that way, maybe I have changed the game. But I'll never sit here and tell you I've changed the game. It's up to the critics to make that determination.

Last year you said, "Enjoy what you see now, because I won't be around forever." Why did you say that?

There have been years when I've won major titles and been number one, and in some ways, it was expected, and maybe taken for granted. It seemed like the only time I made news was when I lost. And maybe I was frustrated for being penalized for not having the [great] rivalry for my legacy, and [thus] not being everything to everybody. So I was saying that once I'm gone, I'm gone. And you might not see a player dominating for years and years like me again. I felt appreciated in some circles. But also in some circles I wasn't appreciated.

In 1998, in recognition of your tennis achievements, you became only the tenth sportsman to receive the MARCA Legend Award, which is presented by MARCA, the best-selling publication in Spain. You have often said you are more appreciated around the world than in the U.S. Which countries appreciate you the most? And how do you explain this phenomenon?

All the countries in Europe. I've felt, especially during the final six weeks of 1998 while I was there, an appreciation from the people when I walked on the court from the response they gave me. It's an American trait to root for the underdog. I've been the favorite pretty much every match I've played for the past few years. I'm not saying people are rooting against me. They're just rooting to see a good match. But I've felt an appreciation in Europe that I haven't really had quite the same in the States. I also feel very much appreciated in Australia and Japan.

The women's tour is loaded with personalities now, but Todd Martin, the president of the ATP Tour Player Council, blames his fellow players, saying: "I don't always feel like players are very approachable, but they sure know how to complain. The problem is, a lot of our guys don't feel pressure to do the sport justice. They feel they've gotten their take." Do you agree with Todd?

Not entirely. There are a couple guys who aren't appreciative and bitch and moan more than they should. What has hurt the men's game is that there are *too many* good players. What sells sports today? I don't think it's personalities. It's more matchups—Davenport playing Hingis, Venus playing Hingis, Serena playing Davenport. It's the rivalries, the consistent rivalries. In the men's game there are so many good players that there are a lot of different winners. There's not much of a men's rivalry other than Andre and myself— whenever we play, which might not be for another five months.

What's the solution then?

Instead of the media taking the easy way out and saying the ladies game is more popular, they should put their brains together and note why this is happening. It's because the men's game today is as strong as it has ever been. It's gotten stronger in the past five years. When the men's game was very popular, Borg, McEnroe, Lendl, and Connors were much better than everyone else. Tim [Gullikson] told me that when he was ranked fifteen in the world, he had no chance of beating those guys. You had the rivalries then, the consistent matchups. And that's what fans and the media cling to. Now you have lots of different guys in finals. This is no disrespect to Corretja and Enqvist. But when they played in the Indian Wells final, they're not going to generate the interest in this country like Andre and I would, or any top rivalry.

Did you know that your semifinal with Andre at the Australian Open broke the all-time record for TV sports ratings in Australia?

Yeah, I believe it. That's because of the rivalry. It's because of who is playing. Our personalities, sure, are different, but it's the sport that will sell. True, the ladies got Kournikova, Venus, Serena, Hingis and whoever else, but it's the consistent rivalries they have. We don't have that. A lot of great players win different titles. And if I'm not playing Andre, people don't seem to be interested.

You've said your Porsche is your most prized possession. What do you like most about it?

The sheer power.

So you're a power player and a power driver?

You got it!

FASCINATING FACTS:

- The subject of Pete Sampras's 1994 how-to article in *Men's Health* magazine was how to successfully swat and kill flies.

- Pete Sampras once said his favorite television program was CNN's *Crossfire* because "I get a kick seeing grown men acting like little kids."

- Pete Sampras won the longest-drive contest at the 1997 Isuzu Celebrity Golf Tournament with a drive of 332 yards.

- Dr. Pete Fischer, Pete Sampras's coach from age nine to eighteen, taught him that the only three acceptable statements on the court were "In, out, and a score."

- Pete Sampras decided he'd like to meet actress Bridgette Wilson, his future wife, when he saw her in the movie *Love Stinks*.

12

John McEnroe: Mac the Mouth Roars on What's Wrong with Tennis
1997

There is no great genius without a mixture of madness.

—ARISTOTLE

In his Superbrat days, he lashed out at umpires, linespeople, opponents, fans, and entire nations. Now, as an outspoken TV tennis commentator (when he's not making music, running his art gallery, and caring for his five children), he Mac Attacks the ATP Tour for damaging the sport he cares deeply about. In this penetrating interview, John McEnroe prescribes thought-provoking remedies for tennis, compares his charismatic contemporaries with today's "robotic" stars, and reveals how fatherhood put him in touch with humanity.

You've said: "The trouble with tennis today is that there's too much money and too many nice guys." Would you please expand on that.

The obscenity of the staggering amounts of prize money has gotten so revolting that I don't think people want to view the top players as personalities. It's hard to relate to them. I got thirty-nine thousand dollars when I won the U.S. Open. Now the winner gets six hundred thousand dollars. We should take 10 percent from the prize money and give it to charity. When I played Davis Cup for the first time [in 1978], we got one thousand dollars. Now these guys get twenty-five thousand dollars per match plus bonuses for winning, and guys *still* don't play for their country. And doesn't it make you sick that Becker and Stich get paid nearly $2 million to play Davis Cup for Germany for one year? And that was after they told the German tennis federation to "kiss off" for a couple of years. You know, the money in Germany has

83

changed the sport. It's not healthy. The Germans insulted the intelligence of tennis fans. I wouldn't play that stupid tournament [the $6 million Grand Slam Cup] in Germany. You can't have a tournament where you win four matches and then you win $2 million.

What about all these nice guys?

You've got nice guys like Pete [Sampras], Jim [Courier], Michael [Chang]. But sometimes you need more feistiness and fire. It's hard to imagine anyone matching Jimmy Connors's intensity, but I think I came pretty close. And some controversy is good for tennis and any sport. That's why Andre is great press—for better or for worse. That's why Andre and Boris are, by far, the most interesting personalities. Pancho Gonzalez was a great personality. You want to set up a sport that encourages that. The way tennis is set up now, it discourages it.

How does pro tennis discourage personalities?

You shouldn't encourage or allow obscene language. But those times when I, or someone else, went overboard, they should default the player on the spot rather than suspend him for an extended period. That ends up hurting other tournaments which have nothing to do with the event where the misbehavior took place. The ATP has this accumulated fines rule where you find yourself figuring out exactly what total you have. There were times when I would deliberately go over the limit because then it would be a three-week suspension, and you needed the break anyway. Otherwise, you'd be playing too much. There's a way of manipulating that. So either you'd find yourself inhibited on the court, which you didn't want to do, or else playing the system.

What else do you object to?

I don't like the way they have microphones set up all over the court. If that were in the best interests of tennis, they'd be doing that in other sports. You have to consider what's best for the kids who watch sports, and they don't [place microphones] on football and baseball fields and in basketball and hockey. You can't hear every word they're saying. Tennis microphones make it appear a lot worse than it is. I don't condone cursing. But it almost seems like the ATP's goal is to catch someone saying something. I also question the twenty-second rule [between points] because there are times when people are stalling, but other times if you strictly enforce it, you discourage human emotion and fireworks and energy and interaction with the crowd between points. That's exciting. We lose that now. It seems like robots are playing now.

Brad Gilbert recalled sitting in a locker room a decade ago with you, Connors, Lendl, and Becker. Gilbert said: "I couldn't believe the electricity in that room. These four guys wouldn't even look at each other and wouldn't talk to each other." What were your feelings toward those guys?

We were waiting for Brad to leave, that's all. You're talking about three of the most intense personalities of the last fifteen or twenty years. You have to put Becker at the top of the list for the last ten years as far as intensity. Connors without question, too. Lendl worked his way up with tremendous fitness and desire because his intensity level was so high. You're talking about three champions you'd learn things from. I hope people would look at me in the same way. To be in that group is something I would feel good about.

Now you speak about them with respect and admiration. But at that time did you dislike or hate them?

Yeah, absolutely! Certainly there were *years* when Jimmy and I would barely talk. Lendl and I *still* barely talk. Boris and I never had the same animosity because there was quite a bit of age difference, but there were moments when we didn't get along, without any question.

You've competed against nearly all the great players of the Open Era, from Borg and Nastase in the 1970s to Sampras and Agassi in the 1990s. In your opinion, who were the greatest?

I would put Borg, Lendl, Connors, Becker, and Sampras and probably Wilander at the top, but not in any special order.

How would the McEnroe of 1984 fare against the Sampras of 1994?

I like my chances, but he'd like his chances probably. Pete is a better-conditioned athlete generally than I was. He seems to learn so well from his past mistakes. I felt my serve together with my serve-and-volley was very solid, but his serve is really fantastic. When Becker came up in '85 and '86, he had the greatest serve I'd ever seen. Pete's ability to serve is terrific. That would be the difference to me. I'd like to think if I had the chance to play with a graphite racket [instead of wood] for a longer period, that I could have developed more power on my serve. But I don't have Pete's phenomenal power.

Many players, administrators, and media have denounced the ATP's "Best 14" rule that counts only a player's fourteen best tournaments and produces inaccurate and unfair rankings. What can be done to rectify this travesty?

The players should just get together and say they refuse to play until the ATP changes the ranking system. Sampras and Agassi and Courier have strongly condemned the "Best 14," but why haven't they done something about it? They talk about it. But talk is cheap! I vividly remember when me, Jimmy, Bjorn, Vitas, and Guillermo got together in 1978 at Boca Raton [Florida] to fight for changes, and we did it two other times in the early and mid-'80s. Me, Lendl, Edberg, and Boris specifically told the ATP that we didn't want a "Best 14" system in 1990, and we got shafted by [then ATP Tour CEO] Hamilton Jordan, and it was installed. We realized then Pete and

Andre were going to be [top] players, and we should have them in our corner, and they should realize this is important. But they weren't really involved in 1990. They were young players and young politically. In a certain way *everyone* seems to be young politically now because no one is doing anything.

You've alleged that the ATP Tour has betrayed the original goals of its 1989 revolution against the establishment, the Men's Tennis Council, and has become a tournament directors' tour and not a players' tour. Would you please elaborate.

Tournament directors want all the top players to play every one of their events. They're going to devise ways to encourage the top players to play as much as possible. That's why you have the "Best 14" system. That is clearly not good for tennis. What's good for tennis is the idea that every time a player steps on the court he is going to give 100 percent effort. I definitely feel the players were betrayed. What was promised to us was not what was delivered. We, the top players, met with the ATP and told them that we specifically did not want a "Best of anything" ranking system. This "Best 14" is a cancer.

The worst thing anyone can say about a pro sport is that its players aren't trying to win. Yet you've said tanking is "epidemic" on the ATP Tour. What evidence do you have?

Watching the matches. I'm not saying that players are going out there deliberately planning to tank before the match starts. My idea of tanking may be a tougher definition. I feel that sometimes you have to figure out ways to be professional. And that means even if you've been away from home for a long time, that you owe it to the people who have come to watch you play—and to yourself as a professional. If you enter the event, you should give it your best shot. Too often these guys who have made airline reservations, if things go well, maybe they'll take the victory. But if things start to go wrong, their effort level drops. That's what you hate to see.

Which guys have been known to tank?

Agassi is a guy you hate to see do it because he's such a tremendous talent. You hate to see it when his head isn't 100 percent into it. He's been guilty of that. But it's also the ranking system that's been set up. It's as guilty, if not more guilty, than the players themselves because it encourages tanking.

Sampras says he'll play Davis Cup in 1997 *if* the United States reaches the semifinal round. But in 1996 Sampras, Agassi, Chang, and Courier all failed to play against the Czech Republic, and the U.S. was upset in the second round. Why can't our four stars agree that two of them will play every Davis Cup tie—which likely would be enough to win the Cup for the rest of the 1990s?

I don't know the answer to that. It seems like an easy thing for them to do. One problem is that the ATP tried to downplay the Davis Cup because they don't have anything to do with it. So the ATP hurts the sport by putting the Hong Kongs [tournaments] of this world the week after the Davis Cup tie with the Czech Republic—and Hong Kong offers these guys a ton of appearance money. So Chang and other guys come up with lame excuses that the schedule is too tough. What's embarrassing is that they get away with it. I personally told every one of them that they're full of crap when they start laying out their baloney excuses about why they are not playing. They don't care enough is what it boils down to.

What about the way the Davis Cup is scheduled?

It's a problem. I used to have to play Davis Cup right after Wimbledon or right after the Australian Open. December is not a good time to play the Davis Cup final when players desperately need rest. The other point is that we want the Olympics to be an important [tennis] event, but it's been received in a lukewarm way by the male players. They should not have the Davis Cup in the year of the Olympics so that the focus can be on the Olympics then. And the Olympics should have a Davis Cup [team] format.

You've often expressed your desire to be Davis Cup captain and recently said: "I think I was the type of guy who should have been named captain." Why hasn't that happened? (In 2000 McEnroe was appointed Davis Cup captain. He resigned after the U.S. lost in the semifinals. His tempestuous behavior was criticized after all three ties.)

People are afraid that I'm going to do my thing, and [USTA officials] want to tell the captain what to do. They want a guy who just toes the line. Also they feel it's their chance to get back at me for the injustices they feel I did by misbehaving or whatever or criticizing people who I felt didn't know much about the sport, like most of the people involved in these associations. Now they feel that this is their big moment and they can say, "We'll show John McEnroe." So that's the price you pay.

Sports Illustrated **called you "defiant, complex, enraged, and rich," and said that "there is a sort of integrity to his negativity." Is that description on target?**

I'd like to think I'm not a negative person. When I was out on the tennis court, I had a tendency to lose my temper, and that's a challenge for all athletes when things go wrong. The key is somehow to try to be mentally strong and stay positive. And in tennis there are a lot of negative things going on around you, at least it felt like that to me. But I don't really understand that quote. Instead of looking at the comments I've made to make tennis a more interesting sport, people regard them as negative

John McEnroe.
International Tennis
Hall of Fame

because I'm just not going along with the status quo. You need people to lay it on the line. My strongest attribute is that I have the courage of my convictions. The great majority of the players today don't have the guts to speak out or get involved. The sport is still pretending that everything is hunky-dory.

You've said, "By having kids, I got my humanity back." What did you mean?

You lose sight of reality when you're on the tennis circuit. That is your reality, but it's not the reality of what most people deal with in the real world. You don't realize how spoiled you are. You lose sight of ways to be productive besides trying to be a good tennis player. [My] having kids made people feel they were more accessible to me, and I felt more accessible to people. It brought me down to earth and made me more patient and generally relate better to people. I feel much more comfortable having kids around. Just today, having lunch with my brother and my baby and just walking around the restaurant, I don't feel totally comfortable. Yet I feel that is something you do as a father. And I wouldn't do it otherwise. I'd be hiding in the corner feeling like I didn't want people to recognize me. Having kids brings out the best in me. Having kids is the ultimate commonality. People have started looking at me as a person instead of this guy who was yelling on the tennis court. They feel this guy is just like we are.

What was your reaction when you were among four men honored as "fathers of the year" by the New York–based National Father's Day Committee for being "great father role models"?

It's pretty tough to get a better honor than that. I felt at least people had seen enough of me to respect what I was trying to do as a father. The Father's Day Committee and the award are about making people more aware of the extreme importance of fathers in children's lives. If it can make people say, "Hey, if John McEnroe can be a good father, I can do better, too," then you feel you're making a contribution to society.

The late Arthur Ashe once said, "Just for the sheer enjoyment of watching somebody play, no one comes close to McEnroe. No one." Why did your playing style so fascinate people?

I'm just thankful that people say that. The style that I played—taking the ball early and on the rise and being aggressive—that's the most exciting way to me. That's what I would like to watch. I don't like to sit back. That's why clay court tennis bores me. It encourages players to stand there and wait for other people to make mistakes. I always believed your best shot at winning the point was at net.

Back in the 1980s people used to say that the best doubles team was "John McEnroe and anybody." You've won nine Grand Slam doubles titles and racked up an 18-2 Davis Cup doubles record. Do you consider yourself the greatest doubles player of all-time?

I don't place myself. I let other people decide that. But I feel I was up there. There's no one up there who I feel was a better player than I was in doubles. But I don't go around tooting my own horn.

John Lucas, a former NBA player and coach and now Lori McNeil's traveling coach, rates you, Connors, Michael Jordan, David Thompson, and Dennis Rodman as "the five greatest athletes I've ever seen, coached, or competed against." Do you consider yourself one of the greatest athletes in history?

I can't put myself in the same class athletically with the basketball players and some of the stars in other sports. But the combination that tennis provides—the physical and the mental and the fact that you're out there by yourself—makes it a tougher game than people realize. I'd like to consider myself a good athlete, but I wouldn't put myself there, no.

You often said that your great ambition was "to take the game to another level, to put tennis players up there on a par with the top names in the NBA or the NFL." Has that happened?

We brought tennis more to the masses in terms of name recognition—although Magic Johnson and Larry Bird and Michael Jordan brought more charisma recently. Connors and myself fired up the game so that the average sports fan became more interested. I wouldn't say tennis, athletically, is quite at the level of some other sports. That would be a longer-term goal. That name recognition is something tennis is missing now. Tennis doesn't have the interest it had fifteen years ago, particularly here in the States. In Europe tennis is still quite a bit more popular. Tennis has not reached the level I would have liked when I first made that statement.

You always liked it when people called you an artist on the court, and now you have your own art gallery in New York City. What do tennis players and artists have in common?

They're both out there by themselves. Artists are pretty insulated and isolated, and so you can practice and practice, but you're really not sure how you're going to do. Obviously there are differences because artists aren't competing against one other person directly. But it's pretty difficult for them. A friend of mine had an art opening last night, and he's got to sit there while everyone is looking at his paintings and deciding whether they like them or not. There's a nervousness and fear of failure you have to deal with. You have to try to put aside the feeling that what you do as an artist or a tennis player directly reflects how people are going to view you. As an athlete, if you lose, you're considered a loser. And if you win, you're thought of as a better person. I found myself getting caught up in that. I think 99 percent of the players do. You could be Jim Courier, who is number fifteen in the world, and he's thinking his career is terrible now. He's a guy who has won four major titles, and he's got nothing to hang his head about. Sometimes he thinks things are awful. Then you catch him off the court, and he's a pretty smart guy, and he feels just fine. They should have full-time psychologists on the tour. They're just as important as physical trainers.

Peter Gold, the owner of the independent label 21 West Entertainment, which will release your album this summer, said in *Time* magazine: "John's playing, songwriting, and singing have all gotten incredibly much better." Please tell me about that and the Johnny Smythe band.

He's the owner of the label so he's going to say that. He's been very supportive which has been nice. He's one of the people that I really try to do the best I can for because there are zillions of people out there who are really great musicians, and I've come into this so late. My goal is to enjoy it, and hopefully, people will say that it sounds like good music. I feel like I've come a long way, but I've still got a long way to go.

Are you striving to be like Eric Clapton?

No. That's like Mick Jagger deciding he's going to be the number-one tennis player in the world. It's not realistic.

In 1995 you said, "I would have loved it sometimes if an umpire or linesman had just said, 'Look, piss off you little shit.' Maybe they should have had more of a go at me." Did you really mean that?

Yeah! What I like when I go to the basketball games is you feel like all the players know all the officials by name. And you hear all the officials talking, "Look, this is it, don't do this anymore." They give the players a hint that a penalty is about to come if you push them too far. That doesn't take place in tennis. I would favor using former players as umpires in tennis. I think players would have more respect for them and their decisions.

The new super camera, dubbed "Mac Cam" after you, has shown that linespeople make mistakes surprisingly often. Do you believe, in retrospect, that many of your protests against line calls were justified?

I believe that they were justified. I believe I went too far in protesting them. If they had just said, "You know, we probably did miss it, John, but we've got to go with it," then you say at least they admitted it. It was the fact that they never admitted it that angered me. No one pretends you can see every ball—the players [also] don't see every ball right. But when ten, fifteen years go by and they don't overrule one line call for me, you know there is something screwed up here. In the NBA, one official will sometimes overrule another when they're not sure, or they'll confer and have a jump ball. I don't know why tour officials were told they can't say they just didn't know. Because when you see Pete Sampras or Boris Becker hit a serve on grass 120 miles an hour, that's a pretty difficult [line] call to make. It would almost be 30 or 40 percent of the time you couldn't tell.

In 1993 Donald Dell, chairman of ProServ management company, admitted: "It is very difficult for me to see how in the long run the huge guarantees can be good for the game.... It is certainly making players and us [business agents] a lot of money, but personally it is very hard for me to justify because I think guarantees eventually dampen competitiveness and desire and intensity." Should the ATP Tour join the WTA Tour and ban *all* guarantees and make tennis an honest sport?

What does that mean—an honest sport? Name one sport that doesn't have guarantees. You watch a pro football game. The players get paid X amount of dollars a year [regardless of how much or how well they play]. It's worse than tennis. This guarantee issue has been presented in such a way that makes tennis players look greedy. How about basketball players?

Michael Jordan is getting $30 million this year. Are people saying he's not trying as hard? Champions are going to compete just as hard, whatever they're making. If I made $30 million a year, I'd feel extreme pressure to show that I was worth it.

But what about the players who don't always put out 100 percent?

Those are the type of people who shouldn't be getting guarantees the next time around. They're the type of people tournament directors should know better about paying money to. The problem is, these [ATP Tour] contracts say if they get two players in the top ten, then the sponsor, Wendy's or whatever, is going to give them a hundred thousand dollars. But if they have only one top-ten player, they get a lot less. Because of that, tournament directors will pay someone who doesn't try hard. Ultimately, that's bad for the game. That's why we're having problems with the sport. Andre gets a lot of appearance money to play a tournament in Memphis, and he loses to [then 419-ranked] Luke Jensen. So that can tell you something right there. If that continued and I were the tournament director, I wouldn't pay Andre the same appearance money.

But do you think it's good for the game that Sampras went to Qatar in 1994 and picked up a reported four-hundred-thousand-dollar guarantee and lost in the first round in singles and doubles, while the first prize there was ninety thousand dollars?

That's another issue. But, yeah, if Pete Sampras sells four hundred thousand dollars worth of tickets. The Paul Haarhuises of this world sell two dollars worth of tickets. I oppose the abolition of guarantees. You already have the Grand Slam events where there are no guarantees. To pretend that every event should be that way, I just don't believe that. What they should encourage is to take 10 percent of all this prize money and give it to charity. There is such huge prize money in sports. Mike Tyson is going to get $25 million and Evander Holyfield is going to get $35 million for their rematch. Actors are getting ten, fifteen, twenty million dollars for one movie. It's the same thing. Why pick on Pete Sampras when it's all over the place?

Only a blond streaker enlivened the otherwise boring 1996 Wimbledon final which, like too many men's matches these days, had too many aces and too few rallies, too much power and too little subtlety, tactical awareness, and finesse. What should be done to remedy the power crisis facing tennis?

That is really *the question.* Grass courts are where the problem is more apparent if a big guy is on his game, like [1996 champion] Krajicek at Wimbledon. It looked boring. For that Sampras-Ivanisevic [1994] Wimbledon final, there was only one rally that went over four shots and something like nine minutes of action in the two-hour match. That's bad. Otherwise, the aesthetic beauty of watching tennis on grass is terrific. Something has to be done. I've always thought that every court in the world should move in the service line a few inches. I think it would make it tougher to get really hard serves in. Tennis shouldn't go to one serve [as 1960 Wimbledon champion and former Australian Davis Cup captain Neale Fraser advocates]. Whoever invented tennis 120 years ago did an excellent job, and that would be a huge alteration. It would take the serve out of the sport. We have to reduce the potency of the serve without destroying it. One possibility is to have a speed limit and ban rackets that, after testing, produce too much power. I still believe though that we should go back to wood. Pete Sampras played with a wood racket at the December [Nike Cup] exhibition at Madison Square Garden [against Agassi, Courier, and McEnroe], and he was serving at 120 miles per hour. The difference is that you can't keep that up for an extended period of time. Pete's arm started hurting. So that's why you wouldn't serve as hard.

Instead of applauding Pete Sampras's courage in his memorable U.S. Open quarterfinal marathon win over Alex Corretja, letter writers to *Tennis* magazine (U.S.)—by a ten to one ratio!—charged that Sampras used his exhaustion and vomiting as gamesmanship and trickery to win. Was Sampras innocent or guilty?

What Sampras did was what Connors did. When Connors was really tired, he'd start stalling. He would talk to the crowd. Pete said afterwards that his conditioning wasn't as good as he'd like. He clearly took well over the [twenty seconds between points] time limit on a number of occasions in the fourth and fifth sets. So he wasn't innocent. He was a champion who used everything he had. When he vomited in the tiebreaker, that was Academy Award material, if he could pull off that kind of acting. There were times when Jimmy and I slowed down. Lendl would take minutes; he'd refuse to play until every person sat down. This is doing whatever it takes to win.

When you were praised as one of the top two or three TV tennis broadcasters, you replied, "That's not saying much." What do you offer that other TV tennis broadcasters lack?

I've been there. I've been involved in a lot of big matches. That's something that can't be overlooked. I've been down in the trenches. I know what it feels like in those situations. And I'm still close enough to it to know what's going on now. Some commentators played twenty-five, thirty, forty years ago. The game isn't even remotely like it was then. The culture of tennis was so different, too. Then it was more buddy-buddy camaraderie. There was really no money involved. Tony Trabert knows a lot about tennis. I have great respect for Tony. Tony, Cliff Drysdale, and Fred Stolle played the game a long time ago. They know the sport. But what matters is how in tune you are with what's going on in the sport now. In all honesty, I don't know if in twenty years I'll know what the hell is going on. Tennis has changed a lot. Commentators are like players. You have your run and then you're dated. Just like I'll be.

One of your more controversial opinions is that athletes don't have to be role models for kids. You've said, "Kids aren't morons. They don't sit there and say, 'I'm gonna copy McEnroe yelling at an umpire.'" Do you really believe that?

I think kids need good parents as role models. They need good teachers. That's far more important than some athlete on TV. Kids are impressionable. They're impressionable watching cartoons or movies where a hundred people are killed in a thirty-minute show. Violence is a huge problem. Yet people are worried about an athlete misbehaving. Some people feel it's very important for athletes to be role models. I don't feel strongly that way. It's not like I go out there and say I want to be a bad role model. I'd like kids to look up to me and say, "I'd like to be like him." I like it when people come up to me and say, "I like what you try to do for tennis and the way you played." That doesn't mean they have to agree with everything I did though. No one is perfect.

But do you really believe eight-, ten-, and twelve-year-old kids can make that distinction?

It's up to the parents to help them make that distinction. As I said, kids are smarter than you think.

When you think about your place in tennis history, will people look at your great overall record, or will they remember the times you told an umpire to screw himself?

I think both. I wasn't as interested as Sampras or Lendl in winning the majors [Grand Slam titles]. I wanted the number-one ranking for that year. Fifty years from now, maybe people will say Sampras was a better player because he won more majors. I don't buy the importance of just counting up major titles, when as late as 1985, guys like Lendl and myself were getting guarantees to [induce us to] play the Australian Open. People didn't even play the Australian much in the 1970s and 1980s. Borg played there once in his whole career. Connors played twice. All of a sudden, you win the Australian, and it's like a major. Nastase played Kodes in the [1971] French Open final, and the stands were half empty. Chris Evert skipped the French Open to play Team Tennis a few times. In my early years, the French didn't have the importance that people make it out to have now. Even though I crossed the line a few times, I'd also like to be known as a guy who fought like a warrior every match.

FASCINATING FACTS:

- In 1981, Australian Davis Cuppers, disgusted by John McEnroe's disgraceful court behavior, vented their animosity towards him by taking potshots at McEnroe's picture with whipped cream.

- NBC, CBS, and USA Network commentator John McEnroe, who now occasionally covers women's matches, once claimed he couldn't comment on women's tennis because he doesn't menstruate.

- At the 1992 Beckenham (England) tournament, 83 percent in a poll of spectators said they preferred to watch someone like John McEnroe blowing his top rather than watching a top-class tennis match.

- The *New York Times* once called misbehaving John McEnroe "the worst advertisement for our system of values since Al Capone."

- Roy Emerson, a 1960s star who owns the men's record for most career Grand Slam titles (twenty-eight), once asked distinguished British journalist Rex Bellamy: Why do players who behave badly receive more publicity than those who play well?

- As U.S. Davis Cup captain, John McEnroe was fined four times for transgressions during the 2000 Spain-U.S. Cup semifinal.

- Tom Hulce studied John McEnroe for his role as the eccentric, half-crazed eighteenth-century composer Mozart in his 1984 film *Amadeus*.

This interview was nominated for a *Tennis Week* writing award.

13

Jimmy Connors: The Tennis World According to Jimbo

1994

Jimmy Connors is telling an anecdote to contrast the charismatic stars of his bygone era with today's colorless breed.

"I was in the locker room recently with five top-ten players," relates Connors. "Not one word was said in twenty minutes. As I walked out, I said, 'It was a pleasure talking with you fellows.'"

Mocking that bristling silence, Connors points out the camaraderie and animation of former top players such as himself, Borg, Nastase, and Gerulaitis, which is present on the new thirty-five-and-over Champions Tour. I caught their entertaining show at the Mentadent Champions event on Cape Cod, Massachusetts.

Connors, now forty-one, still whacks punishing ground strokes past opponents and exchanges wisecracks with spectators. And yes, Jimbo is the same pugnacious, proud, and unrepentant yet genial, humorous, and charming character, as I found out in this memorable interview.

Your two-day exhibition in March in St. Petersburg, Russia, with Borg, McEnroe, Nastase, and Lloyd drew sellout crowds and attracted an amazing 50 million TV viewers. How do you account for your tremendous popularity there?

They've been starved for action. And they've missed out on a lot. Russia didn't allow world-class tournaments there in the '70s and '80s, but the good thing is it's open now. And they're going to take full advantage of it. They have unbelievable players—Kafelnikov, Medvedev, Chesnokov, and Cherkasov, and some women that have been at the top of the game. So they know what the game is all about. But to have the game coming there and being live was incredible. And it was exciting to be a part of it.

Will the Champions Tour stage a tournament in Russia and other foreign countries in 1995?

We're going back to Russia. It's going to be either St. Petersburg or Moscow. And we're looking to go international. We've had interest from people in Germany, Japan, England, and Australia plus South America and other countries in Europe and Asia. If Australia would get in there, that would be even better to give us a nice two- or three-week Pacific swing. We want to get established here in the United States first. Once we do that, it's going to be very easy for us to spread out.

You are undefeated on the Champions Tour, having won all five events you've entered. Do you need both McEnroe and Lendl to give you more competition and the tour more star players?

I would love for McEnroe to come and play. Next year a number of guys are turning thirty-five. Noah will be thirty-five. I'd like to get him interested. Andres Gomez will be thirty-five and has already shown interest. McEnroe would be great. Lendl would be great. Next year it will be important for us to have one or two of those guys, and eventually I hope all of them, and just have a full-fledged circuit. I'm undefeated, but I'd be glad to step aside once this tour really gets going, but I won't do that at least until I'm forty-five in three more years.

You have an enthusiastic full house here. What makes the Champions Tour different from and better than previous senior tours that were only moderately successful?

Because it's real tennis we're selling. We're going out and playing full-fledged two-out-of-three competitive sets in singles and doubles. We're not just playing tiebreakers; we're not just playing one set. We've been giving real competitive, knock-down, drag-out tennis to people. And it's been working so far. With myself, Borg, Vilas, Kriek, Lloyd, Tanner, Gerulaitis, Nastase, Solomon, and Dibbs, we've got a whole host of guys who have been a big part of making tennis over the past fifteen or twenty years. We're succeeding because of their talent and charisma on the court, plus their abilities off the court with the media and corporate sponsors, which is also very important. We've got to be pleased with the marketing which has gotten us the attendance and the attention in the major markets around the country and, we hope, around the world.

You and McEnroe argued and exchanged profanities during your match in St. Petersburg. Even though you're drinking buddies afterwards, you're still fierce competitors and rivals on the court.

Yeah! I'm never going to argue with that. Nobody wants to go out and not give 110 percent. And even though we're all buddies here playing the

Jimmy Connors.
International Tennis
Hall of Fame

Champions Tour, once we get out on the court, it's tennis at its finest and the intense way we've played our matches over the past twenty years. I could never go out against Borg and not give it the competitive drive and desire I gave it against him in the U.S. Open and Wimbledon finals. There's a lot of history there.

About your rivalry with McEnroe, you once called it "ten years of war."

We had some battles. That's why it would be great for him to come and play.

You also used to say, "I still go on the court to kill or be killed. That's what I'd like to be remembered as—a warrior." Do you still feel that way?

Why not! I'm too old to change now. (Laughter.)

In 1981 you commented: "Being on a winning Davis Cup team is important to me, because I haven't done that." If you have any regrets about your

illustrious tennis career, is never being on a U.S. team that won the Davis Cup one of them?

No, not really. I made my decision along the way not to play and only play Davis Cup sporadically. I don't look back and regret anything that I've ever done. I really don't. I made the decisions. I'm big enough to stand up and take the good and the bad. And if that's the way it turned out, I don't think it's going to put any tarnish on my career. I've gone out and played the way I wanted to and had the results I wanted to have.

The late Arthur Ashe, in his 1993 book *Days of Grace*, wrote that you were "the greatest male tennis player, bar none, in the two and a half decades since the Open Era began in 1968. No top player lasted longer as a major attraction or so thoroughly captured the admiration and sympathy of the public for the same length of time." Why and how did you so thoroughly capture the admiration and sympathy of the public?

First of all, Arthur must have been in a very solemn mood at the time to say that about me! I think I was like that because of my feeling toward the game and the way I played it. I went out and was willing to break my back and come off there scarred and bleeding to do whatever it would take to give the people what they wanted from me—and that was great tennis and an all-out effort every time. That helped me to improve my level of play, and it helped me make the crowd a part of what I do and was doing on the court. And because of that, the feeling between the fans and myself mixed and meshed in a way so that we had a really neat thing going over the past twenty years. And I hope it doesn't stop now.

The stabbing of Monica Seles and Jennifer Capriati's drug problems and arrest are tragedies for themselves and for tennis. What thoughts do you have about their plights?

It's hard to say if Seles will ever come back. I didn't think that [the trauma] would last in her mind that long. It's better if you're thrown off a horse to get right back on. The sooner she gets back out there playing, the better. She might have let it go too long. I hope she hasn't. She was great for the game. Her results have spoken for themselves. I would like to see her come back.

What ruined Capriati?

Being pushed from an early age by the father and being put under that kind of pressure from a very early age to compete in an adult world with an adult game. Even though she handled it well at the beginning, it put excess pressure on her. Plus, I don't know if she really played tennis because she loved it. She might have been pushed because somebody was living through her and wanting her to succeed for their own personal gain. And, if that's what happened, she had to give up her childhood, her schooling, and her little-girl life to live the tennis life. And now, if she looks back, she might regret that and, in turn, not look at her father with the admiration and feeling that she should.

Do you think that the WTA Tour should raise the minimum age to play pro tournaments?

I've got a little girl who's going to be ten years old, and I see how she is. And there is no way I would push her to go out and play tournaments and do that now. I really wouldn't. She's small, she's dainty, and very laid back and quiet. Capriati came out [in her pro debut] at thirteen years old, and that's only four years from my daughter's age. There's no way. Thirteen or fourteen is way too young.

Your children seem happy and well adjusted. Are you glad they didn't get seriously involved in tennis?

Yes. I am very glad they stayed away from the tennis. My boy plays a bit of tennis, and I'm glad they're around it just a little bit to play for fun and enjoy themselves. But both of them have gone their own route. Brett is into golf and basketball and loves it. My little girl, Aubrey, takes tap and jazz dance and piano and has done little-girl things. I'm very pleased both of them have chosen their own ways.

Is your family now the most important thing in your life?

They always have been. I really realized it more in 1990 when I was out with my wrist injury and the phone never rang. My family had to get me through that year or so away from tennis. And how they went about it—my wife, my children, and my mother—was great. There were very few friends who really stayed in touch. Anyone who gets in the way of me and my family is in for a hell of a lot of trouble. That's the only thing I've got to say.

Chris Evert has condemned today's players as "unapproachable, defensive, isolated." Recently you remarked: "They say, 'I'm paid to play, not to entertain.' That kind of talk makes me sick." What should they do—or what *can* guys like Sampras and Courier and Bruguera do—to be more entertaining?

I'm not here to give a course or speak for them. They have to find their own way and find out what it takes to make what they do appealing to the masses, as everybody in my era did. I talked to the crowd, but everyone [then] had their own personality and their own identity and their own tennis game. Nobody really played the same, acted the same, reacted the same. Everyone forged their own way. For the *game's* sake, I would hope something like that happens now, but not through circus-like activity through the ATP. You can't have people at the ATP who haven't been involved in the game. They sit back and make big-time salaries and have never been in the trenches playing four-and five-hour matches, yet they're trying to run a game that has become such a big business now.

Jim Courier recently replied to your criticisms, saying: "I've got nothing but respect for Jimmy as a tennis player, but there's no reason for him to be taking shots at us. His day is done. And I think we're doing it pretty well and not with fingers in the air and our hands on our crotches." What do you say to that?

Obviously, he's not doing it too well. He just quit [playing tournaments] for a while. (Laughter.) Maybe if he'd do a little bit of that [entertaining], he'd get a little ink. He'd get a little press in the papers. (Hearty laughter.)

Are there any real entertainers out there? How do you rate Agassi, Becker, and Medvedev as entertaining performers and personalities?

First of all, I'm not taking shots at Courier and guys like that. You asked me my opinion. I'm just giving my opinion. I'm not taking shots at them. I wish them nothing but the best. Unfortunately, they don't look at it that way. And they think they're carrying on where I left off. I took the ball—from the guys I took it from twenty years ago—on the thirty-yard line and got it down to the five-yard line, trying to get it in for a touchdown. These guys should take it in for a touchdown and shoot the game to the moon. Unfortunately, they got sacked behind the line of scrimmage for a loss. But I'm not taking shots at them. Listen, if they think they're doing the right kind of job, more power to them. Good luck.

Regarding the passion and charisma that you, Nastase, McEnroe, and Gerulaitis had, you said: "I know I took things too far many times. We walked a thin line, but what we did was show people we were alive, that craziness and real feelings existed in the game. We weren't robots." Is that basically what it takes to make tennis boom again?

You know, I don't want to take shots at these guys. I'd hate for these guys to really think that I wasn't a nice guy. That would really upset me.

You also said: "We took the game from the country club and gave it to the blue-collar man." Looking back, do you consider that your biggest achievement and greatest legacy?

Yeah. And now I'm taking it back to the country club. (Laughter.) Tennis needed something to grab the imagination of the football and baseball and basketball kind of crowd. And tennis players were very specialized at the time. The TV [tennis] wasn't every weekend. It was only on occasion. So if you got to the final of the U.S. Open or Wimbledon, that might have been your day on television. Then when you walked down the street, somebody would look at you and say, "I've seen him. Where did I see him? Where did I see him?" But nobody was giving you that exposure on a weekly or on a daily basis. Do I like the masses coming in? Sure I do! I would rather have played in front of twenty-five thousand people and another 40 million people on television than play in my backyard in front of my family. And that's really what advanced the game and brought all the money in and all the corporate sponsors in and made the game alive at the time.

I know you hate tennis politics, Jimmy, but what do you think of the new ATP rule whereby it can slap a fifty-thousand-dollar fine on anyone for critical remarks that the ATP considers contrary to the integrity of the game?

Then that just goes to show it right there. It's their way or the highway. I would be broke by now if I went by their rules.

What about the ATP Tour's rule change intended to encourage tournament spectators to yell and scream and emote more? Is that a good one?

They're fishing to try to do something to add a little excitement to it. But far be it for me to make a response about the players, because I don't want them thinking ill of me. I can't have Courier sitting there and thinking ill of me. (Laughter.)

Two years ago Billie Jean King said: "I can always see Jimmy having to be carried off on a stretcher, quite frankly. I can just see him playing until his last breath." Is Billie Jean right?

In some way or another, I'll probably stay around tennis my whole life. Not [always] out playing tennis like this, even though it does keep me young and in pretty good shape. But there's going to come a time when I feel I cannot satisfy my own expectations. And when that happens, it's time for me to do other things. I might be on this tour for another ten years.

Your pro career has spanned twenty-five years, from Laver to Sampras. Who are your top five all-time greatest opponents?

I played against Laver. I played against Gonzalez. I played against Emerson and Newcombe. I played against Borg and McEnroe. I'm not putting them in order. It's too difficult. I played Laver and Gonzalez when they were past their primes. But I played Borg and McEnroe in their primes. And they played me when I was in my prime. If I look back and had to have two guys play for my life, I would take McEnroe and Gonzalez—outside of myself, of course.

FASCINATING FACTS:

- Jimmy Connors occasionally brought brass knuckles to tournaments when he was a junior player.
- When Jimmy Connors was twelve, he declared his real goals were "to play in England and on the Davis Cup team."
- Jimmy Connors played Davis Cup for the United States for a total of three years during his twenty-one-year pro career.
- Jimmy Connors said he invented the fist-pump victory gesture in tennis.
- Chris Evert, who was once engaged to Jimmy Connors, told ESPN Classic: "I remember when Jimmy and I went into confession and he came out a half-hour later and I said, `How'd it go?' He said, `I wasn't finished. The priest said come back next Sunday.'"

14

Bobby Riggs:
Bobby Riggs Keeps
Hustling for the Fun of It
1987

Mention the name Bobby Riggs in mixed company and you're bound to stir up all kinds of emotions. Memories instantly flash back to his celebrated "Battle of the Sexes" match against Billie Jean King in 1973.

The self-proclaimed "king of the male chauvinist pigs" lost, but the hundred-thousand-dollar extravaganza grabbed the public's imagination and helped trigger America's astounding tennis boom. The largest crowd (30,472) in tennis history witnessed it at Houston's Astrodome, and 60 million people watched it on worldwide television.

Riggs, a fun-loving instigator, reveled in all the attention he never had commanded as an amateur or pro star. Ironically, this son of a preacher was always a compulsive gambler. Back in 1939, as a cocky twenty-one-year-old, he collected $108,000 on a long-shot bet by winning three Wimbledon events on his first try.

Now sixty-nine, cagey Bobby is still capturing national titles—including USTA super senior 60 and 65 singles "Grand Slams"—as well as zany big-money hustles.

I caught up with fast-moving, fast-talking Bobby at the Black Horse Motel in West Springfield, Massachusetts. He had already lightened the wallet of the unsuspecting owner with golf hustles and even challenged this scribe to a tennis set (I would have to win 6-3 or better) for one hundred dollars.

Fortunately I had the good sense to decline. Instead I listened to the colorful character Jack Kramer has called "the most underrated champion in tennis history" and "one of the most honorable men I've ever met." Here's what Bobby had to say.

"It doesn't bother me I became more famous for my 'battle of the sexes' matches than for my tournament career. Hey, that was a great achievement that I was able to beat a person [Margaret Court] to bring about 'battle of the sexes' matches. A great player like Don Budge or Jack Kramer or Pancho Gonzalez, it wasn't their style, and it wouldn't have been credible if they were playing the women. But because of my style—everyone knew I had made up handicap matches, and I liked to bet on matches—so it was kind of a natural for me. I'm tickled that they were so successful.

"When I played Margaret Court [in the 'Mother's Day Massacre'], she was the best woman player in the world, and a lot of people think that I psyched her out by giving her the red roses. And I must say it did seem to fluster her. She did seem to get sidetracked. I played extremely well that match, and she, of course, was off her game and just couldn't seem to get her act together. Don't forget that I had the best of my tennis world, a slow cement court. We played at twelve o'clock noon in California so that the Eastern audience, home from Mother's Day at three o'clock, could watch it on TV. So when I lobbed to her the sun was right in her eyes; she had to back up and let the ball drop, and she didn't know whether to attack me, come to the net on everything, hit the ball hard. She just got bewitched, bothered, and bewildered, and I was able to defeat her 2 and 1.

"Of course, Billie Jean King, when she found out I beat Margaret Court so easily, had to come to the rescue for women. She was carrying the banner of women who wanted equal pay, equal prize money at all women's tournaments. I didn't believe in that at the time. I'm really not that much against it now. It's okay. There are only two or three [sic] tournaments where men and women play together. Otherwise the women play separately.

"Everyone should get everything they can out of life: happiness, contentment, and everything is a prize. So if a woman can survive in this world of competition, if she's just as good a businessman or executive as a man, she should get whatever the offer is there. I definitely am not for holding them back. It just always seems to me that men are more capable, smarter, and better and more physical. (The waitress roughly puts Bobby's coffee down on the table.)

"I can't think of anything that a woman can do that a man can't do better. I'm just calling it like it is. There's nothing a woman can do as well as a man except make babies.

"I said that my number-one favorite place for women to be is in the bedroom and number-two in the kitchen, and I like 'em around the fireplace with a pipe and slippers ready for men after a hard day of work. I like 'em on the tennis court, golf courses, and hey, I like 'em out in the business world. I like to compete with women—that's the thing I do best—go around challenging women to all kinds of games. They're fun to play with. Not everyone wants to be a home builder and stay at home. For those who can get out and compete with men, good luck to 'em.

"Jack Kramer wrote in his book [*The Game—My 40 Years in Tennis*] that more than one woman took care of me in Houston [in 1973]. Jack is intimating maybe I wasn't paying too much attention to strict training habits [for the Billie Jean King match], and maybe I was having a little fling with my bosom buddies—they were sort of my guides around Houston. Jimmy the Greek, the guy on TV, has been quoted as saying the same thing.

"Actually it's not true. I trained very hard for that match and was ready for it. I'm not going to use that as an alibi. It will go down as mythology.

"People like Kramer and Jimmy the Greek saw me around town with half a dozen beautiful girls surrounding me all the time. And they just imagined what they would probably like to happen to them thinking it was happening to me—and it didn't happen. The truth is that I did not delve into extracurricular activities."

"There are hustles that you feel good about. And there is the unusual and different and once-in-a-lifetime kind of hustle like the one I had when I bet [renowned daredevil] Evel Knievel twenty-five thousand dollars that I could ride a motorcycle from Las Vegas to Twin Falls, Idaho, and get there in time to see him make a jump. Evel was promoting his jump across Snake River Canyon then.

"Now I won the bet, but it was very difficult because I wasn't very good on a motorcycle. Instead of putting the brakes on, I put the throttle on, and I very nearly got killed two or three times.

"When I saw him go into that water, I said, 'Oh, my God! Evel is gone and my twenty-five thousand dollars is going with him.' I was never so relieved in my life when I saw him get up and come back up. And sure enough, he paid me later for that hustle. That was a funny one. I was never on a motorcycle before, and I never expect to get on one again.

"One of the most satisfying hustles I had [was] when I went to Wimbledon in 1939. I took one hundred pounds and bet on myself to win the singles and let it ride to win the doubles and let it ride to win the mixed doubles. I thought I had a lock to win the singles and mixed doubles [with Alice Marble]. In my mind the only one that was questionable was whether I could win the doubles because we [Bobby and Elwood Cooke] weren't really too strong a team. I knew I had two of them locked up, so why not take a chance?

"So I thought it was pretty good for a twenty-one-year-old to put up a hundred pounds, which was like five hundred dollars, and come back with over $107,000. I hustled those English bookmakers pretty good on that one.

"I had a mule one time, playing the Rocky Mountain [section] ladies champion near Boulder [Colorado], and I had this leash with the mule. Boy, that was the hardest animal act ever because this mule was so stubborn I couldn't make him budge. He wouldn't move at all, and I could only get as far as the leash went because I couldn't move him. I managed to win that match anyway, but that was a tough one.

"In contrast to that, I once played with a baby elephant against the 'All Stars,' the cast of *M.A.S.H.* They were doing a special at Disney World in Orlando, Florida, and I was there. They had me play the whole team. In the zoo there they had a great big mother elephant. It was so big they wouldn't let me have the elephant as a partner because they thought it might break down the concrete court.

"So I took the baby elephant and put a racket in its trunk, and that elephant moved around like crazy, and, see, I had all kinds of chances. I beat the *M.A.S.H.* team easy, all five or six of them. That was a fun thing to do.

"I ran against one of the best distance runners of all time at Death Valley, California, the lowest place in the United States. We ran for twenty-five thousand dollars. I figured this was a real hustle because he was such a great distance runner. He thought I wouldn't even last twenty-five miles, and he had to run twice the distance, fifty miles to my twenty-five.

"So I was walking over the finish line waiting. I had to wait an hour and a half for him to finish the race. That was one of the easiest and best hustles I've ever had."

"I have to disagree with people who claim the game has changed so much. From 1920 to 1930 it was a baseline game—Tilden, Hunter, Lacoste, and Cochet were baseline players. Then from 1930 to 1940 you had players like Vines, Crawford, and Budge who would take the first [short] ball and then come to net, playing a little more aggressively. They played good baseline tennis and combined the net. Then you had Kramer, Sedgman, and Gonzalez and Hoad and Stan Smith, players who served and volleyed just like Tim Mayotte and Edberg, the Swede, are doing now.

"So the game goes in cycles. The game in the last ten years went back to the '20s, reverted back to baseline play, with Borg, Vilas, Connors, and Solomon and Dibbs and Lendl. You could name fifteen or twenty [leading] baseliners. Now with McEnroe and Mayotte and Edberg, we may see the cycle go back the other way to serve and volley.

"The main difference now is that they're hitting excessive overspin on the ball and more two-handed shots with overspin. Topspin is good for the clay courts and lousy for grass. That's why you haven't seen one of these overspinners, except for Borg, win Wimbledon and why Lendl may not win on grass this year.

"Two-handed is a great shot! Hey, would a golfer use one hand on a golf club? Would a baseball batter use one hand? It makes sense to use two hands to swing a racket. It's better for men *and* women tennis players. We got one kid—I love to watch Greg Holmes—who hits two hands on both sides. He hits the ball a ton. I wish I had a two-hander, let's put it that way. I think the shot is here to stay. By the year 2010 everyone should hit two-handed on both sides."

"When we were players [in the 1930s and 1940s] and got a bad line call, we were playing for a cup or a title—no money was involved at all. It's much easier to be a good sport under those kinds of conditions. When you're playing out there and it means fifty or a hundred thousand dollars to you, and you feel that you got robbed because some blind linesman gave you a bad call, these guys have every reason to get upset and be spooked out.

"I do not approve of foul language and calling a guy every name in the book. I never approved of Connors's antics, giving the finger to somebody or lowering his pants and giving him the moon and having umpires removed and calling for the referee. They've carried this a little too far.

"To be upset and to do it in a nice way like Lendl, he goes up to the referee, and he says, 'Are you sure that ball was out? It looked like a bad call to me.' He had a little discussion with him and went back to play. He offered his protest and he had every right to do that.

"But to do what McEnroe does, he gets out of control and just throws a fit on the court, you might say, like a tantrum, that's not right. And it's not good for the sport. A lot of people look at these tennis guys, and they think they're brats and poor sports. Here they're making millions and millions of dollars, and now they're raising Cain out on the court.

"I never liked Nastase's antics. He's a beautiful guy off the court, and I like him very much, he's a fun guy. But on the court, he was dirty pool. I've seen him steal five or six matches from opponents just on gamesmanship, just by upsetting his opponent. He would cause a rhubarb. He wasn't upset; he was trying to get his opponent upset. I didn't approve of that. That's poor sportsmanship.

"These guys got a lot of ink. They gave tennis a black eye and a bad name for having the kind of people who misbehave like that. Some fans said, 'Hey, let's go and look at what that jerk is going to do today.' You have to say that the American public sort of likes that kind of thing. They're disappointed if McEnroe behaves himself and is a perfect gentleman."

"The USTA is well aware of the great strides and great advancement other nations are making. Czechoslovakia, in particular, has had a productive program. The Swedes now are coming along very, very strongly.

"Now it used to be in the old days, you had to either come from California, Texas, or Florida or forget it, because there weren't any indoor courts around the country at all. And you had to have the sun shine to play all year round. That gave anyone playing all year round a big advantage, of course.

"Now with indoor courts, hey, we're liable to get the best player out of Duluth, Minnesota, where there's twenty-six feet of snow on the ground for six months. You never know. Good techniques now are being developed everywhere. So it's even now. I'm surprised that England hasn't developed a top player in years. The next best player could come from Finland. The coaching techniques and indoor facilities make all the difference. No longer do you have to live in California or Australia.

"The USTA is doing a good job. We have ten-and-under tournaments, twelve-and-under tournaments, and fourteen-and-under tournaments. And when you get that early start like Chris did, Jaeger did, and Austin did, you have a big advantage. The idea is to get kids started in competition early.

"Here we have a nation of 240 million and we can't get a dozen top kids started that can compete with the Czechoslovakian kids. It's crazy! It's disgraceful! Look at Sweden. It's got 10 million people in the whole country, and they got ten of the top fifteen players [sic] in the world.

"We got to get this early start in developing kids. There's no such thing as burnout. That's exaggerated. That's somebody coming up with a doctor's degree who is a psychologist or somebody. That's got nothing to do with reality. There's nothing to burnout."

"Generally speaking, I was never my best friend when it came to impressing the media, the tennis writers. I used to delight in taking a player I could beat love and love, and I'd like to let him go 6-4, 7-5. I liked to play cat and mouse with him. I was a little bit of a torturer out there. I'd like to drop shot him and run him around. I knew he couldn't win the match, and I had to have some fun. It was no use beating a player love and love.

"Budge did that, Kramer did that, and a lot of players looked so good, you couldn't believe it. Budge was the most awesome-looking player I've ever seen play. He beat even good players love and one, one and one. I didn't do that. I played just well enough to beat the opponent. That's not very impressive.

"They used to say: 'I can't understand—why is that Riggs winning?' I would try harder when I played Kramer and Budge in the finals. Budge and Kramer would say: 'You can't believe how tough that guy is. You don't understand because you're not a player and you don't play him.'

"So I only played to win, not to impress people on the sidelines. And that is what works against me in being considered as an all-time great player. Except to a guy like Kramer who knows. Or a Gonzalez or a Budge. They know. And Gardnar Mulloy, who is a great admirer of me. He said that if you somehow put the all-time greats from various eras in one tournament, I would sneak through and probably win it.

"Here's the way I'd rate the players: Tilden, BT and AT, Before Tilden and After Tilden. Don't rate him. He was just in a class by himself. I don't want to relate him to present or past stars. He was great; give him his due. He was a beautiful player, a baseline player, he never came to the net. From 1880 to 1930 he was the best.

"After Tilden, chronologically now, you can make a case for Ellsworth Vines being the greatest player of all time. Then Fred Perry, who won three Wimbledons. Many people think Budge *is* the greatest player of all time, and he's maybe the greatest hitter, striker, of the ball. Following Budge was Riggs. I beat Budge to death all around the world for five or six years. Following Riggs was

Kramer. Following Kramer came Gonzalez, Sedgman, Rosewall, Laver, then Connors, then Borg, and now McEnroe. And the next great player is Lendl. Those are the players I think were the greatest of all time.

"If you had to do it on this basis, an elimination contest, with a one-week rest between elimination matches, and there was only one survivor, it might be Gonzalez. Because, under that kind of test, he could get himself up and become inspired, and he had the greatest serve. But if you had to play every day, then I might like Kramer because, as a grind-out guy, grinding out one match after another, he might win.

"For the women, I would have to give the nod to Martina [Navratilova]. She is maybe the best woman player who has ever played on grass and fast courts. As an aggressive player, she sometimes plays a little too risky, takes a few too many chances, and some days she may be off. But she's resourceful, and she has a good enough game to fall back on.

"On clay Chris [Evert] and Maureen Connolly are close. Maureen hardly ever lost a match, winning Wimbledon at sixteen, seventeen, and eighteen. I don't think she ever lost a match until she fell off the horse that bumped her into the walk and ruined her leg and she had to retire. She and Chris are very similar—great, great baseliners. If anything, Maureen might have been a little swifter and quicker around the court than Chris. Maureen would have beaten Martina on clay. It's questionable whether Maureen would have beaten her on a hardcourt. On grass I like Martina."

"Anybody that has to listen to a coach to tell them how to win a match is only going to get in more trouble. It's a lot of hogwash that a coach on the court can help a player. I never had a coach and I never needed a coach. Like Vilas looking up at [Ion] Tiriac and Martina looking up to Renee Richards for help. It's a lot of baloney.

"This [on-court] coaching controversy is way overblown. Tennis players who start at six, eight, ten years old and play tournaments for all their lives are like fighters who start young. You don't have time to think. Tennis is too fast, too quick. It's an instinctive game. If you don't know what shot to play by the time you've played seven, eight, nine years of competitive tennis, forget about a coach trying to tell you to improve your tactics. That's a lot of hogwash.

"The smarter a tennis player is, probably the worse off he is. The higher I.Q. you have and smarter you are, the worse tennis you are going to play. Because tennis is like fighting: you don't get the smartest people in the world fighting, do you? They fight instinctively, and the tennis player is just like a fighter on the court. He's been trained to play, and he's seen the right shot to play on a drop shot a million times, and he reacts instinctively. If you have to have a coach to tell this guy what to do, or if he doesn't know how to play his opponent, you got one guy who is even stupid for a tennis player." (Laughter from the growing audience.)

"My father was a preacher, the Billy Graham of his day. A kid can get too much of something and rebel against it. I've seen a lot of great young tennis players look so good when they are twelve, thirteen, or fourteen, and their parents are pushing them, pushing them, and they rebel against it and say, 'I don't want to play anymore,' and they quit the game very early.

"I had so much church, so much religion when I was young that it didn't 'take' on me. Then I started playing tennis tournaments, and I was in the finals every Sunday, and I couldn't go to church so often.

"I became a Sunday school teacher as an adult. I liked that. I believe in the doctrine. Christianity is great. I didn't teach kids to hustle. I stuck to the text and gave them the best lecture. And I took all my kids to see the [New York] Knicks play basketball. (Everybody laughs.) I was the favorite Sunday school teacher in the whole school."

"It took a long time to get over the disappointment of Billie Jean not honoring her contract [for a rematch]. I considered that a breach of a business contract, and I don't know many men who would do that. But she was so ruthless and so carried away with the cause. She had conquered Bobby Riggs, and she was never going to put that at risk again, and she said so at the time. She said, 'You know what you can do with that contract.' I got a rough idea, see. (Laughter.)

"But there's a chance Nastase and I may play Billie Jean and [Rosie] Casals in a doubles match. There's no way I can overcome the [1973] defeat by Billie Jean King. But this would be a lot of fun and satisfying and make some money, and it would be a good promotion. And I think Nastase and I can beat the dickens out of them.

"The big [1973] match with Billie Jean was a contributing factor to the tennis boom of the 1970s. One hundred million people [sic] saw it around the world. People had never been exposed to the game before, and they saw it and thought: 'An old guy like Bobby Riggs is out there; it must be an easy game. We'll go out and buy a racket and some balls, join a club, and take it up.' So it was a big boost.

"But I think the first Open [tournament] was the big boost in 1968. Big sponsors came in with so much money pouring in, and the sponsors fighting each other to get a tournament on TV. So it became a players' market out there, and they're all making two or three million dollars, which is fantastic.

"I wish I was there now. I wish I was fifty years younger. I'd be getting my share of it. You can bet on that. (Laughter.)

"But I was one of those guys who was able to improvise. I got in on some of that. After all, I made a million and a half [dollars] on the Billie Jean King match. And how did you like Gerulaitis and me playing Navratilova and Shriver for five hundred thousand [dollars]? That wasn't bad either. So I don't let any grass grow under my feet. I don't give up. I keep trying and I'm having fun.

"I got the best hustle of all just coming up now. I'm going to play the 'Great White Shark,' [golf superstar] Greg Norman. And we're going to play eighteen holes for five hundred thousand dollars. And he's giving me fifty yards off the tee, and I get to throw the ball once a hole. That's the only handicap I get. And we're going five hundred thousand dollars winner take all. When we're through with that, he's going to remember Bobby Riggs as the greatest hustler of all time."

FASCINATING FACTS:

- An overconfident Margaret Court said playing Bobby Riggs would be "like taking a stroll in the park" before the fifty-five-year-old hustler slaughtered her 6-2, 6-1 in the 1973 "Mother's Day Massacre."
- Billie Jean King hit 250 overheads a day to prepare for her celebrated 1973 "Battle of the Sexes" match against Bobby Riggs.
- Bobby Riggs took 415 vitamin pills a day prior to the "Battle of the Sexes" match.
- *During* a professional match victory against then world number one Don Budge, Bobby Riggs bet Clark Gable and Groucho Marx and won several thousand dollars.

This interview received a 1996 *Tennis Week* writing award.

15

Arthur Ashe: Blacks Can Dominate Tennis
1988

In his 1981 autobiography, *Off the Court,* Arthur Ashe philosophized: "The ultimate connection between tennis and life is in the doing, not the winning.... Success is a journey, not a destination."

Ashe started his journey as a black boy in legally segregated Richmond, Virginia, where "coloreds" swam at different pools and had to sit in the back of the bus. Ashe would challenge racial barriers at clubs staging junior tournaments, and he won the 1961 USTA Interscholastics and 1965 NCAA titles. He secured his niche in tennis history as the first (and last) black man to capture the U.S. Open (in 1968) and Wimbledon (in 1975).

A near-fatal heart attack in 1979 ended his playing career, but energetic Ashe quickly found new challenges. He became a successful businessman, corporate board member and consultant, author, spokesman for the American Heart Association, and TV tennis analyst. He also served as U.S. Davis Cup captain and co-chaired the USTA Player Development Committee.

As one of the most influential blacks and tennis people in America, Ashe firmly believes that the United States can regain its traditional status as a tennis superpower only if the sport attracts talented, hungry, minority players.

Ashe, 45, explains why blacks are athletically superior and how their eventual domination would dramatically change our sport.

You have asserted that "given the same chance as others have had, blacks would dominate our sport as they have done in other sports." Why do you believe that?

I believe that minority athletes—blacks in particular—would do very well in tennis because the same sets of athletic skills called for in basketball, baseball, and certain positions in football are necessary for tennis excellence. Minority athletes tend to be hungrier because there are fewer perceived occupational options available to them outside of the athletic and entertainment fields. I literally believe that, given the social dynamics of our country at present, minority athletes could dominate tennis in as little as ten to fifteen years, if given the chance, just as they have dominated in some of our other major team sports.

Are blacks genetically superior to whites for sports and, in particular, tennis?

The notion of the inherent black genetic superiority for sports is a very contentious issue. Historic evidence certainly points to an unusually high success rate in physical activities requiring running and leaping. Since I am not a geneticist, I am not expert enough to pass a generalized judgment on this issue. However, the evidence certainly seems to point to "something" that blacks in general have that has enabled them to succeed far beyond their normal proportional percentages in our national population. The evidence going back to the last century is overwhelming, but I am not adequately trained or learned enough to give the appropriate answer. I would certainly like to see someone disprove it; and by that, I mean not a sociologist but a scientist. The last word on this issue certainly is one that bothers quite a few people: the notion that in the past blacks have been all brawn and no brains.

Do inner-city blacks, while economically and educationally deprived, actually have environmental advantages for sports because their lifestyles tend to give them superior physiques?

Inner-city blacks, if given the same opportunities and advantages in tennis that are given to them in other sports, would do quite well with tennis. The important environmental factors include a) natural talent, b) peer support, c) adequate coaching and facilities, and d) the proper level of ego gratification.

Sports Inc. **magazine reported that a new viewership study of network television sports done by BBDO, the New York-based advertising agency, revealed that "tennis, a sport generally considered haughty, gets 12 percent higher ratings in black households than in all others." Also striking was the finding that in the 18–49 age group, black men watched an average of 33 percent more tennis than their non-black age-group counterparts. What are the implications of this high black interest in tennis?**

I am aware of the viewership study. What you may have failed to notice between the lines was that this increased black viewership of tennis is occurring among the growing black middle class. Tennis is, in fact, the number-one participant sport among black professional females. The major implication right now seems to be that most of the future American tennis stars may very well not come from the black underclass—from which the major team sports draw most of their players—but from the emerging black middle class who have the money to provide lessons for their children.

Arthur Ashe. International Tennis Hall of Fame

You have opined that "there is terrific apprehension among some people that blacks will take over the sport." Would you please elaborate.

Yes, I sense subjectively that there is much apprehension that blacks would take over tennis if given the chance. Tennis is a very conservative game with deep roots grounded in Victorian English moral codes and traditions. Minorities—in particular, inner-city minorities—have cultural norms that are diametrically opposite those of upper-middle- and upper-class white American standards. However, it is clear to almost all of us that if the United States is to regain its preeminence in the sport, then we will have to look for our future stars in places that were ignored before—namely, public parks and public schools.

If blacks did take over, as they have in the 75-percent black National Basketball Association, you have predicted "it will create problems because their behavior, speech, and dress is just a completely different culture." What will those problems be?

The problems of an increasingly minority-dominated tennis culture include a) a changing of the cultural norms for the sport in general; b) an increased focus on public facilities for competitions and tournaments; and c) a complete rethinking of the normal, orthodox methods of teaching. Minority athletes resist learning anything by the book. Reggie Jackson, Michael Jordan, Yannick Noah, Walter Payton, and Rickey Henderson all defy conventional approaches to their craft.

As far as the way big-time tennis is played—athletically, tactically, stroke-wise, and in the entertainment sense—how would blacks change the sport?

The major change black players would bring to the sport would be sheer speed. If, say, someone like Larry Myricks or Mike Conley [two long jumpers] had played tennis, we would have seen supernatural court coverage. Within five years of Jackie Robinson breaking the color barrier in major league baseball in 1947, black players dominated the stolen-bases category in the National League. Black players caused basketball coaching techniques to be completely rethought because blacks were so fast as to make the old patterns of setting up [offenses and defenses] obsolete. And, of course, in track and football, the tremendous influence of black athletes needs no further elaboration.

You have said that the nearly completely white USTA will have problems adjusting to an influx of black standouts. Why? Isn't the USTA trying to attract blacks and other minorities now with a variety of programs and increased funding?

I believe the [seventeen] USTA sections will have a difficult time accommodating a growing minority involvement in the sport. The problems crop up all the time, and I see a transition period of about ten years before new norms are established. The USTA is trying to attract more blacks and minorities, but that cannot be done with the cadre of coaches and administrators in place around the country at present.

What then is a faster, more effective solution?

At the Nick Bollettieri Tennis Academy in Florida, the Black Tennis and Sports Foundation is trying to train new minority coaches to go back to their public parks and run programs that will produce advanced players as well as more players who just want to play for fun. Pointedly, our first objective is to create more trained minority coaches, not to concentrate just on the promising young minority players. Most of the obstacles are organizational; it's a matter of persuading some people from various parts of the country that our ideas and programs are credible.

Since blacks have traditionally gravitated toward (so-called) macho sports like basketball, baseball, football, track, and boxing, should local tennis leaders try to lure and recruit excellent varsity athletes in those sports who lack pro potential (because of size or other reasons) to try tennis for a year or two, especially since the aforementioned BBDO survey indicates their predilection for the sport of tennis, at least in TV watching?

No, I do not believe tennis should try to recruit excellent black varsity athletes in other sports as tokens in the beginning. What is needed is a program to produce players the way they are produced now: by having enough programs that would attract players who want to play for fun—and out of this group will emerge those who want to concentrate on the game enough to see how far they can go with it. It is extremely difficult to try from the very beginning, say, at age eight, nine, or ten and produce a Wimbledon champion.

Since Bill Cosby and Sugar Ray Leonard are highly recognizable, popular, and respected, should the USTA hire them to do TV tennis commercials that may prove more effective than those featuring Dick Cavett, William Shatner, and Pam Shriver? Would the proposed commercials be effective in attracting blacks to tennis?

The USTA has given consideration to hiring people like Bill Cosby and Sugar Ray Leonard to do public service announcements for the sport. One of my strongest suggestions was for the USTA to take a different approach in its public service announcements to attract the more athletically inclined youngster who may want to give tennis a shot.

You have asserted that tennis could really use a charismatic American champion. Does eighteen-year-old rising star Andre Agassi fit that description?

We really could use an American champion right now on the world professional scene in the men's competitions. I do not believe that Andre Agassi will fill that bill because right now he has some shortcomings that I believe will keep him from becoming a top four or five player. However, he will improve.

What would your ideal champion be like?

What I would really like to see is a young American girl or boy who, after college graduation, becomes the world's best player. That is the ideal profile that we are looking for because it publicizes athletic excellence and still adheres to our American ideals of education being worthwhile. But I would settle for someone who has the mental toughness of Ivan Lendl, the athletic abilities of Yannick Noah, the personality of Andre Agassi, the smarts of Chris Evert, and the flair of Boris Becker.

Why are you convinced that America cannot rule the tennis world again unless we find and develop talented minority players?

Minority players—especially those from the underclass—tend to be hungrier, take direction more seriously, have already been screened out as being gifted and talented, have a very high level of achievement inherent in their character, and have invested quite a bit of their own ego gratification in the results of their athletic accomplishments. Let's face it. Through whatever combination of factors, black Americans today make up a substantial proportion of America's top athletes in most of the major sports. But that has not been true in tennis because the sport has been organized in ways that have discouraged black participation.

Your opinions have been quite strong. Is this because you want to jolt the tennis world?

No, they happen to be what I believe. And so far, I don't see any holes in any of the arguments that I have put forth.

FASCINATING FACTS:

- When Arthur Ashe first visited the disenfranchised people of Soweto, South Africa, in 1973, they nicknamed Ashe "Sypo," which means "hope."
- The first time that anyone except for a fallen boxer had ever been honored by a bell sounding ten times at a championship fight was when the late Arthur Ashe was honored that way at the Riddick Bowe–Michael Dokes title fight in 1993.
- *NBC Nightly News* anchorman Tom Brokaw said Arthur Ashe was "one of the three or four most impressive people I've met in my lifetime."
- Outside Arthur Ashe Stadium stands a statue of the legendary 1968 U.S. Open champion. A message etched in stone beneath the statue reads, "From what we get we make a living; what we give, however, makes a life."

16

Arthur Ashe: We've Come a Long Way, Racially—or Have We?

Arthur Ashe on Old Segregation in the New South

1990

For years, elitism was a way of practicing racism without calling it racism....
These clubs are one of the last bastions of segregation.

—CHARLES WILLIE, HARVARD URBAN EDUCATION
PROFESSOR AND BROTHER OF LOUIS WILLIE.

The Shoal Creek Country Club controversy last summer exposed golf's dirty secret: an all-white membership policy exists at many elite golf clubs throughout America.

Hall W. Thompson, founder of Shoal Creek in Birmingham, Alabama, unashamedly told a local reporter that "we don't discriminate in every other area except the blacks."

While Thompson's unwitting confession was met mostly with indifference from the touring pros who would soon compete there in the PGA Championships, the indignant media pounced on the story. Civil rights organizations threatened to demonstrate, and six major corporations (including two Japanese) withdrew their advertising from the telecast of the PGA, costing ABC $2 million in revenue.

Only then did Shoal Creek—which Thompson had vowed would not be pressured into accepting blacks because "that's just not done in Birmingham"—agree to admit Louis Willie, a sixty-six-year-old black businessman, as an "honorary" member.

Both embarrassed and jolted by the stunning episode, the PGA Tour announced that, after 1995, it would prohibit tournaments at clubs where membership "raises a question" of discrimination on the basis of race, religion, sex, or nationality. Lo and behold, barriers in the exclusive and exclusionary world of golf were finally coming down.

But what about the Shoal Creeks of tennis? How many are there, and where are they? And what should we do about them?

I asked former Wimbledon and U.S. Open champion Arthur Ashe, who was not allowed to play sanctioned (USLTA) tournaments as a junior in his home state of Virginia because of the color of his skin.

Does America still have any tennis clubs that subtly or not so subtly prohibit blacks from becoming members?

Oh, sure! The tennis world has quite a few clubs like that. I'm not sure [which ones offhand], but if you look at a *USTA Yearbook* and look at the member clubs that make up the seventeen sections, there are a lot of clubs in there that have discriminatory membership policies.

How do you know that?

Some of them are fairly obvious. Some of them don't have minority members and have discriminatory bylaws. Some may not have minority members, but their bylaws would not expressly say that they have discriminatory membership policies. And there are some [clubs] that would just tell you, "Look, we don't have any blacks here or Jews or Asians." And that's the way it would be.

Can you name just two or three?

I don't want to mention names. I'm saying if someone wanted to really research it and go to those clubs and say, "Do you have any Jewish, Asian, Hispanic, or black members?" you'll find dozens of clubs that don't have members who are of minority groups. Dozens.

Dozens?

Dozens.

Which clubs? Where?

I'll give you one that has already been in the news, and I won't be accused of creating a new story. The USTA had two problems. One, at the Orlando [Florida] Country Club, a Jewish women's group filed a protest with the USTA claiming that a women's team there didn't have any minority and Jewish members. The USTA is looking into that. There were two others just three weeks ago involving national junior tournaments. One, I think, was in

Nashville, where they had the boys' 16s. And another was in Asheville, North Carolina. There was a problem involving a black player practicing at a certain place. Locally, it was a big deal. I'm just trying to pick an example, rather than throw names out and put myself in deep trouble.

You just said, "Rather than put myself in deep trouble." Yet you've always been known for having the courage of your convictions.

Look, you're trying to trap me. I would not start anything like this unless I had *all* the facts. Because if this became public, my phone is going to ring off the hook.

Is it bad if your phone rings off the hook if it's an important cause?

It's not as if this thing is new. That's what surprises some people, maybe even like yourself. But this has been a problem for thirty years.

Who then is trying to rectify the problem?

The USTA now has Alexander Associates, which is looking into this thing in a very methodical, scientific way. That, I think, is the best way to do it. In fact, Cliff Alexander was on a CBS show talking about it. Yes, it is being extended to tennis, and it is going to get wider and wider. And it's not going to be hit or miss, a haphazard sort of inquiry. It's going to be very reasoned, very logical, and with an eye toward trying to redress the situation with the least amount of fuss.

Will there be some explosive revelations?

They may be explosive to some; it won't be explosive at all to someone like me. Golf definitely had its head in the sand as evidenced by the statements by some of the leading golfers. Finally, you get someone like [Jack] Nicklaus who was asked about Shoal Creek a lot. He finally came around and really made some—what I thought for him were—good, responsible statements that acknowledged the problem. He acknowledged the sport has to do more about [racism], acknowledged that golf was way behind on this issue and that everyone was better off for its having been exposed the way it was. Tennis is not like that yet, yet the problem still exists. The problem, centrally, is that many of the member clubs that make up the seventeen sections have discriminatory membership policies, and, to the extent that the USTA is a 501 tax-exempt organization, that is an untenable position.

Could these clubs lose their tax exemption?

It's a possibility. If some lawyer really wanted to go after them on that premise, it's a possibility, no question about it. Because, look, they enjoy tax-exempt status, and you can't discriminate by having some of your members specifically deny some other citizens the right to become members.

When was the last time you, personally, were told blacks weren't allowed to join a particular club?

That [scenario] may not arise very often because that is not the way people join clubs. See, that's what a lot of club presidents and club spokespersons are trying to say now: that we don't have a discriminatory policy and that blacks haven't applied. But that's begging the question. That's not the way one becomes a member.

How does one become a member?

Normally, someone asks you to become a member if they themselves are a member and can get someone else to sort of cosponsor your membership. They'll have a few private words with a few key members of the board and invite this person to a few events, like a member-guest golf or tennis event or a social event. You let it be known that this guest of mine would make a terrific member here. Now it just so happens in the normal course of events there are minorities with the same academic credentials, the same solid family background, the same responsible attitude, who never get invited.

Are any pro tennis tournaments staged at clubs that discriminate against blacks?

Membership-wise? I don't think there are any like that in the U.S. One of the big reasons is that very few pro tournaments now are played at private clubs. The problem is not with pro tennis—just as the problem really was not with the PGA too much. The problem was the USGA and the USTA. Those are the ones with the greatest exposure. We are talking about hundreds and hundreds of tournaments and clubs.

Hundreds of USTA clubs discriminate?

You can just go down the *USTA Yearbook* pages and throw a dart and you'll hit one. Obviously, I'm a Southerner, and you would expect Shoal Creek, being in Alabama and so forth [to be a likely offender]. I'm looking on page 553 at places [in Georgia]. I'd almost bet the ranch—although I'm not going to say it publicly—that these clubs discriminate. (Ashe then rattles off five member clubs.) Hey, it wouldn't take a Pulitzer Prize–winning investigative reporter to find problems here if he really wanted to do it.

Why are you soft-pedaling your criticism?

Because I do think the USTA is earnestly intent on trying to do something about it. And I don't want to back the USTA into a corner. I and others could have done that five, ten, or fifteen years ago. Look, you space out these things. But I'm not now going to try to nail anybody to the wall because I see the process has started. I just want to see how it develops.

Are you optimistic the USTA will succeed?

Oh yes, oh absolutely!

Why?

Because golf put everyone else on notice. Tennis would be stupid to go through the same thing golf went through at Shoal Creek. Absolutely stupid.

Isn't tennis much more of a liberal sport than golf and nicer to minorities, anyway?

It's less tradition-bound than golf. Both on the amateur and professional level, tennis draws from a wider range of people, in terms of ethnic groups, race and class, socioeconomic strata. No question about that.

When you won the first U.S. Open in 1968, did you become a member of the West Side Tennis Club?

An honorary member. The reason it wasn't tokenism is because anybody who won the U.S. Open was made an honorary member. What would have been tokenism would have been if I had been made an honorary member not having won the U.S. Open.

But were there any other black members in the West Side Tennis Club then?

No.

Still, you became the first black member, by whatever means.

Well, Althea Gibson won the tournament in 1957. She definitely did not become a member when she won.

Are there any black members at the West Side Tennis Club now?

Oh yeah, West Side has several black members now.

Is tokenism good?

Tokenism is always the way it starts out. Because when anything starts, you're not going to start with waves of people coming in. You start with one or two, and then it will be opened up.

So, tokenism in the short run is acceptable?

To me, it is, as long as there is movement toward broader participation.

Is it either illegal or immoral for a president of a private club to declare: "We pick the people we want to be members?"

It's neither. I would think that one of our basic rights is to associate with whomever we want. And I still respect that right. But there is a price you pay for that. The price is that you cannot be tax exempt, your property has to be taxed on its highest use according to a professional appraisal, and you should not entertain any functions of a public nature like tournaments—PGA of America, USGA, PGA, LPGA, USTA—where you derive revenue from the public.

What about the corporate world? Was the advertising withdrawal by IBM, Toyota, Honda, Lincoln-Mercury, Anheuser-Busch, and Spalding of television broadcasts of the PGA Championships justified, or was it a gross overreaction?

No, it wasn't a gross overreaction. They did what they had to do. They knew it was going to come one day sooner or later. But it had never been made an issue by pulling their sponsorship out [before]. That was the most telling action of this entire Shoal Creek incident. We're talking two million bucks down the drain in twenty-four hours. Boom!

What's the lesson there?

The lesson is that corporate America now has been sufficiently sensitized to recognize a no-win situation quickly when they see it. And they get the hell out.

FASCINATING FACTS:

- From 1950 to 1959, somewhere between two and five blacks were allowed to compete annually at the U.S. Championships (Forest Hills), according to an implied USLTA quota.
- The title of a 1901 book in Arthur Ashe's home library was *Is the Negro a Beast?*
- Arthur Ashe (1993) and Confederate General Stonewall Jackson (1863) are the only two people ever to have their bodies lie in state for public viewing at the Executive Mansion in Richmond, Virginia.
- In 1973 Arthur Ashe maintained that "the overpopulation crisis is the *only* real major issue in the world today."
- In 2001 world number one Martina Hingis called Richard Williams's allegation that there is racism on the women's tour "total nonsense."

This interview received the "Tennis Journalist of the Year—Original Submission to *Tennis Week* Award."

17

Ted Tinling: Talking to a Tennis Legend
1985

The best effect of fine persons is felt after we have left their presence.

—RALPH WALDO EMERSON

When tennis writers want a surefire great interview, they head for Teddy Tinling. His gossipy tidbits, wonderful sense of history, and provocative opinions make him a treasure just waiting to be rediscovered by every new tennis journo on the block.

No wonder, either. Ever since he ballboyed for the flamboyant superstar Suzanne Lenglen on the French Riviera in the 1920s, Teddy has had a love affair with women's tennis that has been mutual.

Eclectic doesn't do justice to Tinling's background, achievements, and prominent positions. "Teddy is our [frame] of reference," says Philippe Chatrier, president of the International Tennis Federation. "Always, when I need advice or have to make a decision, I like to listen to him because he knows so much background."

As a favorite of Lenglen, Tinling umpired 104 of her matches in the Roaring Twenties and umpired the first match ever played at Stade Roland Garros in Paris in 1928. He served as a peacemaker at Wimbledon between disgruntled players and the establishment from 1927 to 1949 and again from 1982 to now. He was just as highly competent and durable as a competitor, having played Bill Tilden and Lew Hoad while both were Wimbledon champions. Another feat only he can proudly point to is working for pay on the staffs of all four Grand Slam tournaments.

An Edwardian Englishman by birth with unmistakably proper breeding, the towering (6'4") seventy-four-year-old Tinling was a colonel in the Second World

War and regrets only that he "didn't move to America right after the war." His enduring notoriety came as the most revolutionary designer of tennis dresses in this century. Most memorable was the dress with sexy lace panties he made for Gussy Moran in 1949 that both shocked and delighted the sports world. The daring move put "Gorgeous Gussy" on the front pages everywhere and got Teddy kicked out of sedate Wimbledon. Now, he is chief of protocol on the flourishing women's tour, an assignment that happily requires all the knowledge of sports, business, media, sponsors, local traditions, and feminine mystique that Tinling uniquely provides.

I interviewed this tennis legend during the Florida Federal Open at the luxurious Innisbrook resort in Tarpon Springs.

As chief of protocol for women's tennis, what are your main responsibilities?

Half-jokingly, I always say that in these international matches my first function is to see that the flags aren't upside down. And then I have to be sure that the people understand certain things, particularly when there are reigning heads of state present, as they often are. Then they have to be a little more formal than when they are playing a tournament for themselves. Generally, it involves just keeping the thing up to standards of international behavior instead of national.

What made women's tennis really blossom in the 1970s? Was it the celebrated Billie Jean King–Bobby Riggs match? The women's rights movement that made sports more acceptable for women?

It was a combination of those plus the enormous dedication of Gladys Heldman, who really invented the women's circuit [Virginia Slims] in her friendship link with Joseph Cullman III, the chairman of the board of Philip Morris. I've summed it up before. All productions need three people. You need an author and an angel and a star. Gladys Heldman was the author. Joseph Cullman was the angel. And the star was Billie Jean King. We had the perfect trio.

There is so much concern now about the "burnout" problem that the Women's Tennis Association is reportedly about to make a ruling about when junior prodigies can join the tour and how often they will be allowed to enter tournaments. What is your position?

I'm not sure if they are about to [make a ruling]. I know they are about to consider it. That doesn't mean that they are about to do it. That's quite a different thing. They're considering limiting the number of times that people under a certain age—hypothetically, say fifteen or sixteen—can compete. That is excellent, very necessary. But there are problems with the American Constitution about inhibiting anybody's liberties. That won't apply in other countries, but here that might prove a problem.

When Martina and Chris and others complained that the press was invading their privacy during the 1984 Wimbledon, you retorted that the public has a right to know all about tennis stars and, indeed, that you would be thrilled that people cared enough to ask what you eat for breakfast. Please explain where the line should or can be drawn.

The line should be drawn by the person who is being questioned, who is never forced to answer. At Wimbledon, where there was the most focus on this situation, there is a member of the committee in every interview, and every time a contentious question is raised, he will warn the person—and did frequently warn Martina—that you didn't need to answer. It's very much as a lawyer does in court. The difference of opinion comes from whether a player subjected to a question should or should not be required to answer. I personally feel that if a player is making a great deal of money from the public, and she can't take care of herself when subjected to questions, then there is something the matter.

Is the current WTA policy of restricting extensive interviews, reviewing questions in advance, and generally being highly protective a result of the prying, sensationalist, and sometimes untruthful Wimbledon articles?

The problem really derives from the average age of the [WTA] membership being so young and the fact that the girls are not instructed on how to handle press interviews, at least not to their own advantage. And when you get the champion of the world [Navratilova] who says the press are really out of line because she doesn't know how to handle them, how do you expect a girl like [thirteen-year-old Miami phenomenon] Mary Joe Fernandez, who is just coming into the public eye, to know about handling an interview? So out of this situation this protective wall for the players has grown up. And I think something down the middle would be more suitable.

Thinking back over your sixty years in tennis, which stars handled—or even manipulated—the press best?

Certainly Suzanne [Lenglen] was ultra-professional in everything she did. She had enough knowledge of public life and repartee to handle the press. In fact, I wouldn't say she manipulated the press, but she always managed somehow—except on two notable occasions, when she retired in the middle of a match—to have a favorable press.

Were there others as skillful as Lenglen?

Well, it's such a different situation [now]. You see, until the Second World War there was hardly a single woman writing tennis about a woman at all. Women's tennis was reported almost exclusively by men, and the men

Ted Tinling. International Tennis Hall of Fame

themselves were all ex-players. There was hardly a leading newspaper in the world with the possible exception of the *New York Times* that employed a feature writer on tennis who hadn't been a tennis star. And a lot of times those players were still playing, so that the subjects of the articles were there on a friendly relationship with the writer. A lot of the problems that we discuss now could never have arisen.

Wasn't there a conflict of interest, though, when a person could be writing and competing at the same time?

Well, eventually Tilden brought that issue to a head in 1928 because it was felt he was advising people how to beat somebody that he didn't want to play. And there is still a rule now that you should not be allowed to write about a tournament in which you are playing. The rule is going to be researched because there have been [recent] breaches of it. You are allowed to write about a tournament as long as the [article] publication is either before or after it. I think that what's been found good and reasonable for fifty years by a lot of people has got to have some merit and has to be very carefully examined before it is discarded.

Let's talk about Martina. You've called her "the greatest ever" and said, "Finally, I have seen someone who can play better than Suzanne." How long do you think she'll dominate the way she has for the past two years?

I've seen Martina play *three times*—against Chris Evert—in a manner that I thought was better than Suzanne. Certainly not every day. Martina will dominate as long as she is motivated to dominate, and that is impossible to forecast. I have been told that she wants to surpass Billie Jean's achievement of six Wimbledon singles [titles]. She's now only got two to go to do that.

Is her total domination good or bad for women's tennis?

The matter of what is good or bad for women's tennis has always produced divided opinion. A lot of spectators feel a good match is 7-5 in the third set. There are just as many people who think it's marvelous to see a tremendous exhibition of skill and see the victim writhe. In most of my younger years, through Lenglen and Wills, people only went to tennis to see how well the victim could do, but they were capable of admiring the marvelous skill of the leading player. That was probably more true then than now because the spectators—before the media greatly increased the number of spectators—were normally much more knowledgeable about the game. That was most especially true in the late 1930s after they had seen Suzanne for years and Wills for years, and they were able to make comparisons.

There seems to be no competition in women's doubles for Navratilova and Pam Shriver, who have lost one match in the past two years and have captured seven straight Grand Slam titles. What has happened to their competition?

They've had little kitty-catty quarrels, silly little vendettas, and broken up. Just three years ago there were eight top teams. At the Bridgestone Doubles in Fort Worth, Texas, there were Hobbs-Durie, Kiyomura and Barker, Casals and Turnbull, Kilsch and Pfaff, Acker and Paula Smith. Martina and Pam are the only survivors from that lot. In years before, top teams like Kerry Reid and Turnbull, Reid and Kerry Harris, and Rosie and Billie Jean broke up over personality clashes. Casals can't get a partner now. The women are too emotional and not practical. Most men submerge their differences. If you're a pro, you're out to win money. If you're a tennis player, you're out to win. Whatever the reasons for these breakups, they weren't good enough reasons. It's very sad.

The concept of femininity has changed considerably in the past twenty years. Now it's okay for women to be muscular, sweaty, athletic, and aggressive. Do you regret all this?

First of all, I don't think it's twenty years. I was the main designer for Virginia Slims until 1978, and it hadn't changed then. That's only seven years, and seven years ago girls were wearing spectacular show-business dresses and being very feminine with a great deal of acceptance and pleasure for everybody concerned. So the trend is only seven years old. I don't have regrets about anything. But I am critical of performers who are not showing their maximum perception of public relations. I don't think the girls understand how to present themselves to their best advantage.

You've often commented how appalled you are by the clothes women players are wearing. What is wrong with them? What would you like to see?

I championed the cause of women being women, which was under the generic heading of femininity on court. I am a man, and since indoor tennis [arrived] in the United States, the proportion of male spectators has grown enormously because they can now watch tennis at night, which they couldn't do for the game's first ninety years. So one is therefore concerned about pleasing more men. I know for a fact that across the world men like, in most instances, a woman to look like a woman. And they don't want to have a woman's physical features thrust down their necks when they don't feel like it. They don't want a woman to show her panties every two seconds, to show her bust every two seconds, and whatever. So I know they like femininity and some sort of mystique about women's clothes.

What kind of clothes, specifically then, should women wear?

You see, you're putting me in a fixed time frame. What I might have liked five years ago, I wouldn't want any more under any circumstances.

Then what do you like today?

Nothing! I'm retired, and so I'm capable of making a judgment call as opposed to a personal opinion. Having seen the 1984 Olympics, I was impressed with the wonderful skating clothes, the wonderful gymnast clothes, and other sportswear. The garments are subjected to more strain than the tennis [outfits], so there is no alibi. And for the first time we've got an athletic fabric in spandex that is acceptable to performers. I think women's tennis clothing looks more anachronistic than that in any other sport in the business.

Is there one unfair criticism about women's tennis—such as "a lot of players are lesbians"—that particularly bothers you?

I don't think there really is. In life I'm a great believer in people getting what they deserve, and that goes for the credits just as much as the negatives. I think you guys in the media report tennis very, very well, and when the players criticize what [reporters] have written, it's at least 50 percent the player's own fault. I feel just as severe about myself. If I have a bad interview, I'll accept at least half the blame for anything that is said that I don't agree with.

I don't know whether there is any lesbianism or not because I've never been in the bedroom [observing]. So I have no idea whether that's true. The bottom line is—as Chris Evert recently pointed out—that women's tennis is pulling in masses of people, huge crowds.

You are very fond of the Japanese people and Japan, but you don't think they are suited for producing top tennis players. Why not?

Tennis is a highly spontaneous game and, having worked with the Japanese, I have observed the fact that they don't exhibit spontaneity. They are the great copiers of the world, but they work for a central system under direction. But in tennis that's impossible. In tennis you've got to make decisions second by second. They find that hard to do.

Which Japanese players have you known best? Would you please tell me about them.

I was on the ship when [Jiroh] Satoh committed suicide, and I had been to Japan at the invitation of the Japanese Tennis Federation in 1933, when I was twenty-three, and I knew the entire tennis federation that year as close friends. In later years I dressed the only Japanese girl ever to win a Wimbledon title. Ann Kiyomura won the doubles. She was my client. I've worked there with dress contracts. I've come in contact with a lot of Japanese manufacturers of that description.

Is there a country or countries with ideal national traits or aptitudes for a fiercely competitive, individualistic sport like tennis?

We've had that question [come up] a lot of times. What used to be called the Gallic flair would lead you into inconsistencies and lack of thoroughness. We've had the dour Germanic temperament called unspontaneous and unimaginative. In the olden days when life was different, the English were quite good at tennis because they were neither one nor the other. I think the tremendous determination to have an identity in America provides a lot of motivation to American players and probably dominates the rest of their behavior.

France, Germany, and England haven't produced superstars since the 1930s. How do you account for that decline?

I don't think it's quite true. The English girls won Wimbledon, three of them, in the '50s and '60s. I don't think you can put down Christine Truman, Angela [Mortimer] Barrett—who won the French, the Italian, and Wimbledon—and Ann Jones. And also Virginia Wade, who won the U.S. Open as well as [the 1977] Wimbledon. They weren't superstars, but they were stars of a very bright magnitude. We haven't had a good men's player since Fred Perry in the super-standard class. Nobody understands why. I think it relates to the educational system where you can't go back to school as you can in the U.S. You have to take and pass your examinations at a certain age: O Levels at sixteen, A Levels by eighteen, and then you have to go to the university, and that's it. It's at that exact moment when, to become a star, you'd be playing your tennis. So you have to make a predetermined choice about whether you're going to risk your time to become a star and sacrifice your education and end up with neither. Americans don't face this dilemma. They can go back to school after they've failed at tennis.

What about your assessment of Germany and France?

I wouldn't expect Germany now [to produce champions]. It is segmented physically and segmented mentally. They have had a great deal of turbulence, and today both East and West Germany are very small countries. I wouldn't expect them to do too much … But France is an enigma. They find it impossible to explain themselves. I have no hypothesis, none at all. But I don't live in France anymore. With the example they had of the [Four] Musketeers and Lenglen, maybe that's what plays against them. They feel they can't achieve those same heights.

Is it true that Suzanne Lenglen always used to serve holding three balls and that one of her breasts sometimes popped out of her dress?

Both were true. You see, the fans were composed of rich, leisured people who were not small-time at all. The world got a little more small-time in the last thirty years in that people object to swearing and, on the other hand, they use four-letter words that they never did. In those days, it was what we called a "gentleman's sport," and if a gentleman was titillated by seeing Suzanne, a brief glimpse of her bust, nobody minded except the women. The women minded a lot. The women used to be very uptight about it.

You've called the famous Don Budge–Gottfried von Cramm Davis Cup match the greatest in history. You were there. What do you remember most about it?

It was 1937. The whole outcome of the Davis Cup depended on it, and it was 9-7 or 8-6 in the fifth [set]. I still have the umpire's blank [scorecard] in my possession. Budge was 4-1 down in the final set but pulled a great comeback. We had two great gentlemen playing each other—one of the things that has become more and more conspicuous in my memory—like two white knights playing each other in a duel. They behaved unbelievably well with all that pressure.

One of your most provocative assertions is that coaches and coaching are overrated, that Chris Evert Lloyd noted that her father taught her how to play, but she taught herself how to win, and that most coaches know little about winning. Would you please explain or justify your position.

You put the word "overrated" in there. I didn't say that. I think they're limited in their scope. The coaches have been a great asset to the tour in providing companions for the girls at a time when they need it. If a girl wants to go out to lunch or dinner or the movies, she doesn't have to traipse around looking for an escort and making herself undignified. She has a paid servant, if you wish, to do what she wants. That's been very helpful to the tour. There is no doubt coaches can teach people how to hit the ball over the net because that's what they're there for. The actual technique of winning a match is a different dimension. Unless they've won matches and are experienced match winners, I don't think you can teach anybody how to win. I don't know many coaches—or hardly any, in fact—that have made a name for themselves as winning performers.

You've remarked that "tennis is an assassin's game," and you also have said how much you lament the decline in grace and respect you see in tennis today. Just a few minutes ago, to your dismay, you saw Pam Casale talking back to the umpire about a line call in her match against Eva Pfaff. Would you agree that if the former statement is true, then the latter is inevitable?

No, I don't think tennis is any more of an "assassin's sport" than it has ever been. When I say it's an "assassin's sport," I'm very basic. That is to say, if you've won, I'm dead; if I've won, you're dead. That situation is unchanged over a hundred years. People used to commit tennis murder with much more grace and charm. There's no need for misbehavior. There never was. Tennis is so much a part of contemporary lifestyle that one of the problems today is the loss of knowledge of the word "respect." Across the world, people do not respect each other and each other's rights as they used to. So perhaps it's asking too much for tennis players to be any different and respect the dignity of the other person.

One of your most fascinating quotes is: "We know what will happen in the world, more or less, don't we? But we don't know what will happen in tennis, and I can hardly wait to find out." If you had to predict, what does your crystal ball tell you?

The technical side will keep on evolving just as it has in recent years, when the rackets got bigger, the covering of the balls got different, and various rules, such as the foot-fault rule, have become more permissive. Variations of that sort will undoubtedly go on. As far as the fundamentals of hitting the ball over the net, it doesn't seem to have changed at all since the game first began. People rush the net more and better than before, but that doesn't necessarily mean that will go on. Chris Evert reversed the whole trend by being a wonderful example of playing tennis without being a net-rusher.

Will the game be able to sustain its tremendous popularity?

There is no way I foresee it dying when it's survived all sorts of turbulence in the 110 years of its history. Tennis' extraordinary mystique has been its capacity to survive, and that is due to its capacity to revitalize and present an image of totally contemporary people in every era.

FASCINATING FACTS:

- Queen Elizabeth once told Ted Tinling: "I had no idea tennis girls could look so pretty."
- Famed dress designer and tennis historian Ted Tinling opined that Helen Wills and Karol Fageros were the two most beautiful women who ever played tennis.
- In a 1996 survey by DMB&B ad agency, tennis (62 percent) was the third most-popular sport among the 25,057 teenagers (ages fifteen to eighteen) in forty-one countries around the world, trailing only basketball (71 percent) and soccer (67 percent).
- The mint green Ted Tinling dress that Billie Jean king wore for her famous "Battle of the Sexes" match is displayed in the Smithsonian Institution.

PART 3

Topical Trends and Burning Issues

18

Does Father Really Know Best?
1998

It is a wise father that knows his own child.

—WILLIAM SHAKESPEARE, THE MERCHANT OF VENICE

When loose cannon Richard Williams fired off false accusations of racism during the 1997 U.S. Open, tennis' newest Bad Dad reminded us how tennis parents profoundly shape the lives of their prodigies—for better or for worse.

Who can forget abusive Jim Pierce, self-destructive Peter Graf, obtuse Stefano Capriati, and unrelenting Roland Jaeger? These well-meaning but fanatical fathers hurt the ones they loved and left behind a wake of misery and embarrassing controversy.

Bad Dads originated long before Open Era megabucks brought out the greed in them. Charles Lenglen, an unfulfilled bicycle racer, got his vicarious thrills by molding his daughter Suzanne into tennis' first female superstar and France's greatest heroine since Joan of Arc.

Unfortunately, nothing short of perfection satisfied Papa Lenglen. If Suzanne practiced poorly, he punished her by denying her jam on her bread. A stern taskmaster, he sometimes scornfully scolded Suzanne on the court in front of others. She became so drained emotionally and physically that she looked older than she actually was. When she turned professional in 1926, she confided to friends, "At last, after fifteen years of torture, I can enjoy my tennis!"

If only tennis parents could guide—or let others coach—their talented kids toward the top *and* let them enjoy their tennis. Pierce, a convicted felon who had spent time in a psychiatric ward while incarcerated, was obsessed, like Lenglen, with turning his little daughter Mary into a champion. Inside the cover of a notebook that Pierce started keeping when she was ten, he wrote: "She will be number one. She will dominate."

When Mary was eighteen, she made the cover of the August 23, 1993 *Sports Illustrated* magazine—but not because she won a major title and was hailed as the next teen queen. The cover showed a beautiful young woman staring forlornly behind a stark headline that blared, "Special Report: Why Mary Pierce Fears for Her Life."

The exposé revealed that Mary filed two restraining orders, traveled incognito, and hired bodyguards to protect her from a dangerous pursuer, her father. In May 1993 Pierce stalked Mary, her mother, Yannick, and brother, David, at a hotel in Italy and attacked Mary's bodyguard with a knife. In June Mary fired her father as coach, and at the same time Yannick decided to divorce him. Both declared in the restraining orders that Pierce had a history of physically abusing them and threatening their lives. Since she was ten, Mary told *Sports Illustrated,* "He would slap me after I had lost a match or sometimes just if I had a bad practice," confirming what many in the tennis world had long suspected.

Psychiatrists would have a field day analyzing the violent, unrepentant Pierce, a battered child himself. In a 1990 *Sports Illustrated* article, "Too Much, Too Young," Pierce recalled the bitter relationship he had with his father. "I carried an ass-whipping with me to school every day." And he ironically added, "I promised that my children would never be beat."

The press aptly dubbed Pierce "The Tennis Father from Hell." His reign of terror started with his yelling "Mary, kill the bitch!" during her junior tournament matches and ended with his slugging two spectators at the 1993 French Open. On July 17, the WTA Tour banned him from attending her tournaments for a year. Since their split Mary has seen a sports psychologist, sometimes partied heartily, and switched coaches a few times, once being fired by Nick Bollettieri for being out of shape.

But power-hitting Mary also captured the 1995 Australian Open and reached the final there in 1997 and the French final in 1994. She credits her father with giving her a strong work ethic and sound game. Mary insists she doesn't regret her troubled past and says, "What happened, happened. Sometimes I wonder if things hadn't been so tough, would I have been the tennis player I am today?"

The soap opera resumed in December 1996 when Pierce, stricken with bladder cancer, sued his daughter, claiming she had promised him 25 percent of her career earnings, now more than $3 million. Recently he said he intends to sue the WTA Tour, arguing that the ban prevented him from earning a living as a coach.

Williams, Pierce's pal in Florida, portrays him as the victim, and, true to form, invokes the race card. "Mr. Pierce is a great human being and a great instructor," vouches Williams. "The WTA did a very unjust service to Mr. Pierce. You wouldn't treat a dog that way. As a matter of fact, they treated him as if he were black."

While 1980s burnout victim Andrea Jaeger commented, "There's no manual to teach them how to deal with being so good so young," Mary Pierce says she uses Steffi Graf as her role model to deal with adversity. Indeed, Steffi has endured her father's two highly publicized scandals and other lesser embarrassments with extraordinary strength and grace.

Ted Tinling, the late tennis maven who knew both the Lenglen and Graf families, once observed, "The similarities between Suzanne and Steffi and their fathers are remarkable. Both fathers built their lives around the daughter. Both daughters adored the father no matter what his flaws."

During Steffi's childhood, Peter Graf did all the right things to nurture her genuine love of tennis and protect her. He patiently taught her the fundamentals, found her the best coach and training facilities, and arranged full medical examinations for her twice a year from the age of ten. He also prevented burnout by severely limiting her tournaments and exhibitions during her early years on the pro circuit and had her take several months rest at the end of each season.

But by the time Steffi became number one in 1987, the former used-car and insurance salesman proved inadequate to manage his daughter's affairs in big-time tennis. His inability to negotiate deals adroitly, as well as greed, a penchant for the limelight, boastfulness (he once claimed 80 percent of the German people knew his name), and poor relations with WTA officials and the media all contributed to his downfall. His alcohol problem accelerated it.

In 1990 Graf's brief extramarital affair with twenty-two-year-old call girl and model Nicole Meissner sparked sensational front-page headlines in the British and German tabloids during Wimbledon. The sordid stories later revealed Meissner and boxing promoter Eberhard Thust tried to extort four hundred thousand dollars from the Grafs, claiming (falsely) that Peter fathered her baby girl. Although the couple was arrested and jailed for blackmail, the revelations devastated Steffi and clearly hurt her performance. After upset losses at the French Open and Wimbledon, she confessed, "These days I am not at my very best. I could not fight as usual because of all the turmoil. Tennis is a game won with the head, and lately my head has not been on tennis."

In the summer of 1995 another shocking Graf scandal rocked Germany and the sports world and tested Steffi as never before. Her beloved "Papa," as she called him, was arrested and imprisoned on tax evasion charges. The Grafs had failed to declare the full extent of her earnings between 1989 and 1993; Peter had funneled more than 20 million deutsche marks through a secret bank account in

FASCINATING FACTS:

- The father of 1996 Wimbledon champion Richard Krajicek sometimes forced his son to walk several kilometers home after being eliminated in junior tournaments.
- The defense attorney explained the actions of Lyle and Erik Menendez during their eight-month trial for the brutal murder of their parents by saying, "Too much tennis and not enough hugs."
- Mike Agassi, Andre's father, once threw Andre's trophy into a trash can after Andre lost a junior tournament final.

the tax haven of Liechtenstein, and he had signed an invalid agreement with regional tax authorities. Although Steffi was grilled by the tax investigators for two days and not arrested, she confided: "The last few weeks have definitely been the worst and unhappiest time in my life." Even so, Steffi remained loyal to her father and used the tennis court as a refuge against the heartbreaking vicissitudes in her life. Almost unbelievably, the resilient superstar won all six Grand Slams she competed in during 1995 and 1996.

If only Stefano Capriati had heeded a 1985 tennis-camp evaluation in the family scrapbook! It ironically reads: "She has potential and should be developed wisely. Keep her tennis 'career' in perspective. Keep it fun! Be careful not to push her progress too quickly."

Jennifer was still playing for fun while making millions in endorsements when she reached the final of her first pro tournament in 1990. Magazine cover headlines like *Sports Illustrated*'s "And She's Only 13!" and *Newsweek*'s "The 8th Grade Wonder" heralded her seemingly certain greatness.

The cute and bubbly ingenue so charmed the sporting public that Tinling exclaimed, "Happiness has returned. Mary Poppins tennis! The next ten years are going to be terrific!" With youthful naivete, Jennifer said, "I learned that it will be fun if it's all like this."

The fairy-tale rookie year ended with Jennifer ranked in the top ten, but the fun proved short-lived. After losing a disappointing 1992 Australian Open match to Gabriela Sabatini, she confided, "There's a lot of pressure on me from every-one. Maybe it's because things are more serious now."

The destructive pressure came mostly from her domineering father, who usu-ally didn't know best. He forced her to practice, compete, and travel far too much, especially to lucrative but meaningless exhibitions in faraway Asia. When questioned about pushing Jennifer into pro tennis too soon, Capriati often replied with an Italian saying: "When the fruit is ripe, you eat it." Everyone but he could see that Jennifer was far from ripe. What about possible burnout? Capriati, even more stupidly, replied, "Kids don't burn out, parents do."

Unrealistically high expectations—such as Billie Jean King's prediction that Jennifer could be world champion before she was eighteen—the intense media coverage, and the demands of her sponsors and the WTA Tour, eager to exploit its hot commodity, further increased the pressure on her.

Jennifer, who craved a normal teenage life, rebelled against all of it, burned out prematurely, and finally dropped out of both the pro tour and school. The downward spiral escalated. Jennifer moved out of her parents' home, was cited for shoplifting, went into a drug rehabilitation facility, was arrested for posses-sion of marijuana, and entered rehab again. She even contemplated suicide. Now twenty-one, she has tried several comebacks, most recently, to the dismay of many, with her father back as her coach.

Like Capriati, Andrea Jaeger surrendered much of her childhood and teenage life as a devoted follower of her hard-driving, one-dimensional father, a German-born immigrant to America. He liked to tell tennis parents, "Your child plays for himself last. First he plays for you, then for his coach, then for himself."

Unfortunately, Jaeger was right. Although Andrea was a wonderful competitor and reached number two in the world, she played and played and played, even when she should have rested and recuperated, until her shoulder simply gave out. Seven surgeries couldn't restore it, and she retired at Capriati's age (twenty-one) without the major titles she had appeared destined for. "I don't think I really reached my potential at all," she says.

Andrea learned a painful lesson from her unfulfilled career. "I wouldn't let my kid turn pro at fourteen," she says. In intimate conversations Andrea has advised Jennifer not to dwell on her lost childhood, suggesting, "I can't replace the years when I was thirteen, fourteen. Neither can she."

Andrea may have discovered the hard way exactly what Billie Jean King has long maintained: women make the best coaches because they are natural nurturers. Melanie Molitor has shown that a mother's tender care and a brilliant coaching mind can produce a happy and healthy champion. After sixteen-year-old Martina Hingis won her first Grand Slam singles title at the 1997 Australian Open, Molitor told *Sports Illustrated,* "Tennis is just a short stage of your life, and it can be good preparation for the rest of it. I want it to help Martina become independent and self-analytical until someday she finds a partner. And I don't mean a doubles partner."

The mother-daughter team have a great relationship and vow not to make the same mistakes that other players and their overbearing, obsessive parents made. Ever-smiling Martina pals around with the other players and leads a well-balanced life with a dazzling assortment of off-court activities—soccer, in-line skating, skiing, boxing, mountain biking, basketball, walking through the woods with her German shepherd, aerobics, and her first love, riding her two horses.

Martina's two falls from horses this year, one serious enough to require surgery, bring back memories of the tragic accident that ended the career of 1950s teenage starlet Maureen Connolly. Will the otherwise nonpareil Molitor some day regret the carte blanche freedom she gives Martina to ride horses?

Meanwhile, her sensible methods—such as limiting Martina's practice time—deserve to be emulated by tennis fathers. Until they are, Bad Dads will bedevil the tennis world.

And the bold message will remain on the sign at one of the courts at the Nick Bollettieri Tennis Academy: No Parents.

FASCINATING FACTS:

- In 1999 Martina Navratilova said that the press should not interview tennis parents.
- Mary Pierce reportedly paid her then-estranged father, Jim, five hundred thousand dollars to drop the lawsuit he threatened her with, claiming he deserved part of her winnings as her father and coach for eighteen years.
- Parents who send their children to Pat Cash's new tennis academy in Australia are required to attend behavior classes.

19

Tennis: From Genteel Game to Serious Sport
2000

Conduct is three-fourths of our life and its largest concern.

—MATTHEW ARNOLD

On the seventh anniversary of the invention of modern lawn tennis, London's *Daily Telegraph* carried a long editorial paying tribute to Major Walter Clopton Wingfield, who in 1874 patented and marketed his "New and Improved Court for Playing the Ancient Game of Tennis."

The editorial critically noted that cricket was a "serious undertaking" which "could not lightly be taken up and put down again." At the other extreme was croquet which "the manlier section of society rebelled against" and provided "no healthy exercise." No such liabilities handicapped tennis, though. It was "an amusement which combined exercise with skill, which could attract and bring together both sexes."[1]

Lawn tennis' growth had been meteoric then. "That which can now fairly be called a national pastime has withstood the test of temper, taste, and criticism; each succeeding year has made it more popular," enthused the *Daily Telegraph*. "Wherever the English language is spoken it is known; it has traveled round the world and back again, visited India, explored the Colonies, and been set up in the backwoods of America."[2]

The editorial lauded the gallant ex–cavalry officer for "the bright faces, the incessant laughter, the health-giving exercise, and the wholesome amusement which have been the outcome of his invention." It concluded that "on the one hand, it encourages the enterprise of competition, and, on the other, the agreeable interchanges of social courtesies...."[3]

That coexistence of competition and social courtesies was based on unwritten codes of honor and a spirit of cooperation and camaraderie. E. Digby Baltzell explored how this glorious tradition of amateur sportsmanship originated and evolved in his didactic, scholarly book *Sporting Gentlemen: Men's Tennis from the Age of Honor to the Cult of the Superstar.*

Baltzell, the late emeritus professor of history and sociology at the University of Pennsylvania and an authority on the white Anglo-Saxon Protestant (WASP) establishment, wrote that between 1588 and 1914 "the British gentleman became a model of civilized man, respected and envied throughout the world."[4] An anecdote illustrated how an upper-class code of conduct had so deeply penetrated the British social structure. When visiting the famous Dartmoor Prison in Devonshire, England, in 1958, Baltzell was told by the warden that a particular inmate was apprehended after he squealed about a break-in. Why? "One of his friends was going to use a gun," the warden replied, "and he knew that was *not cricket.*"[5]

Everyone in the Victorian British Empire—whether in a maximum security prison or on the playing fields of Eton—knew what the phrase "It isn't cricket" meant. It embodied high ideals of conduct and decorum. And to the British ruling class, the sports of cricket and tennis symbolized those ideals. But the lower classes admired them, too; Alexis de Tocqueville contrasted their ambition to "level upwards" with today's perverse egalitarian desire to "level downwards":

> There is in fact a manly and lawful passion for equality which incites men to wish all to be powerful and honored. This passion tends to raise the humble to the rank of the great; but there exists also in the human heart a depraved taste for equality which impels the weak to attempt to lower the powerful to their own level.[6]

Thomas Arnold, an Anglican clergyman and headmaster of Rugby School starting in 1828, stressed religious and moral principles, and gentlemanly conduct. Baltzell wrote that those ideals became the public-school ethos in England. They also greatly influenced France's Baron Pierre de Coubertin, the founder of the modern Olympic Games, as well as the manners and morals of America's new upper class between 1880 and the First World War.

President Teddy Roosevelt, who built the first tennis court on the White House grounds and played there nearly every day, weather permitting, with his "Tennis Cabinet," viewed sports as a means to build character, much like Dr. Arnold, and decried professionalism and commercialism. ("When money comes in at the gate, the game goes out the window."[7]) Endicott Peabody, educated in England where he absorbed Dr. Arnold's values, also greatly advanced the gentlemanly values of sportsmanship in early twentieth-century America as headmaster of the prestigious Groton School. Peabody praised the English approach to games ("The highest achievement of any game can be claimed for the national game of cricket, which is used as a measure of moral quality"[8]) and abhorred the growing American ethic of winning at all costs.

The four families whose sons founded American tennis—the Searses and Dwights, Boston Brahmins, and the Clarks and Taylors from Philadelphia—had aristocratic lineages. Their "upper-class" codes were passed on from generation to generation through institutions such as the church, country clubs, exclusive preparatory schools, and colleges, most typically the Big Three of Harvard, Yale, and Princeton. Dr. James Dwight, the first to play lawn tennis in the United States and the president of the United States National Lawn Tennis Association (USNLTA) for twenty-one years, finished his last instruction book, *A Sermon on Lawn Tennis,* with this advice: "Win quietly; lose quietly; don't get angry."[9]

The self-denying value of these founding fathers' Protestant ethic was exemplified by England's William Renshaw, the seven-time Wimbledon champion who gave his favorite racket to his American counterpart, seven-time U.S. Championships titlist Richard Sears, in 1884. It was young multimillionaire Dwight Filley Davis's strong sense of *noblesse oblige* that inspired him to create the Davis Cup competition in 1900 to promote international goodwill and understanding.

Indeed, many of the early Cup ties showcased splendid fellowship that enhanced relationships among players and nations. Norman Brookes, the father of Australian tennis and its first great player, exemplified that at the 1908 Challenge Round, the first international tennis event staged in Australia. Representing Australasia (Australia and New Zealand), the patrician and normally reserved Brookes walked out of the clubhouse arm-in-arm with America's Fred Alexander, a New York stockbroker. And after their grueling five-set duel, they walked off the court with the same arm-in-arm gesture of friendship.

Two other leading figures in that memorable Challenge Round also bonded as so many highly competitive but friendly Yanks and their Down Under counterparts would for the rest of the century. In his superb history book, *Australia and the Davis Cup: A Centenary Story,* Alan Trengove recalled: "Anthony Wilding had gone to Port Melbourne to farewell Beals Wright, and a newspaper photograph showed them clasping each other like fond brothers. *The Age* wasn't surprised at such manifestations of good fellowship—it was only what one would expect from four representatives of the Anglo-Saxon race!"

Put simply, nearly all the tennis champions of yesteryear were true-blue heroes, paragons of virtue, and not colorful antiheroes, like John McEnroe, or vacuous media-created celebrities, like the young Andre Agassi. The most renowned were R. Norris Williams, a survivor of the 1912 Titantic disaster and the last aristocratic millionaire tennis champion, and 1930s German star Baron Gottfried von Cramm. Williams carried chivalry to the point of refusing to lob to an opponent facing the sun. Von Cramm, handsome and impeccably attired, refused to take match point in the crucial match of the 1935 Davis Cup Interzone Final against the U.S. by saying the ball tipped his racquet. When he was reprimanded for letting down his teammates, he raged: "Do you think that I would sleep tonight knowing that the ball had touched my racquet without my saying so? Never, because I would be violating every principle that I think this game stands for."[10]

The manners and morals of the fair sex rarely caused a commotion, but superstar Helen Wills thought both so essential that she wrote a thoughtful piece titled "Etiquette" in her 1928 instructional book, *Tennis*. Wills, the sedate daughter of a Berkeley, California, physician and a Phi Beta Kappa graduate of UC-Berkeley, discussed such fine points as allowing the visiting player to pass first when meeting at the net during changeovers; never throwing points to equalize an incorrect line call because it is not sporting; and when to shake hands at home versus abroad.

Wills also listed six fundamental rules of etiquette for the tennis audience—such as wearing parasols that do not block the view of other spectators—that also reflected what the game stood for. "While the etiquette of the grandstand at tennis may seem conservative, it is based on sane and logical reasons," Wills wrote. "Tennis is a conservative and dignified sport. The etiquette of both gallery and court conforms to the spirit of the game."

On the West Coast both the spirit and style of the game were evolving. Maurice McLoughlin developed all the year round what would be called the "Big Game" on the asphalt and cement courts of northern California. His daring net attack, leaping smashes, and cannonball serving—a major departure from what had been a gentler, slower-paced pastime—captured the imagination of the masses, many of whom had previously considered tennis a sissy game.

McLoughlin, the amiable son of a Scotch-Irish immigrant, became the first Californian, public parks player, and non–Ivy League American to win U.S. National singles in 1912, retained his crown in 1913, and took the U.S. doubles titles from 1912 to 1914. While "The Comet" or "California Comet," as he was nicknamed, blazed brightly but briefly, his contribution was nonetheless immense.

"It was 'The Comet's' hurricane hitting, cheery smile and flaming red hair that really changed tennis from a society luxury into a national game," wrote Bill Tilden in his 1938 book, *Aces, Places and Faults*. "One may justly criticize McLoughlin's stroke production, but no one can deny he was as dynamic and revolutionary a figure as ever came into the game to mark a definite step in its progress."

According to Baltzell, the controversial Tilden fell in the middle of any spectrum measuring sportsmanship. One side of Tilden, a gentleman by birth and breeding, was obsessively moralistic—"The first law of tennis is that every player must be a good sportsman and inherently a gentleman," he wrote—and he would scold a linesman for making an incorrect call in his favor. (So intimidating was a withering Tilden stare that in 1928 the USLTA proposed, but did not enact, a ban on players' glaring at linesmen.)

That side of Tilden, though, was at odds with the temperament of a genius and a frustrated actor, which was often displayed as an irritating gamesmanship. "Big Bill" also incessantly feuded with the tennis establishment off court and once said, "I must own to a special dislike for amateur sports officials in general." Another dichotomy of this giant of Sport's Golden Age of the 1920s was that he was the last cricket-club-bred champion and the first men's champion to turn professional.

England's fiercely competitive Fred Perry, the first player to win all four Grand Slam titles, was renowned for gamesmanship, rather like the mischievous Frenchman Jean Borotra. Once, playing Borotra, Perry intentionally had a stunning-looking French model seated right next to the court. When Borotra smashed an easy lob, "I took off in the opposite direction, over the wall and on to Helene's lap," he recalled. "She gave me a big red lipstick kiss and the place was in uproar."[11]

Ever the showman, Perry would also jump the net after winning a big match to give the crowd the impression that he was fit enough to play another five sets. This son of a working-class member of Parliament unapologetically confided, "I didn't aspire to be a good sport: 'champion' was good enough for me."[12] A favorite Perry trick to break his opponent's winning momentum was to complain that something was in his eye. He would go to the umpire's chair where neither the umpire, the linesman, or he could find anything. And by then, recalled Perry, "the other fellow would be hopping mad." Though brash by 1930s standards and admittedly "probably the most un-English Englishman at the time," Perry was hardly a court barbarian.

From 1930 to 1949, America also produced a different breed of champion. Like McLoughlin and "Little Bill" Johnston, the U.S. Championships titlist in 1915 and 1919, they came not from the grass courts of exclusive eastern-seaboard country and cricket clubs but from the gritty public-parks hardcourts of California. Ellsworth Vines, Don Budge, Bobby Riggs, Jack Kramer, and Mexican-American Pancho Gonzalez were middle-class at most and reflected the inevitable democratization of the game. All, including the nonconformist Riggs and the fiery Gonzalez, were attracted to tennis' aristocratic mystique and aspired to "level upwards."

Perry Jones ruled junior tennis with an iron hand at the famed Los Angeles Tennis Club in those days and demanded the highest behavior and dress standards. "All close balls are good. If you remember that, you'll never cheat an opponent," he preached. "In tournament tennis, you don't question a call by the umpire or a linesman. You continue to play."[13]

FASCINATING FACTS:

- Bill Tilden averred that the two assets that make a tennis player a gate attraction are sportsmanship and a colorful personality.
- All-white clothing was introduced at Wimbledon in order to hide embarrassing sweat marks.
- Englishman Buster Mottram, a world top-twenty player in the 1970s, once deliberately tried to serve a ball into the Royal Box at Wimbledon.

Riggs, known more for his post-career court hustles and celebrated "Battle of the Sexes" match against Billie Jean King than for winning all three titles in his 1939 Wimbledon debut, was perpetually fun-loving but never unsporting. Kramer, in his 1979 memoir, *The Game: My 40 Years in Tennis,* wrote, "This may sound peculiar, but Bobby Riggs is one of the most honorable men I ever met."

When the highly competitive Riggs lost the 1940 U.S. Championships final at Forest Hills on a dubious line call, he didn't explode in anger or even protest. Forty-seven years later, Riggs told me how much Open Tennis had changed the game's mores. "When we were players [in the 1930s and 1940s] and got a bad line call, we were playing for a cup or a title—and no money was involved at all. It's much easier to be a good sport under those kinds of conditions," he recalled. "When you're playing out there and it means fifty or a hundred thousand dollars to you, and you feel you got robbed because some blind linesman gave you a bad call, these guys have every reason to get upset and be spooked out."

Still, this son of a preacher respected the gentlemanly traditions of tennis and stressed, "I do not approve of foul language and calling a guy every name in the book. I never approved of Connors's antics, giving the finger to somebody, or Nastase's lowering his pants and giving the moon and having umpires removed and calling for the referee. They've carried this a little too far."

The recalcitrant Gonzalez, whose father was a day laborer and his mother a seamstress, fell "madly in love" with tennis as a boy and often played hooky from school. Jones disqualified him from playing junior tournaments after finding out about his truancy record, but Gonzalez disclosed in his autobiography, *Man with a Racket,* that he "bore no animosity toward Mr. Jones" who "simply did his duty."

"My love spread from the first racket to the game itself and its many facets," wrote Gonzalez. Feeling like a social outcast in the still mostly WASP tennis world, Gonzalez wanted to emulate his wealthier, more sophisticated peers, and he especially admired the charming Francis X. Shields, grandfather of actress Brooke Shields.

"He's also a big handsome guy who knows how to wear clothes and is poised and at ease in any kind of company," wrote Gonzalez. "His polish and mastery of the social graces interests me as much as his tennis tips. I watched him carefully and tried to acquire some of his self-assurance."

On the other side of the world, the Australian dynasty of the 1950s and 1960s was similarly inspired in part by stories of "Gentleman Jack" Crawford's courtly manners and old-school majesty back in the 1930s. The concept of the British gentleman lived on through genial yet ultra-competitive champions like Frank Sedgman, Lew Hoad, Ken Rosewall, Rod Laver, and Roy Emerson, who were kept in line by strict disciplinarian Harry Hopman, their legendary Davis Cup captain. Hopman was known to fine his young charges if they didn't use the correct spoon at the dinner table or failed to open a car door for a female player.

The "fair dinkum" Australian spirit also fostered camaraderie, teamwork, and patriotism that lives to this day and is exemplified by Pat Rafter's pronouncement that "There is nothing better than playing for your country."

The Aussies, who played hard and often partied even heartier, were especially gracious losers, too. Their code of conduct brooked no excuses. If you played a match you were healthy, and if you had an injury, you hid it and didn't talk about it, else you'd diminish your foe's victory. Double Grand Slammer Laver's wife, Mary, once secretly treated his injury in a telephone booth.

John McEnroe and fellow miscreants ushered in what Baltzell called "the roughneck age of tennis"[14] (from 1974 to 1990), which paralleled and reflected the prevalent social deterioration and loosening of cultural restraints. The infamous 1979 U.S. Open McEnroe-Nastase match—at which dangerously angry, inebriated fans nearly sparked a riot—symbolized the nadir of that era.

Tournament director Bill Talbert was outraged by the turbulent crowd as much as the on-court troublemakers. "In forty-eight years of tennis, I've never seen anything like it," Talbert told the *New York Times*. "In the box seats, two men were fighting, and their wives were fighting. My wife heard one woman—I wouldn't even repeat what she was shouting to Nastase. The words—I've never heard them in most locker rooms. I used to go to Forest Hills in a coat and tie. I saw somebody the other day in the champions' box without a shirt on. This is all kind of new."

The often tumultuous "roughneck age" was lowlighted again when McEnroe and Connors disgraced themselves and America with their temper tantrums against host Sweden in their losing 1984 Davis Cup final. Connors, still immature at thirty-two, was nearly disqualified by referee Alan Mills for savagely abusing the British umpire as Mats Wilander trounced him. McEnroe gracelessly criticized his hosts for the facilities in Gothenburg and the dates of the final, and angrily smashed balls, rackets, and courtside cups—soaking the prime minister and the king!—during his upset defeat against Henrik Sundstrom.

In a syndicated column titled "America's Punks," former U.S. Secretary of the Treasury William E. Simon censured Connors's and McEnroe's misbehavior as "one of the most disgusting and vulgar displays of childishness ever seen in a world-class sporting event."

Embarrassed by its "ugly Americans," the United States Tennis Association introduced new guidelines for future Davis Cuppers, requiring them to show "courtesy and civility towards competitors, officials, and spectators at all times." Not surprisingly, both culprits scornfully refused to sign the guidelines. So much for the noble Cup ideals espoused by Dwight Davis back in 1900!

The roughnecks infuriated mannerly tennis traditionalists, such as Talbert and U.S. Davis Cup captain Arthur Ashe, but delighted the new rowdy breed of fans that Baltzell condemned as "more interested in incidents and confrontations than in the fine points of tennis."[15] Vic Braden, a noted teaching pro and psychologist, shared Baltzell's disgust for their crudeness and rudeness. "Society has changed. Players know what society wants. So people come to watch it," Braden said in 1983. "If that's what society really wants, it's a porno flick. I want to see someone have the guts to have the offender thrown out."

Officialdom belatedly cracked down on the Vesuvian McEnroe when it ejected him from the 1990 Australian Open for cursing—"Go fuck your mother," he ranted at the supervisor of officiating. In 1995 a retired and somewhat repentant McEnroe faulted tennis authorities for not having taken a tougher stand against him. "I would have loved it sometimes if an umpire or linesman had just said, 'Look, piss off you little shit.' Maybe they should have had more of a go at me."

Ashe, a consummate court gentleman, explained the degeneration of player behavior from his insider vantage point. "There is peer pressure in the [pro golf] locker room that is missing in tennis," Ashe told the *New York Times* in 1983. "Arnold Palmer will tell another player, 'Hey, we don't do that here.' Beginning with my generation, the peer pressure stopped. Maybe it was because we felt tennis had been too much of a gentleman's game. But none of us had the guts or will to go up to Connors and Nastase and say, 'Hey, you don't do that here.'"

Television further accelerated the decline of tennis as a gentleman's game. Feuds, controversies, and especially physical confrontations—such as the famous Venus Williams–Irina Spirlea bumping incident during their 1997 U.S. Open semifinal—were sensationalized with repeated replays during matches and later on popular sports programs, such as ESPN *Sportscenter.* TV sports producers knew these running soap operas of feuds pumped up ratings. Viewers increasingly found hostility between athletes exciting and enjoyable.

The promotion of conspicuous displays of bad manners spawned a new breed of "media brats," such as McEnroe and Connors. "Consciously or unconsciously, athletes recognized that television rewarded uncivil behavior in the sports arena," wrote Benjamin G. Rader in his 1984 book, *In Its Own Image: How Television Has Transformed Sports.* "Television advertisers even capitalized on the negative images of athletes and managers."

When Bic began a series of television ads starring McEnroe in 1982, its press release said: "Bic Corporation has tapped the terror of tennis to tout its disposable shaver." That an ad agency poll found McEnroe "the least liked" on a list of twenty-five athletes and "believable" by only 16 percent of the public didn't seem to matter. "The values of obtaining attention and being number one came before respect for authority, a sense of duty, and self-restraint," wrote Rader.

While "roughneck age" antics such as swearing, obscene gestures, and smashing rackets outraged traditionalists, newer fans argued that court shenanigans actually were desirable because they brought much-needed "color" to the game. Tony Trabert, a highly respected 1950s champion and later a TV tennis analyst, decried that view in his 1988 book, *Trabert on Tennis*: "Any flair, any 'color' in the game, should come from the artistry the players exhibit on court with their tennis skills, from their interaction with the crowd, and from their personality, which shows up off court in television and print interviews."

A recurrent parallel argument justifying wild and crazy behavior held that tennis, as an individual sport, depended on champions with "personality." When

Nastase, Connors, McEnroe, and, later, Boris Becker and Andre Agassi, bestrode the stage, fans packed the stands and enthusiasm soared. But should we excuse their faults merely because they exuded personality?

"There is a 'demand' for 'personalities,' because that's the kind of age we're living in," wrote Martin Amis in a persuasive *New Yorker* article in 1994. "Laver, Rosewall, Ashe: these were dynamic and exemplary figures; they didn't need 'personality' because they had character.... All great players are vivid, if great tennis is what you're interested in (rather than something more tawdrily generalized).... These players demonstrate that it is perfectly possible to have, or to contain, a personality—*without* being an asshole."

Dysfunctional behavior isn't confined to boorish, money-grubbing pros nowadays. George Steiner, the European social philosopher, says that tennis is seldom played for fun anymore. A friendly match at the club or the public courts, Steiner notes, more often than not takes on the air of a monumental struggle for power.

In his breezy but penetrating mini-book *Social Tennis: The Decline and Fall of Manners and Civility,* Jake Barnes argues that the deterioration of etiquette among America's hackers reflects a general decline in decorum for the past forty years. Barnes attributes tennis image mongering, chintziness, cheating, and lack of amiability today to narcissism/survivalism, which is associated with such character traits as repressed anger, a decline in playfulness, a blurring of illusion and reality, and a decline in values and ethical standards.

While tennis has evolved from an English garden-party pastime to a serious international professional sport during its 126-year modern history, it has never fully overcome its image as an effeminate and effete game. Back in 1878 the Harvard *Crimson* newspaper expressed alarm over the growth of lawn tennis clubs on campus: "The game is well enough for lazy and weak men, but men who have rowed or taken part in nobler sport should blush to be seen playing lawn tennis."

Tennis' reputation as a country club and rich man's sport, its quaint terminology such as "love," and the fact that its greatest men's champion of the first half-century, Bill Tilden, was tainted as a homosexual (twice convicted on morals charges) all contributed to that incorrect and harmful image.

When famed couturier Ted Tinling, then a lieutenant colonel in the British Royal Army Intelligence Corps, asked for permission from Allied command to stage an exhibition match for the Red Cross in Algiers in 1943, General Dwight D. Eisenhower sent him a terse memo. It read: "No. This is a man's war and tennis is a woman's game."

In 1970 Billie Jean King, who pioneered the first women's pro tour and founded the iconoclastic World Team Tennis league, complained about tennis' unfair image. "Tennis takes stamina, so much stamina, but you never think of it as a sport. You picture people sipping mint juleps under an umbrella, and it's not that way. People think of tennis as a sissy sport. That's what we must get away from."

For better or for worse, tennis *has* lost much of its original genteelness. It no longer resembles its gentle, pat-ball beginnings, as anyone watching spectacularly powerful and athletic Pete Sampras, muscular Serena Williams, and other leading men and women players can attest. But it also lacks the endearing chivalry and integrity of yesteryear.

Some things haven't changed, though. Early in the twentieth century George Bernard Shaw, the brilliant Irish playwright, suggested, "Tennis should be played only in the long grass in the meadows—and in the nude."

Recently, luscious Anna Kournikova, who would certainly do justice to the idea, predicted, "Within ten years women will play half naked."

Now what would Queen Victoria have said about that?

FASCINATING FACTS:

- ATP tour officials have a list of swear words in fifteen languages to let them know when players are insulting them.
- Australian Davis Cup captain Harry Hopman once fined Neale Fraser for introducing Lew Hoad to beer.
- The U.S. government spent more than a hundred thousand dollars in the early 1990s to study the cause of rudeness on tennis courts, according to Martin Gross's book, *The Government Racket, Washington Waste from A to Z.*

Notes

1. George E. Alexander, *Lawn Tennis: Its Founders & Its Early Days* (Lynn, MA: H.O. Zimman, Inc., 1974), pp. 43–45.
2. Ibid.
3. Ibid.
4. I am much indebted to E. Digby Baltzell's excellent book, *Sporting Gentlemen: Men's Tennis from the Age of Honor to the Cult of the Superstar* (1995), for this and the following quotations.
5. Ibid.
6. Ibid.
7. Ibid.
8. Ibid.
9. Ibid.
10. Ibid.
11. Ibid.
12. Ibid.
13. Ibid.
14. Ibid.
15. Ibid.

20

Records Are Made to Be Broken—and Promoted
1999

The sports record is a kind of substitute for immortality.

—ALLEN GUTTMANN, A SPORTS HISTORIAN.

When baseball sluggers Mark McGwire and Sammy Sosa were chasing Roger Maris's hallowed home run record last summer, another record-chaser was closely monitoring their progress.

"I absolutely hope they break the record. Records are made to be broken," chimed in Pete Sampras, just as captivated by the pursuit of "the record" as the rest of the sports world. "To see McGwire, who seems like a pretty straightforward guy, and Sosa, who seems like a nice guy, it would be nice for them to do it."

"It's a lot of pressure," said Sampras, who in August 1998 was himself trying to smash Jimmy Connors's Open Era record of five straight year-end number-one rankings and Roy Emerson's record twelve Grand Slam singles titles. "Everywhere they go, it seems like there's a lot of media around them. And the whole country knows about it. So it must be tough."

McGwire and Sosa eventually not only broke but obliterated Maris's record sixty-one homers with awesome season totals of seventy and sixty-six, respectively. The drama of their hot pursuit served as a national conversation starter, which immensely benefited baseball. It also highlighted the importance of numbers, and especially the magical numbers that records represent.

Even foreign heads of state paid homage to those records. The prime minister of Japan sent Big Mac a letter, and the president of the Czech Republic invoked the record-breakers' names during his visit to Washington.

While the modest Sampras never expected a similar public frenzy and media onslaught to shadow his quest for Connors's less famous record last fall, he and others were most disappointed at the tepid response when he broke it. Only one American tennis writer crossed the pond to chronicle Sampras's history-making achievement at the ATP World Championships Finals in Hanover, Germany. Tennis has never emphasized numbers—and thus records—the way baseball and other team sports do. Sure, hardcore fans can cite Rod Laver's record of achieving the tennis Grand Slam twice, in 1962 and 1969, and Emerson's record—which Sampras tied by winning his sixth Wimbledon—and perhaps Margaret Court's record twenty-four Grand Slam singles titles and Martina Navratilova's record nine Wimbledon singles crowns. But not many other records are recognized.

The tennis powers-that-be should take a lesson from baseball: one of the best ways to make tennis' stars glitter and to publicize the sport is to play up assaults on the most glorious records.

For example, Joe DiMaggio's amazing fifty-six-game hitting streak and Ted Williams's batting .406 for the entire season (the last time anyone batted .400), has been so ingrained in America's collective sports consciousness that President Bush honored both immortals on the fiftieth anniversary of their famous accomplishments at a White House ceremony in 1991.

Basketball followers still marvel at Wilt "The Stilt" Chamberlain scoring a record one hundred points in an NBA game and the even more mystical mark of thirty-three straight victories by the Los Angeles Lakers.

These classic examples of sublime performance and mind-boggling consistency remain part of sports lore that fans revere and recount from generation to generation. In contrast, few tennis fans have even heard about Martina Navratilova's seventy-four-match winning streak, an Open Era record, or her all-time record (with Pam Shriver) of 109 consecutive doubles matches won.

And who can recall—or even ever knew—that Mats Wilander succeeded in 97 percent of his first-serve attempts when he buried Henri Leconte in the 1988 French Open final? That at a record-shattering age twelve, Martina Hingis won the French Open junior (18-and-under) title? That Goran Ivanisevic served nine aces in one *game* in a 1991 match against Andre Agassi? That the latest teen terror,

FASCINATING FACTS:

- After Chris Evert's all-time record of 125 straight clay-court victories ended with a loss to Tracy Austin at the 1979 Italian Open, Evert amazingly won sixty-four more matches in a row on clay.
- Margaret Court, now a minister in Perth, Australia, said she would have won six Wimbledon singles titles, instead of three, "if I'd known then what I know today about the study of the word of God and the power of it."

Serena Williams, easily smashed a record by beating five top-ten players in her first sixteen pro matches?

Golf buffs treasure Byron Nelson's 1945 record of winning eleven straight PGA tournaments, a feat no one has come close to matching or probably ever will. And how about track superstar Edwin Moses: unbeaten in the 400-meter hurdles for nine years, nine months, and nine days! Easy to remember; impossible to duplicate.

The sixty-one NHL records that hockey legend Wayne Gretzky holds or shares is a stupefying record in itself. But The Great One's nine Hart Trophies (MVP) and 2,857 total career points, an astronomical figure 54 percent higher than the next-highest scorer, Gordie Howe, will likely never be broken or forgotten.

But how can you, the fervent tennis fan, engage in those friendly but fierce debates—like "Who's better: Bird or Magic?" in basketball—if you can't throw around numbers to make your case? And how can you get fired up about potential record-breaking if you don't even know about Court's record and that Graf is within striking distance at twenty-two career Slam singles titles?

Ironically, Graf herself undermines the promotion and celebration of tennis records. The day before capturing her seventh Wimbledon and twentieth career Slam crown, she was asked if she thought about the record books. "No, not at all," replied the super-athlete whom Navratilova hailed as "the best all-around player of all-time, regardless of the surface."

After being honored at the German Open in May for playing her thousandth pro match, the unhistorical German confessed, "I had no clue.... Obviously I'm proud of those numbers, but if it meant more to me, I would know these things."

But that's just the point: "those numbers" *should* mean more to Graf. Just think of the splendid publicity opportunities these record-tying and -breaking occasions present. The reserved, modest superstar could laud tennis' bygone heroines, discuss the phenomenal advances women's tennis has made this century, regale the media with stories of her most dramatic matches, and predict which current teen queens may topple her records some day.

Like all these other sports, tennis owns plenty of spectacular records—single-event, single-season, and career—that we *can* and *should* proudly promote. Many, unfortunately, were never celebrated in yesteryear. When Emerson eclipsed the great Bill Tilden's record tenth Slam title by capturing the 1967 Australian, it brought little fanfare. "Nobody talked about records then," recalls Emmo.

What then are tennis' most important records? Most well-known records? Most compelling records? Most amazing records? Most unbreakable records? Let's review them using the last criterion.

Records That Will Never Be Broken

1. Rod Laver achieving the Grand Slam of tennis twice. In 1962 and 1969, "Rocket" won the sport's four major titles—Wimbledon and the Australian,

French, and U.S. championships. While such luminaries as touring pros Pancho Gonzalez, Ken Rosewall, and Lew Hoad could not enter the then amateur-only tournaments in 1962, Laver conquered the entire tennis world in 1969. Margaret Court pulled off the Grand Slam feat in 1970 and Steffi Graf in 1988, but no man has done it since Laver. Indeed, many cognoscenti predict that just one Slam—let alone two or three—will never be accomplished again because men's tennis boasts too much depth, plus numerous one-surface specialists that Laver didn't have to face when he had only two surfaces—grass and clay—to master. Even 1990s superstar Sampras conceded it would take "an act of God" for him to win Roland Garros.

2. The eighty-match rivalry between Martina Navratilova and Chris Evert. Sharply contrasting playing styles, personalities, and national origin made their extremely long rivalry fascinating, and fans passionately picked sides whenever they faced each other. The Czech-turned-American ultimately prevailed 43-37. There's no chance of another eighty-match rivalry simply because it would take two superstars remaining at or near the top—as Navratilova did for twenty-two years and Evert for twenty—and having most of their careers overlap, as these two champions did for seventeen years. Another factor was pure luck because two teen queens, Tracy Austin and Andrea Jaeger, burned out prematurely in the early 1980s.

3. Connors winning the U.S. Open on *three* different surfaces. Jimbo was able to achieve the fortuitous record because his prime coincided with two historic changes in this Grand Slam tournament. He captured the 1974 event at the West Side Tennis Club in Forest Hills, New York, by routing Rosewall in the final year it was played on grass. Two years later he whipped archrival Bjorn Borg on clay there, and in 1980, after the tournament had moved to the National Tennis Center in Flushing Meadows, versatile Connors stopped Borg again on hardcourts. In 1982 and 1983, Connors added two more titles by beating Ivan Lendl. The odds of the U.S. Open changing surfaces thrice in five years in the future are virtually nil.

4. Margaret Smith Court grabbing eleven Australian singles championships. The tall, athletic serve-and-volleyer cannot be denied her rightful place in the pantheon of tennis greats. However, some of the world's leading players skipped the long, tiring journey Down Under during her reign, from 1960 to 1973. Thus seven of her titles came by beating Australian world top-tenners Jan Lehane, Leslie Turner, and Kerry Melville, all excellent players but none great champions. To her credit, Court also vanquished Billie Jean King, Maria Bueno, and Evonne Goolagong (twice) in finals. With women's tennis booming, its depth better than ever, and both trends likely to continue, no player will ever win any Slam ten times, let alone twelve.

5. Helen Wills Moody going unbeaten for six years. During the zenith of her brilliant career, from 1927 to 1933, "Little Miss Poker Face" not only won *every match* she played but also *every set*! In her autobiography, *Fifteen-Thirty,*

Moody wrote, "I know I would hate life if I were deprived of trying, hunting, working for some objective within which there lies the beauty of perfection." For six years—and at least 158 successive matches—this perfectionist achieved perfection. Tennis will never see her likes and such perfection again.

Records That Probably Will Never Be Broken

1. Roy Emerson's twenty-eight career Grand Slam titles. Emerson undeniably cleaned up by winning all his twelve singles and fifteen of his sixteen doubles major titles just prior to the advent of Open Tennis in 1968, before all the elite players finally competed for all the great championships. However, his all-surface singles and doubles prowess cannot be gainsaid. For example, while grass was his best surface, Emmo still captured two French Open singles crowns and six French doubles titles on clay with an amazing *five different* partners. Since leading singles players seldom play doubles anymore, it will take a men's champion with extraordinary talent, ambition, and stamina to surpass this record.

2. Evert's 125-match winning streak on clay. Evert, known foremost for her consistency, amassed this phenomenal streak that lasted five years and nine months, from August 14, 1973, to May 12, 1979. Little, sixteen-year-old Tracy Austin, another relentless ground-stroker, ended it when she upset (then) Evert-Lloyd 6-4, 2-6, 7-6 (7-4) in the Italian Open semifinals. Ironically and sadly, there were more empty seats than spectators at the Foro Italico for one of the milestone matches in women's tennis history. In an era when many of the leading women players were—believe it or not—serve-and-volleyers, Evert-Lloyd racked up seventy-four love (6-0) sets and lost only eight sets during her prodigious clay streak.

3. Navratilova's 28-0 Fed Cup record. Navratilova defected from the former Czechoslovakia to the United States in 1975 at age eighteen. Starting in 1982, she played sixteen ties in four years for her adopted homeland, and her record was sheer perfection. Navratilova racked up a 15-0 mark in singles and 13-0 in doubles. With a record ninety-nine nations competing in Fed Cup in 1999 and first-rate players being produced by tiny nations such as Croatia and Slovakia as well as awakening giants such as China and India, unbeaten Fed Cup records seem implausible nowadays and into the foreseeable future.

4. Boris Becker's 38-3 Davis Cup record. Before Michael Stich arrived as a top player in 1991 when he captured Wimbledon, Becker carried Germany's Davis Cup hopes on his broad but young shoulders. Showing the maturity and poise of a seasoned veteran while a teenager, Becker amassed a sensational 38-3 career singles record, starting as a seventeen-year-old in 1985. He participated in twenty-eight ties over twelve years, typically playing doubles as well, and led Germany to Cup titles in 1988 and 1989 over powerful Sweden. His 38-3 record and .927 winning percentage, achieved amidst

unimaginable pressure for a nation craving postwar heroes, ranks as one of the most amazing and important yet little-known records in tennis.

5. Evert winning at least one Grand Slam singles title each year for thirteen straight years. Evert will be remembered most for her sportsmanship, popularizing (with Connors and Borg) the two-handed backhand, femininity, and consistency, and for her rivalry with Navratilova. But one Evert record truly epitomizes her championship performances over a time span longer than most other players' entire careers. Neither the opposition, injury, illness, or mental fatigue could prevent this moderately sized and talented American from capturing at least one Slam title (from 1974 to 1986) for an almost incomprehensible thirteen consecutive years.

Emerson and nearly all the Australian stars of yesteryear, whom Sampras idolized as a boy, believe Sampras will surpass Emmo's record of twelve Slam singles titles. What's more, Emerson's rooting for the twenty-eight-year-old Californian. "I couldn't think of anyone I'd rather see break it, because Pete is a terrific ambassador for tennis and a terrific ambassador for America," says Emerson. "All around the world he's very well respected."

Emerson acknowledges that greater depth of talent in men's tennis makes Sampras's task more difficult, but he also cites countervailing points, such as tiebreakers that shorten matches today. "The old days were definitely different," Emerson told the *Dallas Morning News*. "If we got hurt, we had to forfeit. We couldn't get a medical timeout or throw up on the court and start playing again. We could play five sets at Wimbledon, and [on the changeovers] there would not be a place to sit down."

Just before the U.S. Open last year, Sampras was asked what would happen if he won that Open and tied Emerson's record. "Then it gets interesting. I mean, people love to see people break records. I know I do."

But how much attention will his quest for the record command? "I don't think it is anywhere near the same as what McGwire and Sosa are going through," said Sampras then. "The whole country is following them. True tennis fans know what I'm doing and what I'm trying to do, but it is nowhere near the same impact.... If the day comes where I can do something, break the record, I hopefully will have the same impact. But we will see."

And how will the sporting public react? There's little chance that Sampras will receive hate mail and death threats as Hank Aaron did when he closed in on beloved Babe Ruth's career homer record of 714 in 1973. And normally humble Sampras would truly astonish everyone if he exclaimed "I'm the greatest!" like Rickey Henderson after the brash speedster smashed Lou Brock's career stolen base record.

All the same, how the media and public view Sampras's run at "the record" and certain sports immortality and how that climactic Grand Slam final plays out could truly pump up tennis or, conversely, generate little excitement.

And much of that question revolves around knowing what the number twelve stands for.

FASCINATING FACTS:

- In eighty-four tournaments from 1982 to 1986, Martina Navratilova reached the final seventy-eight times.
- Elizabeth Ryan, who often declared that she would rather die than see her record of nineteen Wimbledon titles broken, died from a heart attack at age eighty-seven on the day before Billie Jean King won her record twentieth Wimbledon title in 1979.

21

Overkill! The Power Crisis Facing Tennis
1998

There are some very valuable things of the past that have been lost in the wild scramble for speed and power.

—BILL TILDEN, 1950.

Fast-forward to the 2020 Wimbledon Championships. Ace Jordan, the 6'9" son of basketball legend Air Jordan, is literally taking apart 7'1" Killer Ivanadisco in the fifth set of their vicious final on Centre Court.

Although Killer earned his nickname by beheading a net judge and a doubles opponent with errant 175-mile-per-hour serves, he's taking a terrible beating now. Ace has knocked him down fourteen times—eleven requiring emergency medical treatment—with unblockable rocket serves that smacked him in the groin, mouth, stomach, and eye. Bloodied and groggy, Killer finally throws in the towel after holding serve at 21-all, and Ace, with a record-breaking eighty-three aces, prevails.

The future of tennis? Not if sanity prevails—but perhaps it will be if men's tennis keeps evolving from a sport of diverse styles and stylists to one of brutish power and vanishing rallies.

The warnings come from everywhere—this one from John Barrett, a British Davis Cup player in the 1950s and now a respected BBC-TV commentator and journalist, writing in *ITF World of Tennis:* "Today power is all. On every surface, from grass to clay, the modern game is a one-dimensional slugfest, exciting at times, occasionally brilliant, but tediously one-dimensional.

"Subtlety, finesse, tactical awareness—all those things that made tennis a three-dimensional delight—are, at best, only fleetingly observed. Power has killed the

159

artist. There will never be another Santana, Larsen, Pietrangeli, Nastase, or McEnroe to delight us with their chessboard skills.

"Don't blame today's players. They are simply maximizing the potential of the lethal equipment provided for their use. Yet they, too, are becoming as bored as the spectators by the relentless march of power.

"Unless something is done, and done quickly, the whole fragile edifice of professional tennis could come crashing down in a chain reaction like this: increasing public boredom, leading to reduced TV air time, resulting in loss of sponsors, which will mean fewer tournaments, less income for players and less money for development programs. The scenario is frighteningly possible."

Even diehard fans concede that towering athletes wielding devastating space-age rackets have sometimes turned Wimbledon, tennis' most prestigious spectacle, into little more than a monotonous serving contest. Awesome power may thrill the crowd in many sports—the knockout punch in boxing, the home run in baseball, and the slam dunk in basketball—but an endless barrage of service aces and winners in tennis disproves Mae West's wisecrack that too much of a good thing is wonderful.

In the 1991 Wimbledon final, in which 6'4" Michael Stich upset 6'3" countryman Boris Becker, Stich served a hundred points at an average speed of 112 miles per hour and with a high of 126. Burly Becker managed to return only forty-nine serves. Similarly, Stich returned just seventy-four of Becker's 114 serves. A century ago the serve was merely intended to put the ball in play; now it frequently ends the point. And when it doesn't, sharp first volleys often do. In that terribly dull 1991 Wimbledon final, the ball was actually in play for *nine minutes and twenty seconds* in the two-and-a-half-hour match.

Even the winner, Stich, conceded: "I think high-powered rackets are destroying tennis and making it really boring. When you saw the matches that McEnroe and Connors played at Wimbledon, that was real tennis. With the wide-bodies, it will get worse. If it was up to me, I would like to go back to the old wooden rackets and play real tennis."

Bjorn Borg (who failed dismally in his 1991 comeback bid with an antiquated Donnay wood racket), Martina Navratilova, Steffi Graf, Andre Agassi, McEnroe, and Pat Cash have all advocated, at various times, a return to wood. But that legislation won't happen, particularly in light of the millions of dollars that manufacturers have invested in the current equipment. Those who love the feel of wood, and who lament the disappearance of the touch shots that its slower-paced game allows, will have to satisfy themselves with the wood-only tournaments which have become a recent phenomenon for nostalgic Americans.

If only tennis—like golf, cricket, Formula One auto racing, and baseball—had foreseen the problems that new equipment technology would bring! Each of those sports has regulated clearly and firmly against technology changing the essential nature of its sport. But not tennis.

Arthur Ashe pioneered the new generation of rackets in 1969 with his Head Competition, an aluminum-fiberglass open-throat model. It weighed 12.25 ounces and its racket head covered sixty-eight square inches, which made it about an ounce lighter and three square inches larger than traditional wood frames. Connors's small-headed (sixty-three square inch) but explosive Wilson T2000 gained notoriety when he overwhelmed foes to win three-fourths of a Grand Slam in 1974.

Howard Head changed tennis forever with the first oversized racket, the Prince Classic, in 1976. Pam Shriver, then a gangly sixteen-year-old, used the cartoonishly huge-faced (110 square inches, which was more than 50 percent larger than other rackets) and lightweight frame and shocked everyone by reaching the 1978 U.S. Open final. Borg and McEnroe bucked the trend by winning major titles in 1981 with wood, as did Chris Evert to take the 1982 U.S. Open. But, significantly, Navratilova became the first player to capture a Grand Slam title with a big-headed racket at the 1982 French Open, just three weeks after switching to the elliptically headed Yonex R-7. The following day, seventeen-year-old Mats Wilander became the first man to win a Grand Slam title with a large-headed racket.

FASCINATING FACTS:

- Racket strings can generate up to 60 percent of the power in your shot, according to Tom Parry, who strings for several top touring pros.
- In 1955, Jack Crawford, a 1930s champion, wrote an article titled "Leave Tennis Alone," in which he argued against suggested rule changes to control the power game.

The International Tennis Federation, which had acted swiftly to ban the devilishly unfair double-strung, or "spaghetti," racket in 1978, should have promptly limited the size of racket heads by 1982. At that time, more than half of all rackets sold were oversized. The trend accelerated during the 1980s among the pros, too. Oversized weapons served as "equalizers" for undersized whiz kids like Michael Chang and Arantxa Sanchez, who grabbed singles crowns at the 1989 French Open, and for precocious Monica Seles, the youngest (until Martina Hingis in 1997) Grand Slam champion this century, at Roland Garros a year later.

Siegfried Kuebler created the revolutionary wide-body concept in 1984 and sold it to Wilson, which introduced the first wide-body racket in 1987. Like the oversized head, which expanded the "sweet spot" and thus helped off-center hits, the more powerful wide-body was a godsend for the less competent recreational player and the racket of choice for some women pros, like Seles.

But few leading men have switched to the wide-body. Throughout their pro careers Sampras and two-time Australian and French champion Jim Courier have used a mid-sized (eighty-five square inch) Wilson Original Pro Staff that first hit the market in 1984, and they find it potent enough. "I'd rip holes through wind-screens with a wide-body," quips Courier.

Advances in racket technology have spawned more than just a legion of mega-servers. Baseline bashers, with their two-handed backhands and Western forehands, have also proliferated with the introduction of revolutionary racket materials like Kevlar, graphite, boron, and titanium; longer strings that create a trampoline effect on the ball and more power; and aerodynamic designs that make for much faster swings. Navratilova and Evert lament that development, too. "I'm the last serve-and-volleyer, it seems," said Navratilova after losing the 1991 U.S. Open final to Seles. "But with the way Monica and Jennifer [Capriati] are hitting the ball, there's just not that much variety." Evert agreed: "It's become a power game. No one is thinking out points. No one is using finesse."

How could they, though? As Michael Chang points out, "If someone hits a ball 150 miles per hour, you can't finesse that ball." Former Wimbledon and U.S. champion and twenty-year Australian Davis Cup captain Neale Fraser notes that "today's number 100-ranked player is hitting the ball harder than the top-ranked player of the past."

Back in 1993, a symposium at the Lipton Championships debated whether speed was killing professional tennis. Noted coach Vic Braden suggested that coaches could spend more time developing skills and strategies to counteract the power—as if this power surge were just another cyclical phase in the evolution of tennis. But, as super-returner Agassi admits, you can't do *anything* if you can't even reach a Sampras bullet.

Dr. Carl Morris, chairman of the statistics department at Harvard University, confirms that if you're on the receiving end of a serve that leaves Sampras's racket at 138 miles per hour, you have only .55 seconds, barely the blink of an eye, to return it. It's like soccer's distinctly unsatisfying penalty shootouts: if you can't guess which way the ball's going, you aren't going to be able to get to it. And guessing comes down to a gamble.

Of course, others argue that the big serve is nothing new. Since the 1920s, when "Big Bill" Tilden overpowered "Little Bill" Johnston and other contenders, cannonball servers have wreaked havoc in men's tennis, especially on fast grass and indoor courts. In later decades, Ellsworth Vines, Lester Stoefen, Mike Sang-ster, Colin Dibley (whose 148-mile-per-hour serve in 1963 was the fastest ever recorded in official competition until Greg Rusedski recently whacked a 149-mile-per-hour rocket), Vladimir Zednik, and Roscoe Tanner hammered serves more than 130 miles per hour, all with *wooden* rackets.

What makes today's ultra-powerful serving an unprecedented crisis is that gigantic servers aren't the exception but *the rule.* Rusedski, Mark Philippoussis, Richard Krajicek, Julian Alonso, Marc Rosset, Ivanisevic, and Stich have exceeded 130 miles per hour, and the vast majority of players can regularly hit serves at 110 miles per hour or more. That even includes little (5'9", 160-pound) Chang, who has switched to a longer (twenty-eight-inch) and more powerful racket. Chang recently slammed a 130-mile-per-hour serve, a once-unthinkable velocity for him.

Large ace totals are no longer the occasional aberration of post-match statistics. For example, Philippoussis, the former ATP Tour service-speed record holder at 142 miles per hour, notched an incredible forty-four in just three sets (6-7, 6-2, 6-4) against Byron Black in the 1995 Salem Open in Kuala Lumpur. Goran "The Ace Man" Ivanisevic once belted nine in a single *game* against Agassi. Aces are coming so frequently that players and commentators now dismissively refer to them as "easy" or "cheap" or even "free" points. Aces were once that single unanswerable assertion of dominance or defiance, and were remarkable for the surprise and thrill of their appearance. These days, if they were a golf stroke, they'd be a tap-in.

From a spectator's viewpoint, the nadir of the power game came in the 1994 Sampras-Ivanisevic Wimbledon final, where only three of 206 points lasted more than four shots. Fred Perry, the 1930s star, called it "one of the most boring finals in history." Few disagreed. Sampras proved even more oppressively efficient in the 1995 Big W final, allowing Becker just twenty-four points in Sampras's nineteen service games—and seven of those were double faults.

Only a shapely, blond streaker on Centre Court could liven up the otherwise unenthralling men's singles final at the 1996 Wimbledon—a tournament which opted for reduced pressure in the balls and slightly longer grass in an effort to reduce the big servers' dominance. Krajicek, a twenty-five-to-one longshot, blasted first serves averaging 118 miles per hour to overwhelm American MaliVai Washington in straight sets, just as he had earlier pummeled Stich, Sampras, and unexpected semifinalist Jason Stoltenberg. Not surprisingly, the 6'5", 195-pound Dutch Destroyer pounded a tournament-best 147 aces, including twenty-nine against a shell-shocked Sampras.

It could be argued that the reason for this increase in power is simply that there are more-powerful tennis players today, and they're better prepared than ever before. True enough—and that's another good reason to address the crisis.

To retain its appeal, tennis must remain a sport demanding great skill and will—not one where height and power rule. Take relatively unathletic, 6'7" Marc Rosset, who became an Olympic champion (in 1992) merely because he whacked incredibly hard serves and forehands with extremely powerful rackets. Of course, with less powerful rackets, he'd still hit winners, but *fewer* winners. With less power in his shots, his opponents would be able to call on a range of finesse and touch shots to make him move—and take him apart.

Let's be clear about this. As the late, great Pancho Gonzalez acknowledged, "Today's players would beat the pants off us." But nearly everyone agrees that the reason today's players are "better" can be put down to factors such as the new equipment, improved training methods, and better nutritional information. It isn't because today's players are inherently better athletes. Actually, Rod Laver and Roy Emerson were, in this analyst's view, superior athletes to Sampras and Agassi and Becker—with McEnroe somewhere in between.

While most tennis insiders are disenchanted with slam-bam tennis, the irony is that the public remains ambivalent. A 1994 Prince Sports Group survey revealed

---

FASCINATING FACTS:

- When Dutchman Ricky Molier won a tennis gold medal at the tenth Para-
  lympic Games in Atlanta, some of his serves exceeded one hundred miles
  per hour.
- Ellsworth Vines whacked thirty aces in only twelve service games against
  Bunny Austin in the 1932 Wimbledon final.

---

that 74 percent thought the game was too power-oriented. However, an earlier poll conducted by *USA Today* found that 71 percent opposed limitations on power.

But how to rescue the situation? It's time to take strong action. Already, all manufactured rackets are tested; some pass and others don't. It's now a matter of urgency that tennis' ruling bodies put a limit not on racket size, width, length, or materials, but on racquet *power*. All racquets should be tested—using the same strings and tension—and those that propel the ball beyond a certain speed limit should be banned from sanctioned tournament competition. The issue of how much power to allow can easily be settled by discussion with players and administrators.

This is a feasible and fair solution. Make your rackets as long, heavy, light, or weird as you like—but just make them pass the power test. Leading amateurs and their associations would follow the same rules.

Golf has rules on how far a ball can go, major league baseball and cricket have rules banning bats made of anything other than wood, Formula One has incredibly detailed rules on the amount of power a car can use.

Why not make power the measure of racket acceptability? Why not save tennis?

ANY SUGGESTIONS?

Everyone seems to agree that power is the problem. Here's a rundown on the solutions offered, and why each one is seriously flawed.

1. **Increase the height of the net.** This would merely disadvantage short and medium-height players, who aren't usually the biggest servers. It would also infuriate recreational players—you can't have one net height for pros and another for club players.

2. **Bring back the old foot-fault rule.** Abandoned in 1959, it prohibited players from jumping into the court on their serves, so players had to keep one foot on the ground. Maybe it would slow down a few big servers, but Hoad, Vines, Tilden, and others had explosive serves while conforming to

that rule. More important, this idea doesn't address the problem of ultra-powerful ground strokes. It would be a quarter measure.

3. **Slow down the courts.** Too dangerous. A more abrasive surface would create even more knee, shin, ankle, and groin injuries than a medium-speed hardcourt, an already punishing surface. The Australian Open's controversial rubberized Rebound Ace courts—which Sampras, Becker, Muster, Agassi, Todd Martin, and others have criticized—produce these injuries, and are unbearably hot and sticky on some days. They're so unpopular that seven hundred members resigned from the White City Club in New South Wales between 1991 and 1993 before the club covered the courts with synthetic grass. The decision to go with Rebound Ace—as opposed to a more player-friendly surface—now seems foolish.

4. **Use heavier, slower balls.** And ruin the top half of players' bodies. Shoulder, elbow, and wrist injuries would increase because players would have to swing harder to generate power—even with today's rackets. Furthermore, despite the lower-pressure balls (by 5.6 percent) used at Wimbledon in 1996, the serve was as dominant as ever. Why? Because the problem is so great. As Sampras noted, "I don't care what you put in our hands—we're still going to hit aces on grass."

5. **Return to wood rackets.** It's just not economically feasible now. Also, forcing recreational players to use wood would increase the difficulty of learning the sport. The idea of having the pros play with wood, while millions of others don't, makes no sense. (And the racket manufacturers, who have spent millions on space-age technologies, would be furious, not to mention litigious.)

6. **Ban wide-body rackets.** A belated half-measure at best because most of the most-powerful servers don't use wide-body frames.

7. **Allow only one serve.** This reform, advocated by Neale Fraser, is foolish. It goes to the other extreme and emasculates the serve for the better players—while not addressing the ultra-power crisis for the other strokes. It would also be very unpopular with club players, who typically land less than 50 percent of their first serves in—at *any* speed. Single faults, which would lose the point outright, would abound and completely ruin the fun for the server, receiver, and spectators.

8. **Alter the court's dimensions.** The object here is to move the service line closer to the net (reducing the size of the target), or to mark a line a yard behind the baseline from which players must serve, which 1972 Wimbledon champion Stan Smith advocated in 1992. Like the idea of raising the net, this misguided reform would merely disadvantage the shorter and weaker players. The latter reform would also greatly discourage serve-and-volleying. Again, it addresses the power crisis only for the serve.

9. **Cut the grass longer.** Increasing the length of the grass from the customary 5/16 of an inch would have little impact on the ultra-power crisis and would

cause more bad bounces on a surface that is already criticized for precisely this shortcoming. Also, it fails as a general solution—most courts aren't grass.

THE WOMEN'S GAME

It isn't just the men. The women's game is also on the receiving end of a power overdose. There used to be four categories of women players at the top level: 1) Serve and volleyers such as Martina Navratilova, Billie Jean King, Margaret Court, Althea Gibson, and Alice Marble; 2) Hard-hitting baseliners such as Tracy Austin, Maureen Connolly, and Helen Wills Moody; 3) Light-hitting but strategic pushers and retrievers such as Andrea Jaeger, Francoise Durr, and Lea Pericoli; 4) All-court players, typically superb athletes, such as Evonne Goolagong, Maria Bueno, Pauline Betz, and Suzanne Lenglen. While powerful rackets, admittedly, have lifted the caliber of women's tennis tremendously during the Open Era, they have also greatly diminished this diversity. Now, instead of players being fairly evenly divided among four categories, the "hard-hitting baseliner" group—epitomized by number one Lindsay Davenport, Mary Pierce, and whiz kids Venus and Serena Williams and Mirjana Lucic—has burgeoned on all surfaces. Why? Today's women players hit the ball so hard that it's harder to get to the net during baseline exchanges, harder to volley both wicked passing shots and returns of serve, and harder to retrieve and use finesse against such devastating and increasingly consistent power. Smart, strategic Swiss Martina Hingis, the 1997 queen, is bucking this trend with the most success.

FASCINATING FACTS:

- After an eight-year hiatus from the pro tour, Bjorn Borg came back and suffered an embarrassing 6-2, 6-3 loss to unheralded Jordi Arrese in the first round at Monte Carlo in 1991. Borg was ridiculed for playing with an old-fashioned, unpowerful wooden racket.
- Teenagers Taylor Dent, nineteen, and junior event champion Andy Roddick, eighteen, hit the fastest serves at the 2000 U.S. Open with serves of 140 and 139 miles per hour, respectively.
- Andy Roddick's thirty-seven aces against Michael Chang at the 2001 French Open broke the tournament record for a match by eight aces.

22

Seven Revealing Statistics Tennis Should Use

2000

"Statistics are like bikinis: they show a lot but not everything," quipped baseball manager Lou Piniella.

True enough. Historically, tennis has ranked among the least statistical of sports. That's understandable because its main event, singles, is an individual competition. Measuring a player's worth in a particular singles match boils down to whether he wins or loses. Nothing more and nothing less.

Team sports need individual stats, such as goals, rebounds, points, and assists, because they tell volumes about an athlete's performance and are much written and talked about. However, tennis' little-known stats—such as first-serve percentage and break-point conversions—interest the cognoscenti rather than the typical fan.

Tennis can jazz up its numbers game, though, with enlightening and debate-provoking stats. Here are some that you may like.

1. **Tale of the Tape**—Imagine what juicy stuff we could get from borrowing boxing's pre-bout physical comparisons. The WTA wouldn't permit 35-24-34 for "The Russian Lolita," but almost anything would work for the men. Let's take reach, for example. When Pat Rafter, Tim Henman, and Pete Sampras, all 6'1", do battle, it would be most revealing if one of them possesses a whopping 6'7" reach. Just think of the advantages that provides for serving, lunging for volleys, and scrambling for passing shots. And how about body-fat percentage? Heartthrob Jan-Michael Gambill's awesome 4.6 percent looks like the number to beat. No wonder the sculpted Gambill always goes shirtless on the practice courts.

2. **Ground-stroke Speed**—For twenty years radar guns have measured the speed of serves at pro tournaments. We've got precise proof that the master blasters are Greg Rusedski, who holds the men's record at 149 miles per hour, and Venus Williams at 127. Okay, but inquiring minds want to know who whacks the most powerful groundies. We're talking specifically about returns of serve, passing shots, and baseline-to-baseline winners. Is it Andre Agassi, Marat Safin, Lindsay Davenport, Serena Williams, or some unheralded heavy hitter? And are we talking triple digits?

3. **Pressure Points**—The most crucial points in tennis are match points, set points, and game points, in that order. It takes a bold and talented shot-maker to hit winners in those make-or-break situations, just as lesser lights self-destruct with unforced errors on the pivotal points. So let's figure out who the *best* and *worst* performers are by measuring their winners and unforced errors when it counts most and the pressure is greatest.

4. **Tiebreaker Records**—Tiebreakers, of course, are also tremendously important. But not all tiebreakers are created equal. The stakes are highest when the tiebreaker decides the match, whatever set that may be. However, when the tiebreaker decides the third set of a best-two-of-three-sets duel or the fifth set of a best-three-of-five-sets marathon, the tension is almost unbearable for *both* competitors, unless they have the nerveless mien of Bjorn Borg. Every player chokes on occasion, as even Pete Sampras admitted after winning his seventh Wimbledon title, but champions come through most often at crunch time. More precise tiebreaker stats will confirm that.

5. **Action Time**—Sports fans crave action. The disturbing truth is that men's matches, in particular, provide very little action time. For example, in that rather dull 1991 Wimbledon final in which Michael Stich outblasted Boris Becker, the ball was actually in play for a mere *6 percent* of the total match time! If the ATP, WTA, and ITF leaders keep their eyes on the ball, literally, they'll monitor this extremely important statistic closely. Rather than trying to shorten the total time of matches, it behooves them to find sensible and fair ways to increase the proportion of "action time," which is a far more entertaining 30 to 40 percent in several other leading pro sports.

6. **Delay of Game Protests**—This stat records the average amount of time lost—beyond the allowed twenty seconds between points—when a player protests a line call or other officiating decision, plus the total time lost every year. Most spectators and TV viewers don't mind an occasional argument about an injustice—real or even perceived—*if* it's over and done with within a minute or two. But protestors become nuisances and even villains when they endlessly rant on. Their antics not only violate the "play shall be continuous" rule and often unethically break the other player's momentum but also add more "dead time"—just what tennis doesn't need. Let's identify

the culprits with stats and stigmatize them with the "Boor of the Year" award.

7. **Touch Artistry**—Since power has virtually killed the artist and often turned tennis into a one-dimensional slugfest today (except on clay), finesse should receive statistical recognition. After all, spectacular drop volleys and drop shots require exquisite touch and rate high among the most delightful and sublime of tennis shots in the complete player's repertoire. John McEnroe once said that being called "an artist" was one of the highest compliments he ever received. So let's create a stat called "Touch Shots" and record players' points-won percentage on drop volleys and drop shots attempted. At the end of the season, the men's and women's leaders in this category (with a minimum of two hundred attempts) will receive the "Golden Hand" award, a beautiful painting of them at their finesse best.

These new statistics, just like bikinis, will show a lot about some interesting areas previously ignored, but not everything. And that's all sports fans can ask for.

FASCINATING FACTS:

- Jan-Michael Gambill does one thousand sit-ups daily to maintain his 4.6 body-fat percentage.
- Three hundred women were wedged into a corporate hospitality tent with Jan-Michael Gambill at the 2000 Hamlet Cup. Early in the question-and-answer session, they unanimously called for Gambill to lift up his shirt to expose his famous abdominal muscles.
- After bringing home a runners-up trophy at age fourteen, Patrick Rafter took out a hunting rifle and shot it full of holes.
- In 1999, rabid fans of Patrick Rafter got sexy posters of Rafter—clad in Ray Ban sunglasses and little else—by breaking into bus shelters throughout Australia and stealing them.

23

Will Blacks Dominate Tennis?
2001

Obviously blacks have walked into basketball, baseball, and football, and they are tremendous athletes. If tennis is anything like the other sports, whites won't be able to compete with them.

—JOHN McENROE, 1990.

Richard Williams, the father-coach of Venus and Serena, likes to crow that "tennis is a black sport. They [just] decided to go into tennis a little later."

His equally controversial and entrepreneurial soulmate, Nick Bollettieri, always wanted to galvanize black participation. And Bollettieri found the perfect partner in tennis immortal Arthur Ashe.

"Ashe's words to me—read *Days of Grace* [Ashe's 1993 memoir]—were, 'Nick, what are we going to do for the thousands of boys and girls who are potential champions who will never get a chance to hit the ball?'"

Ashe told Bollettieri and others that if blacks were given the opportunity, they would dominate tennis the way they have several other sports. "I agreed totally," recalls Bollettieri, "and that's why I started the Ashe-Bollettieri Minority Project in 1988."

So what's become of Bollettieri's affirmative action program? And now that Venus Williams *is* dominating women's tennis, with little sister Serena close behind, who and where are the next black tennis stars?

Bollettieri raves about fourteen-year-old Jamea (pronounced "Juh-mee-uh") Jackson, calling her "one of the best athletes we've ever had at the academy." Jackson's superior athletic genes come from her father Ernest, a speedy cornerback for the New Orleans Saints and Atlanta Falcons in the 1970s.

Her inspiration comes from—you guessed it—Venus. She grew up with a poster of the Wimbledon, U.S. Open, and Olympic champion in her room. And she chatted with both Venus and Serena when the famous sisters trained at the Bollettieri Tennis Academy in Bradenton, Florida. Jamea was most impressed by their work ethic and unwavering concentration.

Three years ago the entire Jackson family (Jamea has a twelve-year-old brother) moved from Atlanta so her parents could stay involved with her education as well as her tennis. Only in 2000, says Bollettieri, has her talent really started blossoming. "A year ago she had a Western [forehand] grip and wasn't sure of herself. Since then she's become one of the best students I've ever had."

Jackson showcased that great leap forward by winning the USTA Girls' 16 Super Nationals at age thirteen to earn a berth in the U.S. Open junior event. There she knocked off third-seeded Ioana Gasper of Romania 6-3, 6-4, highly regarded American Tanner Cochran 6-4, 7-5, and, on her fourteenth birthday, led thirteenth-seeded Matea Mezak of Croatia 7-6, 5-4, before painful leg cramps forced her to retire in the third set.

"Jamea is a superb volleyer, has huge ground strokes, runs like a jet, and loves to come in [to net] and take it to you," enthuses Bollettieri. "Jamea has it all."

How far can Jamea go? "She could be a [world] top-ten player within three years," predicts Bollettieri.

Michael Green, a sixteen-year-old African-American from Port St. Lucie, Florida, intrigues Bollettieri, despite his late start in tennis. "He's 6'3" and built like Kobe Bryant. He's a great athlete and does everything well."

Continuing to honor his pledge to the late Ashe, Bollettieri says that in the next six months he'll conduct a talent search for minority kids from ages eleven to thirteen. "I'll try to get three or four kids, give them scholarships, and let them train here, and see if I can get another Jamea Jackson," says Bollettieri.

The Evert Tennis Academy also boasts hot African-American prospects, most notably Shadisha Robinson, fifteen, and Natalie Cedeno, fourteen. Shadisha, the daughter of Charlie Robinson, a sixty-year-old retired railroad worker from Queens, New York, obtained individual and corporate sponsors so she could pursue her tennis dreams and move to Florida for top-notch coaching and competition.

"Shadisha has the best hand-eye coordination of any player we have," says Rodney Harmon, the United States Tennis Association (USTA) director of multi-cultural development. "Despite limited training opportunities until recently, she's had very good success in tournament play. She works a lot with Chris Evert and hits the ball as cleanly as any junior around. She's just very gifted. She has everything to be a top-fifty pro player."

Harmon calls six-foot tower-of-power Cedeno a "wild card" among African-American prospects because of her very limited tournament experience. "Natalie hits the ball as hard as any player on the women's tour," says Harmon. "She's got excellent technique on all of her strokes and a very, very big serve that could develop in the Venus Williams range of 120-124 miles per hour."

Cedeno is coached by recently retired French Davis Cupper Guillaume Raoux, who says, "She has great, great potential. She is very powerful. But she needs to control her power and learn to pick the right opportunity to rip the ball. And she is not moving that well. When she can do that, she will have no limits. Natalie can be in the top twenty, the top ten, and then you never know."

Despite—or perhaps because of—her public parks background, fifteen-year-old Asha Rolli, of Miami, believes she has no limits. "My goal in tennis is to be number one in the world," she says matter-of-factly. "Venus and Serena have inspired me. They've done what I want to do. Right now, athletically, I think I'm better than all of them [on the pro circuit]."

If you're tired of watching hard-hitting, one-dimensional, double-handed baseliners, you'll love 5'9", 135-pound Asha. "She plays an exciting, very aggressive style, like Navratilova and Novotna," says Harmon. "She volleys extremely well, has really good hand-eye coordination, and hits a beautiful topspin, one-handed backhand. Asha is going to have tremendous results in doubles, and on faster surfaces in singles, she'll be very dangerous."

Lacking a sponsor and receiving minimal USTA financial assistance, the Rolli family has sacrificed considerably for their prodigy. "Unfortunately, tennis is an expensive sport," says Leo Rolli. "That [thousand-dollar USTA stipend] doesn't go far at all when you talk about traveling to national tournaments in California, Arizona, Tennessee, Pennsylvania, and New Jersey."

Rolli doubts blacks will dominate tennis, at least in terms of sheer numbers, because they just don't have the money for the long haul. "It takes a lot of money to become a top player, and that's usually the determining factor as to whether a kid gets a chance to travel and compete at all these different venues," says Rolli. "The USTA is not making that [financial] commitment, and I don't see any other organization stepping up to make that commitment. From my experience when I travel around, I see [only] two or three other minorities doing the things you need to do to get to that next level."

Undaunted by those odds, Asha, an all-A student, is supremely dedicated, training five to six hours every day. Home-schooled and energetic, she gets up at 5:30 every morning, runs and exercises for two hours, and then practices at the courts from ten to noon and returns for two more hours in the evenings. "She really loves the game," says her father.

FASCINATING FACTS:

- In 1990, sociologist Jay Coakley, in "Sport in Society," calculated the odds of a black or Hispanic female having a professional tennis career as one in 20 million, compared with one in 285,700 odds for a white male.
- In 1995, none of the United States Tennis Association's 120 Area Training Centers were located in a black community.

Megan Bradley, the number-one-ranked girls' 16 player in 1999, is another African-American blessed with athletic genes. Phil Bradley, her father, played baseball for the Seattle Mariners, Philadelphia Phillies, Baltimore Orioles, and Chicago White Sox. And his competitiveness has rubbed off on Megan, who Harmon says "is a fierce competitor." "She has a really good all-around game, highlighted by her serve and her backhand." Bradley has signed a letter of intent to attend UCLA in the fall of 2001, a decision that will advance her education but likely retard her tennis progress.

Natalie Frazier, fifteen, from Riverdale, Georgia, and Shenay Perry, sixteen, from Coconut Creek, Florida, also impress Harmon. Frazier whacks two-handed groundies off both sides, while Perry pounds big forehands and, like Rolli, loves to get to net and pressure opponents.

African-American males have never achieved the tennis success that their female counterparts have, and with the 1999 retirement of MaliVai Washington, they've virtually disappeared. At the 2000 U.S. Open no black players made the main draw on the basis of their world ranking, and even worse, none of the four in the 128-player qualifying event did either.

"It's a terrible thing. When I play, 99 percent of the time, I'm the only black male out there," thirty-six-year-old Ronald Agenor told *Black Tennis* magazine. "It seems almost normal. But it's not normal because tennis is the perfect sport for black people. There is a lot of athletic ability needed to play tennis now, and I think blacks would make it so much more entertaining."

Black male athletes have traditionally excelled in five sports: basketball, football, baseball, track, and boxing. That's why we'll never know the answer to the rhetorical question Ashe once asked: "What if Michael Jordan had chosen tennis instead of basketball?" Or Carl Lewis or Sugar Ray Leonard or Walter Payton or Ken Griffey Jr.?

Ashe knew that black role models—such as those in the above sports—are required for black tennis success to mushroom. Despite being a paragon of dignity and humanitarianism and capturing the Wimbledon, U.S., and Australian titles, Ashe lacked the personal charisma to inspire a new generation of black youngsters to take up tennis. "What we need is an American Yannick Noah. In many respects, I wasn't a very good role model," Ashe acknowledged in 1987. "We need someone who's got flair and can play in-your-face tennis. And he should comport himself like Julius Erving."

As Washington told *Black Tennis* magazine in 1991, "It's very difficult for a young, black kid to identify with a white tennis player. I mean, who are they going to relate to, Michael Jordan and Walter Payton or Boris Becker and Ivan Lendl? If you're talking about exposing young, black athletes to tennis, you can't underestimate the importance of having black role models."

The dearth of blacks in tennis won't likely change in the foreseeable future. Besides the fact that tennis has no black male role models now and is much more expensive than other sports at the more advanced levels, peer pressure also dictates why there aren't more young black males playing tennis. "Many black youths want to do what the rest of their friends are doing.... Tennis is not viewed as macho enough for most black boys," wrote Ashe in a *New York Times* column.

Levar Harper-Griffith, a gifted nineteen-year-old black satellite player who was raised in the rough-and-tumble Fort Green section of Brooklyn, New York, used to be teased by his inner-city friends about his passion for tennis. "When I played basketball, they would go, 'Hey, here comes Arthur Ashe,'" he told *USA Today.*

That participation trend seems to belie fascinating findings from a 1999 ESPN Chilton Sports Poll in which 11 percent of African-Americans said they are avid tennis fans compared to only 4.7 percent of whites. Even more revealing is that tennis ranked fourth in sports popularity among African-Americans—behind only the NFL, NBA, and MLB—in the same survey.

Those numbers are undoubtedly pumped up by the high-profile Williams sisters and their ghetto-to-Wimbledon "Cinderella" story. "Venus and Serena—and their father, Richard, you can't leave him out—have done something that neither Althea [Gibson, the first black champion] nor Arthur did," David Dinkins, a former New York City mayor who is a member of the USTA board of directors, told *USA Today.* "Through their charisma and style, they've captured the imagination of a lot of people."

Richard Williams, who once proclaimed that he was the third-most-famous personality in tennis (after his two daughters, of course), frequently makes headlines, too, albeit with provocative and even inflammatory comments. "Richard copied Muhammad Ali. He promotes himself by attacking people," explains Cesar Jensen, a longtime friend and admirer from Boca Raton, Florida.

"He made fun of Hingis, saying she has short legs and can't run fast. He creates controversy, and the American people love controversy," asserts Jensen. "People love to see two players hate each other. McEnroe and Connors were like that. We haven't had that controversy since then. It's very good for women's tennis."

Whether that notoriety will translate into more black youngsters, especially boys, playing tennis is unclear. Harmon, a U.S. Open singles quarterfinalist in 1983, remains cautiously optimistic about producing world-class male competitors. "If we are able to get some of our most talented African-American males opportunities sooner [when they are younger], and we are able to stick with them longer—because it takes longer for men players to develop—then you could see a lot more success on the men's side, too."

Philip Simmons, fifteen, from Reston, Virginia, ranks as Harmon's top black prospect. "Philip is a big, strong young man who can do a little bit of everything around the court," says Harmon. "He can attack, he can stay back. It's going to be interesting to see how he develops long-term because he got very good very quickly and had some excellent results at national events. He's very physically gifted, not only with hand-eye coordination but also athletically."

Harmon's other picks to click are Robbie Poole, Jonathan Howard, and Jarmaine Jenkins. Poole, a rapidly improving fifteen-year-old from Jackson, Mississippi, "is a really, really good athlete who is trying to learn more about how to play the game," says Harmon. "He's got speed, strength and a tremendous competitiveness that sometimes gets him in a little trouble."

Howard, a lefty from Waskom, Texas, who ranked number nine nationally in the boys' 14 in 1999, is a 5'9" baseliner who uses his forehand to control the action. "As Jonathan gets taller and stronger, he'll control points even more," says Harmon. Jenkins, sixteen, from College Park, Georgia, also is loaded with potential. "Jarmaine is a physically gifted backcourt player now developing a more attacking game," says Harmon. "He's strong and has a great vertical leap, and like [Atlanta Braves star] Andruw Jones playing centerfield, has tremendous acceleration and catch-up speed."

Whatever the USTA has done at the grassroots and elite levels for African-American players with its $2.2 million Multicultural Development Program (out of its whopping $160 million budget), it amounts to little more than a "cover-up" to hyper-critical Richard Williams. In his *Florida Tennis* column, he charged: "The cover-up is the USTA's superficial interest in discovering tennis talent in America.... From appearances, it seems like a blatant plan to lock out, shut out and close the doors on inner-city kids.... The NJTL (National Junior Tennis League) needs to become more serious because for a certainty the USTA has failed. It seems that the USTA has made a complete example of how not to embrace poor people in America."

If black male stars don't emerge in America, perhaps the continent of Africa will fulfill Ashe's and McEnroe's prophecy. After all, Ashe discovered Noah as a talented eleven-year-old in Yaounde, Cameroon, in 1971 and had him sent to France for advanced training. Twelve years later Noah captured the French Open to become a hero in both nations.

But can sub-Saharan black Africa—where AIDS, war, starvation, and abject poverty have devastated some countries—produce tennis champions, or even world-class players?

If past results are any guide, then one can't be optimistic. After Noah came Nduka "The Duke" Odizor, another beneficiary of a *deus ex machina*. Dr. Robert Wren, a University of Houston professor, happened to watch the enthusiastic, athletic, fifteen-year-old Nigerian play while on a visit to Africa in 1983 and offered to sponsor him in Texas. Odizor went on to become a three-time All-American player for the University of Houston and attain a career-high number fifty-two world ranking.

However, Senegal's Yahiya Doumbia, who attended Hampton University and Lander College, and Paul Wekesa of Kenya are the only other black Africans to crack the men's top one hundred in the Open Era.

The women have fared even worse. Only Dally Randriantefy, of Madagascar, achieved world-class status, rising to number eighty-six in 1996 at age nineteen.

Just when Randriantefy was coming into her own, though, she dropped off the WTA Tour. She couldn't find enough sponsorship, either from the ITF or her country, to meet expenses. After assisting Randriantefy financially for more than two years, the ITF had to focus its limited budget on up-and-coming juniors.

The fate of Randriantefy, who showed considerable promise at the 1996 French, U.S., and Australian Opens, exemplifies the formidable challenge confronting black African prospects. "Dally was out of money, and she returned to Madagascar. It's a big tragedy," says Nicolas Ayeboua, executive director of the Confederation of African Tennis (CAT) and ITF development officer for Africa. "We've lost a lot of players like that. She might have been in the top fifty or top thirty now if her career had not been interrupted." Randriantefy hopes to rejoin the pro circuit in 2001, starting with some Futures tournaments.

The upbeat Ayeboua notes that sub-Saharan Africa is blessed with an ideal climate, plenty of land for tennis facilities, and an abundance of gifted athletes who could become professional tennis players. "Every year we discover new athletic talent in the 12, 14, and 16 age categories," says Ayeboua, formerly Togo's top junior and senior player and Davis Cup captain.

"Blacks are athletically stronger because they are naturally built like athletes and do not require much physical training at all," says Ayeboua. "They also learn sports quite easily. Thousands of African athletes have never taken lessons from a teacher or coach to develop their natural talent, yet they still perform at an impressive level."

Indeed, the empirical observations Ayeboua makes about the innate physical abilities of African athletes echo those of legendary American pro football coach Vince Lombardi and track superstar Carl Lewis. "I think Negroes are more naturally endowed. I think physique has a great deal to do with it," said Lombardi. "Blacks—physically in many cases—are made better," believed Lewis.

The opinions of Ayeboua, Lombardi, and Lewis are supported in the well-researched and reasoned book, *Taboo: Why Black Athletes Dominate Sports and Why We're Afraid to Talk About It.* "Since the first known study of differences between black and white athletes in 1928, the data have been remarkably consistent: in most sports, African-descended athletes have the capacity to do better with their raw skills than whites," writes Jon Entine.

Entine noted that blacks with a West African heritage generally have numerous physical and physiological advantages, such as "a higher percentage of fast-twitch muscles and more anaerobic enzymes, which can translate into more explosive energy … faster patellar tendon reflex … relatively less subcutaneous fat on arms and legs and proportionately more lean body and muscle mass, broad shoulders, larger quadriceps, and bigger, more developed musculature in general."

These and other relative physiological and biomechanical advantages, writes Entine, are "a gold mine for athletes who compete in such anaerobic activities as football, basketball, and sprinting, sports in which West African blacks clearly excel." Those advantages also count heavily in tennis, where explosive energy used for running and jumping separates elite athletes from lesser ones.

Superior genes still must be nurtured through vigorous training and a competitive environment to produce top athletes. Ayeboua confidently predicts, "If Africans have a third of what Europeans or Americans have, they will dominate tennis for sure."

Unfortunately, African tennis resources don't even come close to that. The ITF is striving to help this Third World continent take a more prominent position within the tennis world through its five-year African Plan (1999–2003). The ambitious plan has already achieved its goals in three areas: introducing many more boys and girls (103,700) to the sport through its School Tennis Initiative in many countries (twenty-five), organizing more men's tournaments (thirty-three weeks worth), and increasing the number of internationally qualified African umpires and referees (sixteen) and White Badge officials (sixty-seven).

Coaching can make or break any program, so every two years the ITF co-organizes regional workshops for coaches to upgrade their knowledge and skills. According to Ayeboua, the best coaches include Rotimi Akinloye of Nigeria, Lamine Diedhiou of Senegal, Christian Bemba of Congo, and Kevin Smit and Dermot Sweeney at the ITF/SATA training center in the Republic of South Africa.

The general level of coaching in Africa, however, isn't good enough, and some of the better coaches aren't utilized most effectively. "Sometimes a national tennis federation has a good coach, but he's not used because they don't like him," says Ayeboua. "Instead they use someone who is a friend or someone they can manipulate. That's the case in 90 percent of Africa."

Getting enough competition to hone their games poses another problem for up-and-coming African players. The ITF/CAT African Junior Championships attracts players from thirty countries every year, and the African prize-money circuit, from May to September, offers thirteen tournaments in thirteen different countries. "This should be multiplied by three to begin making an impact," says Ayeboua. "The problem is, even at the national level, not much is organized. Some players don't even have the opportunity to play two tournaments a year at home."

Ayeboua believes the ITF Touring Team Program, which was dropped three years ago, is extremely important to develop world-class players: "The ITF discontinued it because they thought it was too much money being put into the leading junior players. Now we believe we need the program again. It would be like what the Swedes and Spaniards have and create excellent competition and camaraderie."

Zonal training centers, another key part of the African Plan, haven't gotten off the ground yet. Africa's vast size makes them necessary. The only existing ITF training center is located in remote Pretoria, South Africa, where young black Africans often experience a culture shock. "You take a kid of fourteen or fifteen away from his family for a whole year, and they aren't happy going to South Africa because it's a different life, like European or American life," says Ayeboua. "They can't even play in the clubs, which are closed to them, and they don't have any contact with the population."

Ayeboua recommends that the ITF build training centers in Nigeria and Ghana so that West Africans can easily travel there by road, paying a modest twenty or thirty dollars. "Life is much less expensive there, so besides the geographical proximity, we can reach many more people."

The $1.5 million the ITF allots to forty-five African countries—thirty of which are very active in tennis—seems like a pittance. "When you ask for a facility grant, the ITF cannot give more than twenty thousand dollars. In Africa, generally speaking, to build a good tennis court costs thirty thousand dollars," explains Ayeboua. "Here's another example. In Mali, the biggest tennis club has only three tennis courts. It's a scandal."

Still, Ayeboua maintains that "the ITF is doing a great deal, the best it can because they had to decrease 7 percent of their budget in 2000. It can't do everything. But it has the power to tell the rich countries, like Germany and France: 'You really have to help Africa.'

"The ITF should also put pressure on the national association presidents who are in charge of tennis in Africa," says Ayeboua. "When we meet with them in London or Paris, we never have the courage to tell them, 'You are not doing well!' "

Ayeboua, in fact, charges that some presidents are "terrible" because they lack motivation and competence. "Some are politicians and are appointed by a friendly minister. They are more interested in the position to achieve social status than developing the game," he says. "Their lack of motivation also comes from their disappointment that the game is not producing money. Many of them never play the game and don't know much about its organization, and they don't want to learn from others.

"The ITF should be much stricter with the association leaders in Africa," insists Ayeboua. "It shouldn't trust them. We shouldn't just give them money and say, 'It's your money, just take it.' This subsidy should be conditioned by good work in the countries."

The association presidents can't be blamed for everything, though. While tennis is the fifth most popular sport in Africa—behind soccer, track and field, basketball, and handball—governments put very little or no funding into tennis programs. "Ninety percent of the money for sports goes to soccer," says Ayeboua.

Nigeria, Cameroon, and Ivory Coast, three of the continent's most prominent sports nations, illustrate the assorted problems plaguing African tennis. "The sports administration is terrible in all of these countries," says Ayeboua. "Until two years ago, Nigeria, which is such a big country, hadn't been able to organize a single satellite tournament for years. There was no competition, no development program.

"I've been to Cameroon many times, and there's no development program going on. That's incredible," says Ayeboua. "That's why no players are coming out of these two countries. In Ivory Coast, they do have good players. The problem there is they used to have a policy of elitism. They used to pick two guys and put all of their money into them and not take care of the rest of the juniors."

Despite all these obstacles, a handful of highly promising African juniors are emerging, albeit more slowly than they would in a more fertile environment. Togo's Komlavi Loglo, a six-foot, 168-pounder just turned sixteen, boasts the most potential. "Loglo technically is very, very complete," assesses Ayeboua. "He has all the strokes. He can serve very well, he can play ground strokes, he can volley. He's a hard worker. I'm also most impressed with Loglo because he displays the most professional approach to the game."

The muscular Loglo, who reached the Orange Bowl boys' 16 doubles final with Algeria's Lamine Ouahab, epitomizes the physically superior West African athlete. In track Loglo ranked as the fastest fourteen-year-old in Africa in the one-hundred, two-hundred, and four-hundred meter races.

"Everybody in Togo is a good athlete," the soft-spoken Loglo says. "I'm 100 percent sure I can be the next tennis champion from Africa. I can be number one in both singles and doubles."

A rare serve-and-volleyer, Loglo backs up his confident words with 115-mile-per-hour serves, lightning-fast reflexes at net, and cleanly struck service returns. Not surprisingly, he most admires Pete Sampras and Patrick Rafter. But Loglo would most like to meet Noah. "I'd ask him for tips about anticipation and how to chip and charge," says Loglo, who has trained under ITF coaches in Pretoria for the past three years.

Ayeboua also likes South African Raven Klaasen and Benin's Arnaud Segodo, both eighteen. "Klaasen is very talented and also has all the shots," says Ayeboua. "Segodo is very intelligent, sort of a magician who plays tricky shots like [Hicham] Arazi, but he doesn't serve or volley well yet."

Among the girls, South African Aniela Mojzis, currently number sixty-two in the ITF junior rankings and number one in the CAT and competing in satellite and Futures tournaments abroad, "has the most potential. She has the game it takes and is already very professional-minded."

Ayeboua believes Africa's problems are exacerbated because the outside world has largely written it off as a lost continent. "When you see the image on television projected from the outside, of AIDS and war, you think Africa is a catastrophe," says Ayeboua. "It's not at all. If you come to a country like Senegal, or many countries, [you will see] we are very optimistic, life is very upbeat."

Why isn't there an outcry from the international tennis community to help struggling Africa? "I cannot imagine a great tennis championship like Wimbledon, like the U.S. Open, like the French Open, where you don't see anyone from sub-Saharan Africa," says Ayeboua. "And nobody cares! Nobody says, `What can we do for you?'

"They [tennis leaders] are just happy to be with us, have a drink during an international meeting. That's all," says the frustrated Ayeboua. "They never make any real attempt to help us in terms of [offering]: 'Can we help you build some courts? Can we invite some of your best players to play in our tournaments?' They never do that."

Enter Alain Limbo, hoping to become the latest *deus ex machina* to advance black tennis in Africa. Alain who? Limbo, born in Cameroon but also raised part-ly in France and Switzerland and now living in the United States, believes African tennis is in limbo in terms of turning out world-class players.

Limbo avers that there's a goldmine of black athletic talent in Africa waiting to be discovered and developed "if only people would give them that chance. Africans are hungry for resources. They are raised with a bare minimum, so with the bare necessities they develop high survival skills. When you transport those guys—say a guy like Hakeem Olajuwon—to America or Europe, with the intellectual and street-smart skills they've already developed, they end up excelling."

Multilingual Limbo, twenty-nine, played satellite-level tennis after college and then worked at Octagon in player management, was a "clinician" introducing tennis to minority youngsters for the USTA's Northern Section, and worked in the media department at the ATP.

His diverse background has shaped his worldview. "Africa is a very slow continent by nature," explains Limbo. "Africans walk slowly, work slowly, and do things slowly. Something drastic has to be done if you want to energize tennis in Africa."

Limbo believes he has just the plan: a commando-type operation. "I want to assemble a team of advisors, the best African coaches that are U.S.-based, entrepreneurs, and people with money with the same approach that I have," explains Limbo. "We would find ten of the most promising African players between fifteen and eighteen and train them for the next two or three years. We could do it faster and better than any of the ITF programs."

Limbo's commando-like vision is based on the highly successful Team SIAB of twenty years ago. The six-player Swedish squad, which included future stars Mats Wilander, Anders Jarryd, Kent Carlsson, Joakim Nystrom, and Henrik Sundstrom, traveled together, ate together, practiced together, played golf and hockey together, and, above all, always supported each other. "That's how that wave of Swedes excelled for a decade and dominated tennis," says Limbo. "We'll have a pan-African team with players from several countries with the same *esprit de corps,* and I guarantee we'll produce a bunch of top-twenty players.

"John McEnroe once said, when asked how we can reform tennis: 'Put the rackets in the hands of the best athletes,' " recalls Limbo. "This project would do just that. I promise you that you will see African athletes do amazing things from the junior level to the professional level. And this sport would change."

But would blacks, if given the chance, actually take over tennis?

"You bet your life they would," predicts Bollettieri. "They're going to whack ass."

FASCINATING FACTS:

- Nigeria's Nduka Odizor received written death threats when he reached the fourth round at Wimbledon in 1983.
- No Caucasian woman won a singles, doubles, or mixed doubles title at the 1999 U.S. Open.

This story won 1st Prize in the United States Tennis Writers Association 2001 Writing Contest in the Hard News/Enterprise category.

24

True Confessions
2001

They say confession is good for the soul. That's good, because tennis stars confess a lot. It's also good for their legions of fans, who are ready to empathize with them and forgive their sins. Of course, some confessions are so shocking or silly that they serve as juicy grist for critics.

So, let's get right to the most provocative quotes that may change the way you think about the players you love or loathe.

After having taken a course in media relations in 2000, Martina Hingis made a rare public admission about behaving like a spoiled brat in the 1999 French Open final. "I did things I should not have done. But people make mistakes, especially at my age, when you feel you are so smart, but in fact you are an asshole," confided one of the sassy "spice girls" of tennis.

Another "spice girl" apparently had a compulsion to set the record straight on something inquiring minds wanted to know. Anna Kournikova, then eighteen, disclosed: "I am still a virgin. I do not let anyone have even a peep in my bed." What a slap shot this public confession must have delivered to the egos of Anna's macho pro hockey boyfriends.

At twenty-two, tall, dark, and handsome Mark Philippoussis let the cat out of the bag and disappointed female admirers when he confided: "I don't want a girlfriend right now. They're hard work and they're very dangerous."

Andre Agassi wasn't always the single-minded workhorse that has ground out four major titles since he turned twenty-nine. Back in May 1992, two months before he captured his first Grand Slam crown at Wimbledon, Andre confessed: "My accomplishments do not live up to my tennis game. Most people have to work really hard and win some big matches, and then they get money and popularity. For me it has been the reverse of everybody else. The exact opposite."

Four years, two more Slam titles, and a $100-million Nike contract later, the education of Andre Agassi was progressing rather gradually, as he admitted, "Even though I'm on a salary, I still don't have a comprehension of what the real world functions like." And dazzling everyone with Australian, Indian Wells, and Ericsson Open titles in early 2001 at nearly thirty-one prompted the still-haunted American to confide, "I have taken off some years that I have spent a lot of nights regretting."

No one captured the paradox of fame better than Patrick Rafter. After winning his second U.S. Open in 1998, the Aussie hero revealed, "When you haven't got it, you really want it; when you have it, you really don't want it."

A decade earlier, French star Yannick Noah, who also got more celebrity worship than he bargained for, said: "Becoming a champion, one learns many things, but nobody teaches you how to deal with the sudden glory." This sensitive soul dealt with it by fleeing fame in the City of Light for anonymity in the city that never sleeps.

After winning his second French Open last year, unpretentious Gustavo Kuerten confided, "I don't want to be promoted. I am already too much promoted. I want to be unknown." No such luck for "Guga," in Brazil anyway, where the national hero is besieged by admirers whenever he appears in public.

Disillusionment hit Mats Wilander just when he least expected it. "All my career I had dreamed of being number one. But when I finally achieved it [in 1988] and the initial excitement wore off, I felt nothing," he recalled. "I had no sense of elation or pride. I was the world champion but so what? It got to the stage where I got more satisfaction out of cutting the grass than playing tennis."

Coaching during matches is illegal on the pro tour, but that doesn't deter zealous coaches. "Over the years I've probably broken the [coaching] rules more than anyone else," Nick Bollettieri confessed in 1989. You've got to hand it to this controversial coach. At least he's honest about his dishonesty.

An on-court beneficiary of illegal coaching came clean, albeit unapologetically, in her autobiography. "If Betty [Stove, her coach] has something to say, I need to be able to digest her coded message," wrote four-time Slam champion Hana Mandlikova. "Coaching is an illegal practice during a match, but everyone does it. It's just that some do it smarter than others."

In her 1983 autobiography Billie Jean King fessed up to something even more serious: "You may be shocked and I won't name the match, because I don't want to deprive my opponent of anything, but I absolutely tanked the final of a Grand Slam tournament once." Say it ain't so, Billie Jean! Could a competitor so feared—Chris Evert once revealed she never looked at Billie Jean during changeovers because she didn't want to be intimidated—do such a thing? I *am* shocked. Did this travesty occur, of all places, at her beloved Wimbledon in the 1978 mixed doubles final when BJK and doubles standout Ray Ruffels lost to Frew McMillan and Stove by the suspicious score of 6-2, 6-2?

But, hey, no one's perfect. Certainly not John McEnroe. An over-the-hill McEnroe once lamented, "I want to be remembered as a great player, but I guess it will be as a player who got angry on a tennis court."

Arthur Ashe, the consummate sporting gentleman, once divulged a secret desire. "I would like to go out on the court for one match and be a complete jerk. It would be extremely out of character for me, but it would be interesting to experience what it's like." The legendary Ashe trash-talking and racket-throwing? It actually might have done him some good, though. Ashe's brother, Johnnie, and others who knew him well have speculated that his heart problems were caused by repressed feelings.

Another famous repressor, Bjorn Borg, renowned for his extreme stoicism on court during his extraordinary eleven-Slam winning career, unloaded a bombshell in 1998 when he revealed, "I was never that cold inside. It was always an act—an act I came to perfect—but an act just the same. It was part of my armory. I felt if my opponents did not know what I was thinking, how I was really feeling inside, then I was invincible." Boy, he sure had the tennis world fooled.

Chris Evert was dubbed "The Ice Maiden" for her stoical on-court demeanor, but behind that facade swirled powerful emotions. On Evonne Goolagong, her immensely popular 1970s rival, Evert once revealed: "I never resented the fact that the crowds were for Evonne. But I was envious and wanted to shout, 'Don't you know I'm feeling something inside?'"

Issues of self-esteem often elicit powerful confessions. In 1998, Lindsay Davenport said, "The other night I saw myself on TV and ran out of the room. Some people love being a star. I'm not one of those people." Considering she possesses stylish strokes and was leaner and more mobile after losing twenty-five pounds, Lindsay seemed overly self-critical.

Not even gaining an Olympic silver medal and the U.S. Open semis made well-adjusted Elena Dementieva completely happy last year. The comely Russian blonde revealed: "I would like to play tennis like a queen, but right now I am a queen without a great forehand."

Thomas Muster, whose killer instinct on court far surpassed his people skills and left him unpopular among his peers, confided: "I can look at myself in the mirror and know I'm a fair competitor on every surface and not a bad guy out there. But people never believe me."

Way back in the 1950s, Pancho Gonzalez, the child of Mexican immigrants, explained in his autobiography why he shied away from parties: "At a cocktail party I was like an olive that found its way into a glass of bourbon. In short, I was a misfit." Now that's real candor from a fierce and charismatic champion who envied the social graces and sophistication of many of his well-bred fellow players.

Some superstars disdain the limelight, while others have mixed feelings about it. "I never wished to live this life. I just wanted to play tennis, not to become a public person," revealed twenty-two-time Grand Slam winner Steffi Graf. "That is why I can be quite bitchy toward people." Perhaps retirement and romancing Agassi will bring out Steffi's sunnier side.

Larger-than-life 1920s great "Big Bill" Tilden, an enigmatic bundle of contradictions, confided: "I can stand crowds only when I am working in front of them, but then I love them."

Child prodigies and their ambitious parents provide plenty of telling confessions. "I really got into tennis so I could get a million dollars," frankly admitted Richard Williams, the controversial father-coach of Venus and Serena, in 1998. "I didn't have the right motives in the beginning at all. I was just like any other [tennis] parent then." Williams, a Louisiana sharecropper's son who picked cotton as a boy, today orchestrates a dynamic duo that has already amassed a reported $150 million in prize money and endorsement contracts.

Dr. Paul Berger, the father of former world top-tenner Jay Berger, had a far different background from Richard Williams but a similar mentality. "You feel like a big shot if your kid is number one," Berger disclosed in the 1992 book, *Tough Draw*. "The parents get *very* involved. I don't care what the other parents say. The parents have a lot of expectations with their kids in tennis. If they tell you differently, that's a lot of bull."

One of tennis' first teen queens, France's legendary Suzanne Lenglen, paid a high price for the pressure her well-meaning but Svengali-like father and amateur officials heaped on her. After turning professional in 1926, Lenglen graphically confided: "The nightmare is over. I have escaped from bondage and slavery. No one can order me about any longer to play tournaments for the benefit of club owners. Now I will be able to make some money, have some fun, and see the world."

The saddest confession comes from Jennifer Capriati, a teenage burnout victim. At her personal nadir in 1994, she told the *New York Times*: "I really was not happy with myself, my tennis, my life, my parents, my coaches, my friends.... When I looked in the mirror, I actually saw this distorted image: I was so ugly and fat. I just wanted to kill myself." Now twenty-five, she happily conquered her demons and rebounded to win her first Grand Slam title at the 2001 Australian Open with impressive victories over Monica Seles, Davenport, and Hingis. Capriati then put an exclamation point on her extraordinary comeback by capturing the French Open.

Not all world-class players are motivated by a quest to be the best. Temperamental Marat Safin, who led the circuit in smashing rackets and was fined at the 2000 Australian Open for not trying, confessed, "I was never a fighter until this year." Soon afterwards, the maturing twenty-year-old Russian grabbed the U.S. Open for his first Grand Slam crown.

In 2000 Philippoussis, another big bomber whose competitive flames sometimes flicker, wistfully admitted: "I'm twenty-three and I've had at least sixteen cars. I've had everything you could possibly have. Now I'm a little sick of it, which is good. I got it out of my system. I'm ready to concentrate on tennis."

Compatriot Lleyton Hewitt clearly suffers no such motivation problem. Believing his fervent fist-pumping and primal screams of "C'mon!" weren't enough evidence, young Hewitt last year announced, "I'm not backing down from anybody. You don't play this game to win. You play to kill people out there." The bloke sounds just like a pugnacious, twenty-first century Jimmy Connors.

Profound emotions produce telling confessionals from even the most tough-minded competitors. "It's not easy for me to live with, knowing that I'm number one because she was attacked," Graf said in 1994, referring to her former archrival, Seles, who was stabbed in the back a year earlier.

Croatia's power-hitting Mirjana Lucic, who fled her physically abusive father and went with her siblings and mother to America in 1998, exposed exploitation of young players on the women's tour when she revealed: "It's not just my case. I know it is still going on with a lot of other players. It's just not right. A lot of other players say the same things happen to them."

Great moral and political issues hit some players hard. In 1999, King confided, "I had a hard time playing tennis during [the] Vietnam [War]. It really upset me." That the war affected King's results is doubtful, however, since it lasted more than a decade and coincided with her brilliant career.

Becoming a teenaged German icon overnight following his incredible 1985 Wimbledon triumph made Boris Becker almost paranoid. In 1991, he disclosed: "It became twenty-four hours a day. When I slept, I suspected a secret camera under the sheet. The more I worked to live up to my nationalistic obligations, the more harassed I became. It's tough to handle at age twenty-three, but much harder at seventeen or eighteen."

Life has proved quite adventurous for Martina Navratilova ever since she defected from the former Czechoslovakia as an eighteen-year-old rising star in 1975. Apparently it became dangerous, too. In 1991 she revealed to a British newspaper: "I used to carry a gun with me on tour because of the IRA threat [to kidnap me]."

Some confessions are far less earth-shattering. Last year Fernando Vicente, a twenty-three-year-old Spaniard ranked in the top fifty, admitted that he stole Andre Agassi's T-shirt and Goran Ivanisevic's racket from locker rooms when he was a mischievous teenager. And in 1999, Alexandra Stevenson told Barbara Walters on *20/20* that she was eighteen and had never been kissed. With a fetching smile, she added, "So any cute guys out there who want to date me, go ahead and call me."

You can't help but like humble and honest confessions from down-to-earth Australians. When asked in 1999 about his status as a sex symbol, Rafter replied, "Would you complain if the chicks wanted to go after you? It's nice having that image. I remember when women wouldn't look twice at me." He added that American women treated him with the most indifference.

Another fair dinkum Aussie, all-time great Rod Laver, also gets high marks for honesty when he admitted, "I didn't find out who were the best [players] until I turned pro and had my brains beaten out for six months at the start of 1963." Laver, who had captured the Grand Slam as an amateur in 1962, lost nineteen of his first twenty-one pro matches against Ken Rosewall and Lew Hoad.

Occasionally players actually confess they'd like to speak more candidly, but they just can't pull the trigger. Last year Tim Henman, a proper Brit, explained to the media why he hedged: "There are times I'd love to be honest, but most of the time I have to give the right answer rather than the truthful one. I know you want more substance, but it has backfired on me before."

Choking is a subject few world-class players enjoy talking about. But Pete Sampras, having squandered six match points before finally beating Gustavo Kuerten 6-1, 6-7, 7-6, 7-6 in the 2000 Ericsson Open final, made a clean breast of it. "My nerves were getting the best of me," admitted the greatest player who ever lived. "It happens to everybody. Anybody who says they don't choke, they're lying."

Before I forget, sex symbol Kournikova has something else she wants to get off her chest—and it's not her "no bounce" bra. "Boyfriends have to understand me, and my needs ... and my strict regimen. I go to bed at ten at night, and no later, unless I'm playing in a tournament. And I shower four times a day, after training and matches," she informs us. I've duly noted all that, Anna, just in case I make the cut.

The fabulous Williams sisters are never short of pronouncements. But they don't do confessions. After all, as Serena last year said: "We're strong, we're very strong. We're making it happen in different ways. We're bringing in new power. We can run fast, we can jump high, we can last. We have it all."

FASCINATING FACTS:

- In the 2001 book *Venus Envy,* Sonja Jeyaseelan, the highest-ranked Canadian player, revealed: "You can look at a men's draw and find maybe three players who have had a [dysfunctional] relationship with their father. With the girls you might find three who don't."
- In July 2001, Martina Hingis confided that she hasn't won a major singles title in two-and-a-half years because "My head is always off in the clouds."

PART 4

The Great Controversies

25

Equal—Not Sequel— Prize Money

1996

Equality consists in the same treatment of similar persons.

—ARISTOTLE

At the first "open" Wimbledon in 1968, Lady Spencer Churchill, Sir Winston's widow, strongly condemned the great disparity in prize money for the men and women in a letter published in *The Times* of London. Ten years later, my first essay advocating equal prize money for men and women in all Grand Slam tournaments appeared in *Inside Women's Tennis*. I envisioned complete equality by the 1990s, if not earlier.

I certainly never envisioned that only one Grand Slam, the U.S. Open, would offer equal prize money in 1996. Nor did I foresee that the Australian Open, after five years of equality, would take a step backwards and give $390,000 more to the men this year.

I wonder: What does it take to convince Wimbledon's hidebound traditionalists—whose favorite rationale is "We've always done it that way"—and the French and Australian Opens that women *deserve* equal prize money?

Maybe they're not using the criteria that I use. Maybe they don't even *know* the criteria that I believe matter most. So, hoping that they're paying attention, I'd like to tell them why I favor equal prize money at their great tournaments.

1. The "more work deserves more pay" argument holds less water than people think.

    Reason number one: Women actually take far shorter breaks between points than men. Many women, such as Graf, Seles, and Capriati, take only eleven to fifteen seconds between points, whereas most men, legally or illegally, dawdle for twenty to thirty seconds. The average "rest time" between points in the 1991 Wimbledon final between Stich and Becker was 27.36 seconds. So more total court time often does not constitute more total work.

Reason number two: Although best-of-five-sets men's matches do average more total games than best-of-three-sets women's matches, women tend to play *more points per game* because they have much more trouble holding serve. And because they hit far fewer aces and service winners, many more games are exciting, fluctuating, and unpredictable.

Reason number three: Since women possess less devastating knockout power, they also play *longer, more strategic points.* In sharp contrast, the men descended to an ultra-boring low during the 1994 Sampras-Ivanisevic Wimbledon final. Though the match lasted one hour and fifty-five minutes, the actual playing time (when the ball was in play) totalled a measly eight minutes. Only one of the 206 points lasted more than four strokes. Nothing tiring—let alone exhausting—about *eight minutes of work.*

2. What about the entertainment value of men's five-set matches versus that of women's three-set matches? It can be summed up with a rarely mentioned truism: Five-set matches have a greater potential for spectacular drama, *but* they also make for tedious debacles. I would have loved to watch Steffi Graf's sensational 4-6, 6-1, 7-5 victory over Arantxa Sanchez Vicario in the 1995 Wimbledon final continue for five sets. I also savored the riveting 7-6, 0-6, 6-3 Graf–Monica Seles final at the 1995 U.S. Open and wanted more, much more. On the other hand, John McEnroe's 6-2, 6-2, 6-2 massacre of outclassed Chris Lewis at the 1983 Wimbledon and Ivan Lendl's 6-4, 6-2, 6-0 rout of dispirited Miloslav Mecir at the 1986 U.S. Open proved to be dismally boring Grand Slam finals that would have pleased everyone had they lasted one set less.

3. Do women deserve equal prize money for *doubles*? This question is mistakenly overlooked in the current debate. Here women's "star power" far exceeds the slim pickings on offer in the men's game. Only one male player, Yevgeny Kafelnikov, was ranked in the top fifteen at the end of 1995 in *both* singles and doubles. In sharp contrast *seven* women ranked in the top fifteen in both singles and doubles. Many potential men's doubles stars—such as Sampras, Stefan Edberg, Boris Becker, and Michael Stich—have abandoned doubles, and the 1995 men's doubles top-ten rankings include Mark Knowles, Daniel Nestor, Patrick Galbraith, and Cyril Suk. Nice players, but hardly household names that draw big crowds.

4. Which side of pro tennis boasts the better competitors? In my view, the three ultimate warriors in tennis are Graf, Seles, and Sanchez Vicario. All are driven by intense passion, pride, and love of competition. Do they always

give 100 percent effort? Do they play even when ill and injured—even when they'd be well advised not to? Yes and yes. Besides them, women's tennis offers relentless Rubin, resourceful Martina Hingis, industrious Iva Majoli, tenacious Capriati,and tireless Anna Kournikova.

Win or lose, these and other diehard fighters *guarantee* crowd-pleasing performances. Compare that to the men's game—which does offer some (but not enough) day-in and day-out warriors such as Michael Chang and Thomas Muster. According to John McEnroe, tanking matches on the men's tour is "epidemic."

5. What about tennis "whiz kids" who captivate the sporting public? Even with the new age-eligibility rules designed to limit teenaged play and prevent premature physical and mental burnout, women's tennis produces far more prodigies than the men's game. In fact, virtually every recent female champion—Hingis, Graf, Seles, Sanchez Vicario, and Capriati, for starters—has displayed her genius as a teenager. Super-athletic sisters Venus and Serena Williams, Hingis, and Kournikova loom as the next teen queens. The women enjoy a big and important advantage here.

6. Doesn't men's tennis have more depth, though? It undeniably does although the gap has greatly narrowed in the past ten years because of the development of so many outstanding European and Asian female players. But the depth issue cuts *both ways*. Depth—as defined by the number of close matches and upsets—matters most for the first two rounds, which eliminate 75 percent of the draw at Grand Slams events. Those upsets can damage tournaments, however, when middle- and lower-ranked men upset high-seeded players. If the game's giant-killers run out of gas (and talent?), we often wind up with the likes of Chris Lewis, Cedric Pioline, Petr Korda, Henri Leconte, and Mikael Pernfors in lackluster or even abysmal finals. Contrast those with the dynamic "heavyweight" finals that Graf, Seles, Evert, Navratilova, and other women stars—who are less often upset—have given us.

7. Does men's tennis really have greater fan appeal and drawing power than women's tennis? Some studies have indicated that men's matches—usually more numerous but less important early-round matches—do attract more live spectators and higher TV ratings. But, ongoing discrimination likely accounts for some of that.

Example 1: *None* of the four women's quarterfinals at the 1995 French Open was showcased on the 16,500-seat Court Central. Not only did fewer spectators get a chance to see those important matches, but the impression left is they don't really matter that much. That's unfair and deprived many fans of seeing quarterfinal matches involving Sanchez Vicario versus Rubin, Majoli versus number nine Kimiko Date, Conchita Martinez versus darkhorse Virginia Ruano-Pascual, and Graf versus Sabatini.

Example 2: For years American TV sports viewers had to guess what time the U.S. Open women's singles final would be played because it was sandwiched between the two men's singles semifinals. For the many tennis fans who missed part or all of those women's singles finals because of the poor, indeterminate scheduling, it wasn't "Super Saturday" but "Stupid Saturday." Those who question what ratings all those women's singles finals would have attained—if given a definite time and thus a fair chance—need only look back at the 1995 U.S. Open final. Graf and Seles, two superstars who also were faced with compelling human-interest adversity, met in the most eagerly anticipated women's match since Suzanne Lenglen beat Helen Wills in Cannes, France, in 1926. They produced an enthralling 7-6, 0-6, 6-3 masterpiece and renewed their great rivalry.

At long last the "brain trust" at the U.S. Open has decided to partly abolish Stupid Saturday and schedule the women's singles final on Sunday and *prior to* the men's singles final. Now the men will get stuck with the indefinite starting time and will have to eat bagels and "cool their heels" while impatiently waiting for the women to finish. All's fair in love and tennis! Not quite. "Stupid Saturday" has become "Semi-Stupid Saturday." With the women's singles semifinals now scheduled on Friday—sans prime TV time—and the men's singles semifinals on Saturday—denying them sufficient rest for their Sunday best-of-five-sets final—*both sexes* are victimized. (In a landmark change to the television coverage for the 2001 U.S. Open, the women's singles final was staged at 8 P.M. on Saturday, September 8, making the U.S. Open the first Grand Slam event to schedule a prime-time final on network television.)

Example 3: Despite unequal prize money at the recent Australian Open, which again left the impression that women's tennis is an inferior product, the five most thrilling matches there—with the possible exception of upstart Mark Philippoussis's shocking upset over number one Sampras—were not only played by women, but played by *one woman,* Chanda Rubin. The rising black star from Louisiana outlasted Sanchez Vicario 6-4, 2-6, 16-14 in a scintillating quarterfinal that set tourney records for time length, most number of games in a set, and most number of games in a match. Rubin then led top-seeded Seles 5-2 in the third set before the eventual champion barely escaped with a 6-7, 6-1, 7-5 semifinal victory. Rubin also paired for the first time with Sanchez Vicario and upset teams seeded one, three, and four in exciting three-setters for the doubles title.

Fair-minded observers—even those relishing Becker's terrific play en route to his second singles title—would have to conclude that women's tennis flourished more than the men's at the 1996 Australian Open, just as it did at the 1995 U.S. Open, which Edberg called "the Seles Open." With superstar Graf and comebacking Capriati returning for the French Open, the women could easily outshine the men again. That should further clinch the already powerful case for equal prize money at Grand Slam events.

FASCINATING FACTS:

- At the 1970 Italian Open, women's champion Billie Jean King received six hundred dollars, while men's champion Ilie Nastase collected thirty-five hundred dollars, nearly a six-to-one disparity.

- In 1971 President Richard M. Nixon phoned to congratulate Billie Jean King when she became the first woman athlete to earn a hundred thousand dollars prize money in one year.

- In 1976 the Women's Tennis Association gave Wimbledon an ultimatum that the women pros would not compete the following year unless they received equal prize money with the men.

- At the 1978 Australian Open the men's prize money was 8.6 times greater than the women's prize money.

- According to a 1991 survey by American Sports Data Inc., 91.8 percent of Americans over thirteen recognized Chris Evert—more than those recognizing Magic Johnson (89.0 percent) and Joe Montana (88.8 percent).

- In 1999 Chris Gorringe, All-England Lawn Tennis Club secretary, dismissed WTA demands for equal prize money at Wimbledon by saying, "If we paid the women more, we wouldn't have so much to spend on petunias."

- In 2000 tennis was the sport with the most athletes (six) listed in "The Forbes Celebrity 100"—chosen and ranked according to their income and media buzz they generate. They were: Andre Agassi, Martina Hingis, Anna Kournikova, Venus Williams, Monica Seles, and Serena Williams.

- At the 2000 U.S. Open, more women's matches were played on the Stadium Court than men's matches for the first time in the tournament's history.

26

Twenty Reasons Why Women's Tennis Is Better Than Men's Tennis
1999

Let's face it. Most of us always preferred watching men's tennis over the women's game, even when Chrissie and Martina provided great drama. The guys were just so much more athletic, rugged, and gladiatorial. But that all changed when trash-talking teen queens fired up passions and controversies and backed it up with terrific tennis that pushed their elders' games to the next level. When macho guys such as Becker, Borg, Leconte, McEnroe, Lendl, and even former male chauvinist Krajicek (who once said "80 percent of the women are fat, lazy pigs") confessed they now like women's tennis more, I had to agree. On Eurosport, the women's television ratings were on average 35 percent better than the men's during all tournaments broadcast in 1999. Why do so many tennis fans love the ladies more than the gents? Here are the reasons why.

1. The women exude personality. Sure, the Spice Girls sometimes turn into spite girls, but they're forever fun and often funny. Venus brashly predicts she'll be number one by the end of the year and fails (but does reach number three). Serena challenges men, gets whupped by number 203, chain-smoking Karsten Braasch, vows revenge, and even requests a wild card to compete at an ATP Tour men's event in Stuttgart. Hingis claims that she has "nothing to learn" from Graf because Graf is past her prime, and that new rival, openly gay Amelie Mauresmo, is "half a man." Jelena Dokic accuses overseas tennis officials of rigging tournament draws and attacks an opponent by saying she "has never been a player and never will be." Kournikova brags she's beautiful, famous, and gorgeous and has a boyfriend in every city she visits.

2. The ultimate warriors—Serena, Venus, Seles, Dokic, and Sanchez Vicario— are women. They don't brood, whine, or tank. They compete fiercely. In fact, Mauresmo is so tough that when three knife-wielding thugs tried to mug her and her girlfriend on a Caribbean beach, she punched and knocked them down.

3. The women don't fiddle and diddle and dawdle for twenty-five seconds between points like the men. Give 'em balls, and they serve 'em right up.

4. Frequent aces and unreturnable rocket serves sometimes make men's tennis a snoring bore on grass and indoor courts. Women's tennis offers more rallies, finesse, and strategy, not just brute force.

5. Fewer tournaments mean more of the best players fill up women's draws. Unlike the quantity-crazed men's game, they never have three tournaments in the same week or two big tournaments conflicting with each other.

6. The chicks dress with class and sex appeal. "Babe Alert!" Compare Lucic's dazzling black dress, Venus's midriff-baring outfits, and Kournikova's blue super-short shorts with Sampras's and Agassi's baggy, wrinkled, super-long shorts that look more like used underwear.

7. We get rivalries with the women. Graf versus Seles was the highlight of the early 1990s. Davenport versus Hingis, Davenport versus Venus, and Venus versus Serena are growing now. In contrast, Pete Sampras won thirteen of his sixteen Grand Slam finals, which included only one five-setter.

8. Many of the women play doubles, so we can double our spectating pleasure. No top-ten guy, except for Kafelnikov, regularly plays doubles, and he grouses that doubles "has played a negative role in my career in recent years."

9. Admit it. You love to hate the Bad Dads of women's tennis. Damir Dokic, Jim Pierce, Marinko Lucic, and Richard Williams outrage you even when you root for their daughters. And let's not forget Samantha Stevenson, Alexandra's vocal mother, whom Davenport says "has offended nearly everyone" on the women's tour.

10. Most games in women's matches are close, hard-fought, and exciting, with ad-in and ad-out fluctuations. The men's booming serves enable them to hold serve routinely and predictably.

11. Women's tennis has no Marcelo Rios, who complains, "In this job, it's like beasts of prey in a cage."

12. The season-ending Chase Championships feature the best sixteen women singles players with a fair-and-square, single-elimination format. The ATP World Championships include only eight men, with a wimpy round-robin format that allows the eventual winner to lose one or even two matches.

13. Physical contact. Where else but women's tennis do you get The Bump Seen 'Round the World? When Irina Spirlea intentionally collided with and kneed

Venus in their riveting 1997 U.S. Open semifinal, sparks and accusations flew.

14. The women nearly always play Fed Cup for their countries, and when they don't—as in the case of Davenport—they regret it. The men unapologetically and shamelessly skip Davis Cup, whether in preference to minor tournaments (Chang), out of grudges with national association officials (Philippoussis), out of exhaustion from playing ATP Tour events (Sampras), or when Davis Cup conflicts with non-tennis functions (Agassi).

15. Some men players have great-looking models and actresses for wives and girlfriends. The women players themselves—especially Kournikova, Kandarr, Lucic, Cristea, Coetzer, Dementieva, and Sanchez Lorenzo—are often as beauteous and sexy as models.

16. The women revel in and relish the one-on-one battles that tournament tennis presents. They wouldn't think of copping some help by proposing an on-court coaching rule change the way the men did.

17. The women have more and better Web sites. Kournikova alone is the focus of thirty-eight sites—some with catchy names like The Annamaniacs Page and Amazingly Adorable Anna. What's more, "The Russian Lolita" is the "most searched for" and "most downloaded" athlete on the Internet, according to search engines Lycos 50 and Yahoo!

18. Men players get phone numbers and obligation-free sex (!) from tour groupies. Women players get marriage proposals from smitten fans. The downside is that some champions, such as Graf and Hingis, also get stalked.

19. Men gutlessly duck tournaments on grass and clay if they're lousy on them. Women typically play all the Grand Slams no matter what the surface.

20. The women, at least most of them, smile. In particular, Hingis, Seles, Venus, Serena, Capriati, Dementieva, Sugiyama, Majoli, Sanchez-Vicario, Rubin, Kournikova, Schett, Pierce, and Lucic enjoy themselves. To them, tennis is fun and games as well as serious competition.

FASCINATING FACTS:

- Muhammad Ali asked Monica Seles for her autograph at the Atlanta Olympics.
- When Martina Hingis was voted "Swiss Personality of the Year" in 1996 in a Swiss opinion poll conducted by *Schweizer Illustrierte* magazine, she beat out Rolf Zinkernagel, the Swiss winner of the Nobel Prize for Medicine.
- One of the fourteen tips on a list given to ball boys and girls at the 2000 Ericsson Open was "Do not stare at Kournikova."
- Seven of the top ten most-searched athletes on the Internet for the week ending July 7, 2001, were women tennis players.
- The five highest-paid female athletes (including endorsements) in the world in 2000 were tennis stars—Martina Hingis, Anna Kournikova, Venus Williams, Serena Williams, and Lindsay Davenport.
- A 2000 MSNBC survey reported that 70 percent of respondents preferred women's tennis to men's.

This column received 1st Prize in the United States Tennis Writers Association 1999 Writing Contest in the Commentary Category.

27

Why On-Court Coaching Is Bad for Tennis
1998

Much of tennis' enduring appeal derives from its one-on-one challenge where competitors pit their athleticism, skill, fitness, strategy, and courage against each other. On-court coaching would distort this distinguishing feature of the game. Matches could come down to two-versus-one (in the case of players who can't afford a coach) or, as in basketball, coaches stealing the limelight from their charges. The Association of Tennis Professionals (ATP) experimented with limited on-court coaching at five World Series tournaments this year, allowing the coach on the court during the first two-minute changeovers after the first and second sets. Interestingly, the ATP estimated that about 90 percent of the players used coaches during the beginning of the trial, but by the summer events, that number dropped far below 50 percent. The view here is that on-court coaching of *any kind* is an idea whose time will never come for the individual sport of tennis. Here are the reasons why.

The Faulty Premise—"The only reason they are doing it [on-court coaching] is to try and make the sport more popular in the U.S.," says Britain's Greg Rusedski. "It's not lacking any spectators in Europe," where tennis is the favorite televised sport, according to the research company U.F.A. Nor does it lack popularity Down Under, where eighteen of the twenty-three sessions at the 1998 Australian Open broke attendance records. Nor in South America, where Gustavo Kuerten's French Open heroics and Marcelo Rios's April takeover of number one have ignited tremendous tennis enthusiasm. In Japan, tennis is the number-one participant sport. Worldwide, a 1996 BrainWaves survey of twenty-five thousand teenagers in forty-one countries reported that tennis ranked third in popularity (behind only soccer and basketball). The good news extends to the United States, too, with winter-spring 1998 TV tennis ratings for ATP Tour events up a whopping 58 percent. So it's no time to panic with an ill-advised rule change.

Tennis' Unique Battle of Skill and Will—Much of tennis' historical appeal comes from its fair and complete test of athleticism, skill, stamina, courage, and strategical acumen. And that unique test is achieved without on-court coaching, substitutions, lengthy halftime or between-period breaks, or being "saved" by a game-ending clock. Put differently, self-reliance makes the individual sport of tennis singles a highly respected and entertaining battle of skill and will between two finely tuned and mentally resilient athletes. On-court coaching would diminish those virtues. As former world top-tenner Jimmy Arias says: "A better coach shouldn't determine who wins the match. This is an individual sport—*mano a mano*."

Spectator Appeal—The idea that watching a coach and a player speaking inaudibly to each other during a two-minute changeover is a boon to fans is ridiculous. What's worse, the chitchat adds yet more "dead" time to a sport already bogged down by ninety-second changeovers and dawdling by men players between points. Fans want *action*—not matches where the ball is in play sometimes a shockingly low 10 percent of the total match time.

The Competitive Fallacy—ATP Vice President of Communications Peter Alfano says: "The objective [of on-court coaching] is to make the game more competitive. That is, if a coach can help a player who is being beaten easily to become more competitive, we would have fewer one-sided matches." However, men's tennis could hardly be more competitive *now*. Tiebreakers, three-set matches, and upsets abound in every round of ATP tournaments. In Grand Slams, unseeded players amazingly filled nine of the sixteen men's semi-final spots last year; twelve of the men players making the 1998 Australian Open round of sixteen were unseeded; and at the 1998 French Open, only one of the top eight men's seeds reached the third round of a Grand Slam tournament for the first time in the Open Era. Sure, a coach can sometimes help losing players; but if better (read: richer) players generally have better coaches, then lopsided matches can get even more lopsided.

Enforce the Current Rule—The "Everyone's coaching [illegally] anyway, so let's just legalize it" argument is intellectually absurd and morally wrong-headed. The ATP and WTA need only increase the penalty for illegal coach-ing and stringently enforce the no-coaching rule without fear or favor. That policy would sharply reduce violations and stigmatize violators.

Media Desperation—A few print and electronic media people claim that a rule change would be justified because on-court coaching would add another dimension to their stories. As a veteran tennis writer, I can assure you that fascinating and timely stories about players, events, issues, and trends *already* abound—even on the slowest news day. The more enterprising media seek and find them. Furthermore, for pre-match and/or post-match strategy stories, tour coaches typically are quite cooperative, knowledgeable, and opinionated. And, significantly, only a small minority of them apparently favor on-court coaching.

The Spotlight Factor—Does anyone want the tours' most self-aggrandizing coaches telling everyone how clever their coaching strategy is after their players pull out tight matches? Or Nick Bollettieri dashing up to the microphone after matches and exclaiming, "*We* played great today!"—as he did early in his career? The last thing tennis needs is ego-driven, attention-seeking coaches taking the spotlight and glory away from the real stars.

Frankly, the ATP's coaching crutch experiment is embarrassing. Real players don't need or want on-court coaching. As teen queen Martina Hingis rightly says, it "is a way to help players who can't think for themselves." Chris Evert further debunked this nonsense when she told the *New York Times:* "When you go down in history as the world champion, you'd better have done it yourself. You can get all the coaching you want before the match."

FASCINATING FACTS:

- Martina Navratilova said that her only regret is, "I wish I had hired a coach earlier in my career."
- All-time great Pancho Gonzalez took no tennis lessons during his amateur and pro careers.
- Father-coach Peter Graf claimed that the only reason Steffi had problems beating Martina Navratilova in the 1988 Wimbledon final was that "she misunderstood my signals."
- Grand Slammer Maureen Connolly, a natural lefty, became a right-handed player because her coach, Eleanor "Teach" Tennant, told her that no left-hander in the twentieth century had won a top women's singles championship.

This story received 2nd Prize in the United States Tennis Writers Association 1999 Writing Contest in the Enterprise Category.

28

Let the Service Let Rule Stay
1998

*Truth is the proper and sufficient antagonist to error and has nothing to fear
from the conflict, unless by human interposition, disarmed of her natural
weapons, free argument and debate.*

— THOMAS JEFFERSON

Billie Jean King, tennis' Joan of Arc when she pioneered the women's pro tour in
the early 1970s, now has radical visions of our sport in the twenty-first century. If
revolutionized her way, tennis would replace the traditional scoring system with
no-ad, put coaches on the court during matches, and abolish the service let.
"Tennis is the most antiquated, backward-thinking sport," she claims. "The only
change in seventy-five years has been the tiebreaker. We need to be innovative, on
the cutting edge. Tennis has got to make some huge changes, especially in the
United States."

Fortunately, the World Team Tennis league that King created has experimented with those and other major reforms in recent years. So we can fairly
judge her laboratory. By any criteria—such as attracting top players, big crowds,
international venues, stable franchises, significant prize money, sponsors, and TV
and print coverage—the month-long WTT season has proved a small success, at
best. And few of even its most ardent fans have clamored to change the main
game into the image of WTT.

Nonetheless, the irrepressible King, John McEnroe, and Martina
Navratilova—marvelous champions all and now TV tennis analysts—staunchly
advocate abolishing the service let. The International Tennis Federation debated
the rule change at its annual general meeting in July and withdrew its
controversial proposal pending further research and consultation over the next

twelve months. Given the ITF's sixteen-year obsession with this issue, it's unlikely that this is the last we've heard on the subject.

The All England Croquet Club formulated the traditional service-let rule in 1880, six years after Major Walter Clopton Wingfield patented "Sphairistike," the earliest version of modern lawn tennis. Impassioned but polite debate followed the game's public introduction, and articles and letters analyzing the new game's controversial rules frequently appeared in *The Field, The Country Gentleman's Newspaper*, a very popular journal.

Henry Jones, alias "Cavendish," didn't fancy Rule Sixteen of the May 24, 1875 "Laws of Lawn Tennis—Revised by the M.C.C." This rule decreed: "It is a good service or return although the ball touch the net or either of the posts."[1] Jones, a physician who regularly had articles published in *The Field*, is *the* nineteenth-century authority on games, and it was he who suggested the staging of the first Wimbledon tournament. Dr. Jones had perceptively pointed out in his November 21, 1874, piece that "Such a stroke [service let], it seems to me, must nearly always be a fluke. No one would play for it intentionally, and in a game of skill I am not inclined to grant more favour to flukes than can be possibly helped."[2]

The following major arguments and rebuttals show why the traditional service-let rule—which has stood the test of time since the AECC heeded Dr. Jones—should *not* be abolished.

Argument 1—Service lets, which require serves that hit the net and land in the service box to be replayed, both slow down the match and increase its length. Player arguments about service lets further delay play.

Rebuttal—Service lets are *very* infrequent, and the delays they cause are quite minimal. A survey taken during the 1982 U.S. Open revealed there were only 1.83 let serves per hour of play. At the 1996 U.S. Open, precisely 5.0 service lets per match occurred in forty-five senior matches surveyed. A recent two-year International Tennis Federation study of 715 matches reported an average of only 4.1 service lets a match. (The no-let rule was used in 1997–1998 NCAA Division I men's competition. It is also being tried in Davis Cup Zonal Group III and IV ties, and the ITF will release its service-let findings at the end of 1998.)

Empirical evidence further indicates that arguments about service lets are even rarer, especially when compared to disputes about line calls and other controversial rulings (even though Cedric Pioline was kicked out of the 1998 Nottingham Open for using an obscenity in arguing that a service let should have been called).

Therefore, it's fair and reasonable to conclude that eliminating the service let—especially when ball kids are on duty—would have a negligible effect on speeding up tennis.

We can speed up the game without tampering with the rules, however, by enforcing the present time limits between points, during changeovers, and whenever arguments threaten to violate the "play shall be continuous" rule. We can also reexamine whether rules allowing bathroom breaks are necessary and fair.

Argument 2—Abolishing the service let, some proponents claim, would push athletes to a higher level of performance.

Rebuttal—The contrary is true. Playing without the service let actually lowers the caliber of play for *both* the server and receiver. Why? How? The two criteria for evaluating a serve are quality—its power, depth, accuracy, effective spin, and variety—and consistency. Allowing the flukish service let rebounds—balls that dribble meekly over the net, pop straight up, or fly wildly after hitting the top of the net—diminishes serving quality as well as inadvertently and wrongly increases consistency. And that de-emphasizes the importance of a sound and effective return of serve and thus further encourages mediocrity. Andre Agassi, formerly world number one and a superb service returner, after experimenting with the no-let at the Nike Cup in December 1996, noted: "It's ridiculous. It just makes the game a lottery." Even worse, it makes tennis a *dangerous* shooting gallery. Returners could powerfully smash high-popping service lets from inside the service box directly at serve-and-volleyers in singles and at both opponents in doubles. That would cause injuries and animosity.

Argument 3—Since service lets are unpredictable and often bizarre, legalizing this element of luck would add spice to the sport. "It just makes for more drama," says King.

Rebuttal—Tournament tennis and national team events, such as the Davis Cup and Fed Cup, are and should remain wonderful tests of skill and will. The present rules offer a fair test of superiority, a *sine qua non* of any athletic competition. The odds are excellent that the more skillful and stronger-willed player will eventually prevail. This is not to say that luck plays no role. Net cords, mis-hits, bad bounces, bad line calls, and bad weather can all make things rather interesting without materially (except rarely) affecting the outcome. However, any rule change as drastic as abolishing the service let would clearly debase the game's intent, beauty, quality, and fairness. As sensible Stefan Edberg, former world number one in singles and doubles, averred: "It's crazy. If the ball hits the net and drops [barely] over, it's an ace? It would be a matter of luck. It's totally unnecessary." And, it is important to stress, when such unnecessary and excessive luck occurs on game points, set points, and match points, its unfairness and foolishness are magnified.

Argument 4—Since play continues after net cords (when the ball hits the top of the net and then lands in the court) *during* the point, why not continue play after service lets that *start* the point? What's the difference?

Rebuttal—Here, a Ralph Waldo Emerson maxim and a simple baseball analogy are appropriate to sort things out. "A foolish consistency is the hobgoblin of little minds," Emerson wrote in his classic essay, *Self-Reliance*. Emerson meant that while consistency has its virtues, if applied uncritically or taken to mindless extremes, consistency is counterproductive.

You can apply Emerson's wisdom to the rules for baseball's foul ball, which is quite analogous to tennis' service let and an integral part of the duel between the pitcher and the batter. An unplayable (not caught on the fly) foul ball counts for the first two strikes, but *not* for the third strike *unless* it's an unsuccessful bunt attempt. Baseball people rightly do not consider this inconsistent or illogical, but rather a brilliant piece of rules-making and also a time-tested and beneficial tradition. It's impossible to imagine baseball's lords ever doing away with third (and successive) foul balls—which, incidentally, often add to the tension—merely to "speed up the game." Many tennis people feel the same way about the service let. They correctly maintain that since the service let *starts* the point—and the server usually starts with an advantage—and the net cord happens *during* the point, the two situations differ considerably in this crucial sense.

Argument 5—"The only thing that concerns me is that the tensions of the nets would have to be standardized," says Stan Smith, who favors abolishing the service let. "At Wimbledon, the nets are loose so balls hit the net and trickle over. At some indoor tournaments, the net is like a cable and net cords bounce the ball up into the air and turn into overheads for the receiver." So, just standardize net tensions and all will go well.

Rebuttal—Not so fast! Since we presumably don't want balls that trickle over the net for undeserved aces *or* balls that pop high into the air for undeserved overheads, what exactly are we striving to achieve here? The relatively rare "neutral" service let. As McEnroe used to say, "You cannot be serious!"

Besides being absurd, Smith's so-called solution isn't feasible. Throughout the world, many nets and net posts are antiquated and damaged and lack net straps and certainly aren't adjusted daily—or even capable of being adjusted—for a precise net tension. In America, for example, about 70 percent of our tennis is played on public courts, and many of these courts are in mediocre to deplorable condition.

Navratilova blithely declares, "You have to adjust [to playing service lets]. And the better athlete will adjust to it." I doubt Navratilova or other service-let abolitionists have even begun to consider how adversely this proposed rule change would affect the millions of recreational players around the world. They certainly aren't top athletes, and the game is difficult enough for them already. The ITF and its 196 member national associations should care profoundly about how this (and every) rule change affects *amateur* players—unless they foolishly envision entirely different rules for the pros and the masses.

Argument 6—"It [the no-let rule] doesn't really give anyone advantages, the server or the receiver," claims Navratilova. Some surveys report that service lets do not give either the server or receiver a significant advantage 75 percent, or even 90 percent, of the time.

Rebuttal—All of the above claims are preposterous! Aside from rare "phantom" (hard to detect) service lets, the vast majority of service lets consist of 1) balls that dribble a few inches into the court and would be certain aces if the rule were changed; 2) balls that pop up high into the air asking to be put away either by overheads or powerful ground strokes; 3) balls that lose some speed and thus help the receiver; or 4) balls that, due to spin, swerve in an unpredictable direction and thus help the server.

King, in fact, concedes these all-important points: "It [the service let] is just like a net cord during the rally. I mean, that's not fair, either. What if the serve hits the top of the [net] tape and bounces up for the person who is returning? He or she has a much better opportunity to do some damage." King apparently doesn't care that the "damage" is "not fair" to the server—as if two wrongs somehow make a right.

Argument 7—"It's hard to imagine another sport where there's been only one major rule change in seventy-five years," says WTA chief executive Bart McGuire. ITF communication manager Alun James insists, "It's about whether people are prepared to accept any change at all." The thinking apparently goes something like this: since change might be good, we should welcome it.

Rebuttal—As neither a hidebound traditionalist nor a rabid reformer, I would merely offer the truism that we should favor sensible and fair traditions *and* reforms—and oppose bad traditions and bad reforms. Secondly, I would suggest to Mr. McGuire that certain other sports actually *needed* several major rule changes, while tennis does not. Furthermore, those who talk of "growing the sport" and "borrowing from other sports" and "making tennis a team sport" (Billie Jean King) need to appreciate that tennis will never be the NBA or Major League Baseball in the United States, nor soccer in the rest of the world. If tennis tries to be all things to all people, it will lose its brilliant uniqueness and end up being nothing much to anyone. Thirdly, Mr. James should understand that many proposed tennis rule changes—such as abolishing the service let—are seriously flawed and thus *should* be rejected. His attacks on the motives and acumen of service-let supporters reflect his seeming frustration rather than the free argument and debate that Jefferson wisely championed.

Summing up, the no-let rule is not just a non-solution to a non-problem. It's detrimental to the game. Tony Trabert, the world's top amateur player in 1955 and a highly respected TV tennis analyst, says, "It's foolish to even consider abolishing the service let." Steffi Graf ridiculed it as "stupid." Jimmy Connors criticized it as "nit-picking." Boris Becker warned, "It's not a wise change." Pete Sampras blasted it as "ridiculous." And Agassi, believing that the proposed rule change would exacerbate the huge advantage already enjoyed by today's explosive servers, called it "horrific."

Patrick Rafter and other players had vowed to boycott the 1999 Australian Open if the time-honored service-let rule were abolished. These players deserve praise and support for their sound judgment and courage. The ITF and other tennis authorities should heed the warnings of these champions. They are right.

FASCINATING FACTS:

- Ivan Lendl once claimed that "There are more rows over let serves than anything else in the game."
- Andre Agassi advocated that the service let be ruled a fault.
- The World Championship Tennis (WCT) circuit experimented with abolishing service lets in 1968. The experiment didn't last long because the players objected.
- When the abolition of the service let was debated at the 1992 Lipton Championships, an overwhelming majority of the players opposed the proposal.
- The no-let rule was used in the thirty-five-and-over doubles event at the 1993 U.S. Open, and nearly all the former champions taking part hated it.

---

1. George Alexander, *Lawn Tennis: Its Founders & Its Early Days* (Lynn, MA: H.O. Zimman, Inc., 1974), p.107.
2. Ibid.

29

Splendor in the Wimbledon Grass
2000

During the Vietnam War, an American officer infamously said, "It became necessary to destroy the village in order to save it."

Such stupefying illogic recently visited tennis when John Lloyd, the 1977 Australian Open finalist and a current TV commentator, suggested in *Tennis Week* that in order to save itself, Wimbledon should destroy its grass. He proposed that it be replaced by a carpet or hardcourt surface.

Lloyd's thinking, while fortunately representing only a tiny tennis minority, runs in the family. In 1992, his older brother David, later to become Britain's Davis Cup captain, wrote an *Evening Standard* column about his "radical solution—to abandon grass and turn Wimbledon over to clay courts." He also predicted: "Wimbledon will soon fade into insignificance unless the All England Lawn Tennis Club is prepared to act."

Since then Wimbledon's prestige and popularity haven't faded, although some fans have complained about men's singles matches marked by too much brute power, especially rocket serving, and too little rallying, finesse, and strategy. Even so, does this trend, chiefly afflicting some matches in only one of the five Big W events, justify killing grass forevermore? Let's test the Lloyds' thesis using several critical criteria.

Wimbledon's Unique Mystique—Make no mistake about it: Wimbledon, without grass, simply would not be Wimbledon. Its 123-year-old tradition and spirit and ethos are embodied in natural sod. Tennis would lose one of its most significant roots (excuse the pun) if Wimbledon's lush lawns were torn up.

"There can be no greater argument for keeping the grass than the ineffable experience of sitting on Centre Court or Court 2 during an upset or Court 13 during a mixed doubles match in the twilight during the British summer," says Tim Mayotte, who reached five quarterfinals and a semifinal at Wimbledon. "The image gives me goose bumps—goose bumps I would not get thinking about the same match being played anywhere else on any other surface."

John Barrett, an authoritative British writer and TV tennis analyst and former world-class player, emphasizes the importance of tradition in his superb book *100 Wimbledon Championships—A Celebration.* "The grass itself adds to the garden party atmosphere. Without it ... the atmosphere is lost. It is just another tournament on the tour."

Pete Sampras, the incomparable seven-time Wimbledon singles champion, believes replacing grass with vastly different clay or a hardcourt resembling your asphalt street or cement sidewalk "would be the biggest mistake for tennis." (Big edge to grass.)

> **A True Test**—"Grass tennis is the height of skill, for on grass, spin, change of pace, speed control, placement, and steadiness all play their true part and carry the correct value," wrote legendary champion Bill Tilden in his 1925 classic, *Match Play and the Spin of the Ball.* "Grass tennis may be won by strength, finesse, subtlety or a combination of all. There is no stroke in the game that is seriously handicapped on grass. Therefore, grass tennis has been and still is the standard of championship play."

As Tilden affirmed, grass not only serves up a fair test of tennis skill and will—a *sine qua non* of any sport—but, in one important sense, provides its truest test. How? Grass is the *only* surface on which powerful shots go faster than on other surfaces, *and* soft, touch shots go slower than on other surfaces.

Put differently, *both* power and finesse are rewarded heavily, as they should be. Of all the game's immortals, three-time singles and five-time doubles champion John McEnroe best exploited both areas. (Even.)

> **Athleticism**—Arthur Ashe, the 1975 Wimbledon champion, extolled playing on grass as "the ultimate tennis experience." Grass demands exceptional athletic ability because it puts a higher premium on volleys, overheads, quick reactions, agility, and improvising to handle the occasional bad bounces. Players must also adapt to the changing conditions—such as slickness, deterioration, etc.—of the grass during the fortnight.

As the late, great Pancho Gonzalez once observed: "Grass is not the surface where the best tennis player wins. It's the surface where the best athlete with a lot of tennis talent wins." And the dynamic athleticism of Rod Laver, Roy Emerson, Sampras, McEnroe, Boris Becker, Billie Jean King, Martina Navratilova, and Steffi Graf showcases tennis at its exciting best. (Edge to grass.)

> **Aesthetic Appeal**—Only grass can seduce the senses with its visual beauty, pleasant smell, soothing footing, and the hush of the green-stained ball. Some Wimbledon contestants of yesteryear have even competed barefoot so they could *feel* the soft, sensual blades of grass.

"I remember a few matches I played on Centre Court—the 1983 quarterfinal against Kevin Curren comes to mind—when the sun fell across the lawn in a way close to religious," recalls Mayotte. "The competitive met the aesthetic in a way that no other surface can match."

Clay's attractive reddish-brown hue and softness afoot get good marks, while soulless hardcourts rate a complete washout. (Edge to grass.)

Injury Factor—Soft, forgiving grass reportedly produces far fewer injuries than hardcourts and also fewer than clay. In an era when serious leg and foot injuries are sidelining players more and more and shortening careers, grass provides at least a brief respite from potentially harmful surfaces. It's no surprise that Becker rarely tried his adventurous dive-volleying on hardcourts. (Edge to grass.)

The Mental Game—While points are shorter on grass, this surface is the most psychologically demanding in one crucial sense. You have to contend with the rarity of opportunities to break serve and thus constantly deal with the huge pressure of converting those super-big, but infrequent break points. That means you must patiently wait for your chances and play aggressively, but not recklessly, when you get them. (Even.)

Surface Diversity—Grass gives tennis much-needed diversity in playing surfaces. Clay is touted as a "slow" surface requiring superior ground strokes, patience, stamina, and strategy; "medium-speed" hardcourts reward an all-court game and give various playing styles a decent chance to win; grass is a "fast" surface that most benefits skillful serve-and-volleyers as well as excellent service returners. This variety in courts not only offers a difficult but fair challenge for players to master, but it also increases the entertainment and appeal for fans.

"I would hate to see it [changing the surface]," Don Budge, the 1937–1938 champion who passed away earlier this year, told the *Los Angeles Times* in 1991. "It's a challenge to the players to play on different surfaces. It brings out the true test of a tennis player."

Abandoning grass courts at The Championships would also cause the death of all four pre-Wimbledon grass tune-up tournaments, too, leaving only the popular grass event at Newport, the site of the International Tennis Hall of Fame, as a quaint relic from the past. (Even.)

Style Diversity—A corollary of surface diversity is style diversity. As Budge, in 1939, wisely pointed out: "The great beauty of tennis is the inexhaustible variety of playing methods to which one may make recourse." The death of grass at Wimbledon would likely portend the eventual extinction of Eastern grips and strokes because they are somewhat less desirable on other surfaces. It would also likely hasten the decline of the volley, the game's most spectacular shot, which is already "in grave danger," according to 1987 Wimbledon champ Pat Cash.

Thus the likes of such stylists as McEnroe, Laver, Sampras, Bill Tilden, Budge, King, Navratilova, Graf, Suzanne Lenglen, and Maria Bueno might never be seen again. What a dreadful prospect, since their stylistic brilliance has always broadened tennis' appeal!

"If you went for what is convenient, then you would put hard surfaces on every court in this whole world and it would be awfully boring," asserted nine-time Wimbledon singles champion Navratilova. "There would be no variety at all then. It would hurt the game in the long run because everyone would play in the same way." (Edge to grass.)

The Ultimate Challenge—What could be a greater challenge than switching from the slow clay at the French Open to the fast and often changeable grass at Wimbledon with only two weeks in between? It may be unfair to players and unwise for tennis schedulers, but it's been a fact of life for decades. (In June 2001 the International Tennis Federation announced that it was seriously considering a major change in the calendar to put Wimbledon a week later and allow more time for players to adjust from clay to grass. Although the All England Club, ATP, WTA, player organizations, and television networks voiced support for the reform, Bill Babcock, ITF executive director and Grand Slam administrator, said the schedule would not likely change before 2004.)

To his everlasting credit, Bjorn Borg, who was forced to improve his serve and attack more to capture an amazing five straight Wimbledons, won those two back-to-back "European" Slams three straight years (from 1978 to 1980). In the Open Era, Laver (1969), Margaret Court (1970), Evonne Goolagong (1971), Chris Evert (1974), Navratilova (1982 and 1984), and Graf (1988, 1993, 1995, and 1996) also pulled off the feat. Tennis only benefits from such awesome challenges. (Edge to grass.)

It is difficult to imagine that tearing up Wimbledon's beloved manicured lawns is even a subject of debate. After all, nearly a half million fervent fans attend The Championships every year—and thousands more wish they could—and a billion people worldwide watch the finals annually on TV. Wimbledon's Web site peaked at 145,000 hits in one minute in 1998, then a record for an IBM-managed site.

Doing away with Wimbledon's grass courts would destroy not only the world's premier championships, but also a surface that has gloriously stood the test of time and showcased much of tennis' many-splendored diversity.

Who would want that?

FASCINATING FACTS:

- The Nice Lawn Tennis Club in France does not have any grass courts.
- During World War II Wimbledon's Centre Court suffered bomb damage, and the famous lawn courts were used for the unseemly duty of raising pigs.
- While grass court tennis and all prestigious American tournaments on grass have been centered at posh clubs along the eastern seaboard, the oldest lawn tennis club in the United States was founded December 15, 1876, as the New Orleans Lawn Tennis Club.
- In 1974, a year before the U.S. Open at Forest Hills switched from grass to clay, only about twelve of the ten thousand tennis clubs in the U.S. had grass courts.
- In 1975 the United States Lawn Tennis Association voted to drop the "Lawn" from its name, and the International Lawn Tennis Federation did the same in 1977.
- Ivan Lendl built a grass court—with the same sod used at Wimbledon and costing more than five hundred thousand dollars—on his Greenwich, Connecticut, estate to help prepare him for the only major championship he never won.
- Eighty percent of the players polled at the 1987 Australian Open said they wanted grass for the surface at the new Australian National Tennis Center, the site of future Australian Opens.

30

Let's End the Rankings Insanity
2000

It is quality rather than quantity that matters.

—Seneca

Imagine how invalid the NBA scoring title would be if it did not count Shaquille O'Neal's twenty least-productive regular-season games, or how meaningless the baseball pennant race would be if the New York Yankees' forty worst games were thrown out.

Believe it or not, that's how pro tennis handles—or rather mishandles—its widely criticized rankings. Throughout the 1990s the otherwise flourishing ATP Tour scandalously counted only a player's best fourteen tournaments during the previous fifty-two weeks for the official rankings. Since the top hundred players averaged about twenty-five tournaments a year, eleven of their tournaments, or 44 percent, weren't counted. Poof, they disappeared!

Many leading players, former stars, the media, tournament directors, and the International Tennis Federation denounced the infamous "Best 14" rule, which produced inaccurate and unfair rankings. Pete Sampras and Andre Agassi suffered the most because they competed in far fewer tournaments and had fewer early-round losses, while others, like Yevgeny Kafelnikov, exploited the bogus ranking system by playing thirty or more tournaments. Indeed, when trying to justify his undeserved number-two ranking during the recent Australian Open, Kafelnikov conceded: "The real numbers one and two are Agassi and Sampras.... [But] I played a lot more tournaments than those guys."

Kafelnikov, you may remember, gained headlines and notoriety by ascending to number one last year after six straight first-round losses. The ATP's embarrassment only worsened when the shameless Russian announced he didn't care about those defeats because only Grand Slam tournaments mattered to him. Tour CEO Mark Miles called him on the carpet and told him to compete and talk like a champ, not a chump. But the damage was done. Sports fans figured: Why should I care about tennis if its top-ranked player doesn't? And why follow a sport where losing often and early doesn't hurt you in the standings?

"Every time you step on the court, it should count," rightly contends Sampras, who reigned as number one for a record six straight years, from 1993 to 1998. "[Now] you can play twenty-five or twenty-six events, lose in the first round of a number of them, and still have a pretty high ranking. That's not good for the game."

Archrival Agassi, who ranked number one for thirty weeks in 1995 and finished 1999 in the top spot, agreed: "To me, the ranking system is like giving a professional golfer mulligans. They could hit a bad shot and say, 'You know what, let's just not count that one. But we will count it if you hit a better one.'"

Despite the fierce protests of leading players back in 1989, the ATP dropped the point average system—which counted all tournaments but had a minimum divisor of only twelve—because players, especially greedy superstars McEnroe, Connors, and Lendl, were shunning legitimate tournaments for unofficial, big-bucks special events and exhibitions. And that meant too few big-name players for the official worldwide tour.

The ATP also contended that the rankings penalized tour workhorses who played twenty to thirty events because their points totals were always being divided by their total number of tournaments. Since many of those tournaments were neither Grand Slams nor other premier events, fewer points were awarded for each round.

True enough. But what the ATP failed to mention—and it's crucial—is that since these middle-echelon tournaments generally have much weaker fields, it is much easier to advance to win those points. In retrospect, the ATP needed only to increase the minimum divisor to eighteen tournaments. Sadly, the ATP didn't and instead butchered the ranking system.

The new ATP Champions Race, which started January 1, 2000, radically departs from time-honored (pre-1990) ranking systems in important ways. Every player starts at zero at the beginning of the calendar year, and the player who accumulates the most points by season end is the world number one. This points race, explains the ATP, "is designed to make the game easier to follow, more fan friendly and to boost the worldwide popularity of the sport."

The ATP concedes, however, that "to determine seedings and tournament entry status, it is not practical to use the ATP Champions Race." So both entries and seedings are based on a fifty-two-week rolling ranking system.

Sound familiar? It should. Because it's the old ranking system format. Although initially this one was to remain secret, now it is merely downplayed in the hope that you, the fan, will concentrate on the so-called "race." Why? Because the ATP figures fans would get confused by having *both* a points race and rankings in the newspapers.

Still confused? You should be. Because for the first few months of the year (and probably even longer) the true rankings, seedings, and entries will sometimes differ considerably from the publicized points race. And that's laughably akin to the Los Angeles Lakers being in *both* first place and third place in the standings *at the same time.*

Case in point: Lleyton Hewitt, the eighteen-year-old rising Australian star, won his first two tournaments of the year to lead the points race. But number one Hewitt was unseeded at the Australian Open. Meanwhile, the top four players from 1999's year-end rankings—Agassi, Kafelnikov, Sampras, and Thomas Enqvist—competed in an exhibition tournament that awarded no points. So, despite being at the bottom in the points race, they received seeds number one, two, three, and six at the Oz Open.

Confused? Don't worry. By the end of the year, if you're still interested, the leaders and the followers in the points race and the real rankings will eventually coincide. And there are also individual doubles rankings *and* team doubles rankings. If you still want more lists, check out the prize money, which combines singles, doubles, and mixed doubles earnings, for what it's worth.

The ATP did make one commendable reform, though, which should both strengthen fields and produce more matches among marquee players at the premier tournaments. Henceforth, all players eligible to play in the four Grand Slam and nine Tennis Masters Series tournaments (formerly Super Nine) must count the points from those events, even if it is a zero because they missed the event due to injury, mental exhaustion, or fear of losing on their poorest surface. Surface "chickens," calculating that a first-round loss would get them only one point anyway, will likely still skip some major tournaments.

In addition to this "Mandatory 13" feature, players count their best five other results from the International Series events for a total of eighteen performances in their ATP Champions Race total and for the real (Entry System) rankings.

Put differently, with this "Best 5" feature—intended, as before, to bribe players to globe-trot until they drop—only eighteen tournaments count, no matter how many you play. That means if players continue to enter about twenty-five tournaments a year, an average of 28 percent of their official tournaments *still* won't count in the rankings.

That violates the time-honored and fair principle that *all tournaments must count in the rankings.* Furthermore, the invitation to "tank" at middle-echelon International Series tournaments—where, regrettably, guarantees are legal—remains because the results of some of these events are thrown out anyway. Players lacking a sense of pride and shame can "take the money and run" and suffer little loss in money and points.

Alas, players and tourney directors allege that tanking and halfhearted play have become more common. In a May 9, 1999, column for the *Sunday Telegraph* (UK), Patrick Rafter charged: "There is no doubt that some players 'tank' or deliberately lose sets. I've seen it happen a lot. There have been some really obvious tanks…. Some players take [guarantees] from tournaments regardless of how they've performed, and the figure sometimes runs into hundreds of thousands of dollars."

Although the points race and the real rankings still do not include Davis Cup results—a glaring mistake—for the first time players will be shooting for world ranking points as well as medals in the men's tennis event at the 2000 Sydney Olympics. That overdue reform is highly commendable. However, the gold medalist will earn a ridiculously low eighty points, less than the hundred points collected for winning Tennis Masters Series events.

All things considered, the ATP continues to make a mess of its rankings, as does the Sanex WTA Tour, which uses a "Best 18" ranking system. (Martina Navratilova once rightly called the "Best 14" formula "the worst rule in sports," but the WTA copied it anyway. In 2001, the WTA switched to a "Best 17" system.) Both tours should be required to put a "truth in advertising" message on scoreboards and TV screens, that, when applicable, reads: "The match you're watching may not count in the rankings for one or both players."

The rankings solution is simple. Both tours must count *all* tournaments and require players to compete in the major ones. With a minimum divisor of eighteen, both tours can rest assured that nearly all players would still enter at least twenty events, which historically was the men's tour's highest priority. A return to the tournament point average system would produce accurate and fair rankings as well as an easy-to-understand "race" throughout the year for the coveted number-one ranking.

Then the ATP would hear praise instead of Sampras's memorable 1999 blast: "Just because you're number one on the computer doesn't mean you're the best player in the world."

FASCINATING FACTS:

- After a past-his-prime Ivan Lendl ranked number eight at the end of 1992, he objected: "How can you have a lousy half year and still be number eight? It's a bunch of baloney. We're the only sport where every game doesn't count. You should not be allowed to have fifteen lousy results and they don't count because you have fourteen better ones."

- In July 1994, Michael Stich was ranked number three despite winning only one match in the previous four Grand Slam tournaments—because those very bad early-round losses did not count in the ATP rankings.

- In 1997 Monica Seles urged her fellow players to sign her petition protesting the WTA Tour's new ranking system, which was based on quantity play (the accumulation of total ranking points) rather than on quality play (a per-tournament point average).

31

Why Players Should Play the Game
1990

Think how much better [pro tennis] could be if the top players played twenty-five events instead of eleven or twelve.

—BOB KRAMER, JACK'S SON AND TOURNAMENT
DIRECTOR OF VOLVO TENNIS/LOS ANGELES.

ATP Tour CEO Mark Miles recently said, "What we need is a system that penalizes people for losing any time they step on the court, but still encourages them to play."

Fair enough. We can all agree that players should be penalized in the rankings—and receive less prize money—when they lose. But must "the system" find a way to encourage pro players to play?

I, of course, may be terminally naive. I actually believe today's players already have quite a few reasons to play. Without undue mental strain, I've thought of these:

1. Even without unsanctioned exhibitions and immoral guarantees, the prize money for sanctioned tour events now is huge, immense by almost every standard. And we know the players love money.

2. The thrill of victory. Remember: You can't win if you don't play.

3. Fame. Same as number two. All that ego-stroking comes from—like it or not—the media. And they focus on winners.

4. Travel. Okay, so it has its grueling downside, too, but all things considered, seeing the world a few times over is some kind of life.

5. You've got to be and stay "match tough." Of course, you don't want to over-do it, but stay away too long and you'll suffer the rusty consequences. Just ask John McEnroe.

6. Support the tournaments on your own new tour. Remember: You wanted control over your own destiny. You'll have it as long as you don't abandon tournaments, the lifeblood of our sport.

7. Be true to your fans. We care about you. Some fans, for reasons I'm not always clear about, even adore you. Anyway, we'd like to see you in more action, rather than less.

8. Television. TV helped ignite tennis booms around the world. However, network sports executives understandably tend to lose interest in televising tennis when ratings fall because of weak, starless tournament fields.

9. Believe it or not, athletes in other sports, with rare exceptions, don't need to be encouraged to play. And, when they compete, they really seem to enjoy it. I bet you would, too.

10. Your sponsors pay you big bucks to be seen often using their products. You just can't let them, or your hardworking business agents, down.

11. In your heart, you really do want to do the right thing. I just know it.

FASCINATING FACTS:

- Former ATP Tour Chief Executive Officer Hamilton Jordan used to refer to the top-ten ranked players as "those selfish assholes."
- Ivan Lendl—who claimed he was overworked from Grand Prix tournaments—played fifty-six exhibitions ("fourteen weeks averaging four a week," he disclosed) during 1987.

32

Grand Slam—or Grand Sham?
1984

If Martina Novratilova wins the French Open in June, she will capture the Grand Slam of tennis. Or will she?

Until 1982, when the International Tennis Federation (ITF) reportedly[1]—and when the Men's International Professional Tennis Council (MIPTC) *actually*—broke ranks with forty-nine years of tradition, tennis' Grand Slam could be achieved by winning the four major tournaments—the French Open, Wimbledon, U.S. Open, and Australian Open—in *one calendar year.*

The MIPTC heretics, abetted primarily by some British tennis writers, declared that henceforth the Grand Slam need not necessarily be won in the same calendar year. Four consecutive major titles, *whenever,* would be good enough for them.

Well, diluting something as cherished and time-tested as our Grand Slam wasn't good enough for much of the tennis world, which reacted with predictable fury. The fight to save the traditional concept was spearheaded by the United States Tennis Writers Association (USTWA) which, after a near-unanimous vote, promptly denounced the blasphemy in a much-publicized September 12, 1982, letter to ITF President Philippe Chatrier and General Secretary David Gray.

Let's discuss the issues from various angles and weigh the competing arguments.

The Origin—Allison Danzig,[2] the distinguished *New York Times* sportswriter, first penned the term "Grand Slam" on the eve of the 1933 U.S. Championships. Jack Crawford's bid for a "Slam" failed in the final against Fred Perry. But Danzig's "Grand Slam" tag caught on and became a challenge—many believe the ultimate tennis challenge—for all the top players.

Five years later, Don Budge captured the first Grand Slam, and later all-time greats Maureen Connolly (1953), Rod Laver (1962 and 1969), and Margaret Court (1970) won the "Big Four" championships. Grand Slams have also been recorded in doubles by Frank Sedgman and Ken McGregor (1951) and in mixed doubles by Court and Ken Fletcher (1963).

John Parsons of London's *Daily Telegraph* has argued: "The point is there never has been a rule. There has been an understanding.... It's just that when you stop to think of it, there is no logical reason to object to the new definition."

Sorry, John, but while the Grand Slam has always been "unwritten," it happens to have represented tennis' greatest individual accomplishment for a half century. Its definition may not have been etched in stone, but our hearts and minds have embraced it just the same.

In his April 28, 1984, letter to me, Danzig unequivocally wrote: "I am entirely in accord with you in standing for the concept of a Grand Slam requiring that the four major championships be won in the same calendar year. There is no question that this was the understanding all the way until the International Federation and the Men's International Professional Tennis Council voted in 1982 that winning four major titles consecutively sufficed, whether or not they all fell in the same calendar year.

"I could not believe that the British lawn tennis writers supported the ITF and the Council. The English are usually sticklers for convention and tradition.

"Had Martina won the French championship and her name been added to those of Budge, Laver, Margaret Court, and Maureen Connolly as having achieved the Grand Slam, it would have been a reflection on the integrity of tennis. The game has enough for which to apologize in the court conduct of some of its high-ranking players."

Fairness—If a rule or concept or understanding is not fair, its chances of passing the test of time are slim indeed. Players, fans, administrators, and media rarely turn a blind eye to this basic yardstick of any legitimate sport. There can be no dispute that changing the Grand Slam rules would diminish—and unfairly so—the sport's pinnacle of achievement. Just as disturbing is what cheapening the concept would do to past Grand Slam champions.

"Changing the traditional rule makes a nonsense of the whole Grand Slam concept," maintains Owen Williams, executive director of World Championship Tennis (WCT). "I think it's a travesty, and I think it's a tremendous insult to the people who have actually achieved the Grand Slam, a great sports accomplishment." As Danzig has said: "It's the last thing I'd like to see done. It would really hurt tennis."

Analogies—Analogies to other sports may not be perfect, but they can be rather useful and instructive. You can't win baseball's Triple Crown by leading the league in home runs and runs batted-in one year and then batting average *the next year.* Nor can you win horse racing's coveted Triple Crown by taking the Kentucky Derby, Preakness, and Belmont in *different* years. However difficult and rare the Grand Slam in golf has been (the legendary

Bobby Jones last did it in 1930), golf's sensible leaders wouldn't for a moment contemplate tampering with it.

The "year" concept must remain a logical benchmark in tennis as well. When Parsons asks: "What's wrong with starting anywhere?" I answer: Plenty, because the "year" framework is clear, understandable, reasonable, and fair. Not to mention memorable. How would you like to reminisce about a Navratilova 1983–1984 Grand Slam *and* an Evert Lloyd 1984–1985 Grand Slam? Who was the superior player in 1984, if they both won two Slams, anyway?

Feasibility—Occasionally one hears the theory that pro tennis is so brutally competitive and deep in talent that no one can possibly win the Grand Slam again. Therefore, we are told, we must do something drastic fast—like devalue the game's premier individual feat.

Just how valid is their premise? Jimmy Connors ruled the tennis world in 1974 when he grabbed Wimbledon, U.S., and Australian titles. His Slam bid was frustrated when our sport's politicians wrongly forbade him from playing the French Open because he had taken part in World Team Tennis. Bjorn Borg also had his chances for a Slam because he won on Wimbledon's fast grass five times and on the slow clay at Roland Garros six times, although he never could master the U.S. Open's hard courts. The closest shot, though, came in 1983 as mighty Martina Navratilova lost just one singles and one doubles match (with Pam Shriver) all year!

Yet Navratilova failed. Maybe she'll consummate a Grand Slam in 1984— fair and square. Maybe she won't. Maybe John McEnroe will. Or maybe Stefan Edberg, the Swedish teenage sensation who won the *junior* Grand Slam in 1983, will in 1989. If it's legitimate, I can wait—and eagerly watch all comers valiantly give their all.

Tradition—Statistics and records—or facts and feats, if you will—help make any sport's lore the grand talking point it is. For years even the casual baseball fan knew Babe Ruth's sixty home runs was the all-time record for a season. They also knew Joe DiMaggio hit safely in an unbelievable fifty-six straight games. Basketball buffs can tell you that no pro has ever (and probably will ever) match Wilt Chamberlain's hundred points in an NBA game.

Unfortunately, memorable numbers are much rarer in tennis. For example, few are aware that Court's sixty-two career major titles far surpass her nearest rival. Still, most fans know what the Grand Slam is. And most of them can rattle off at least some of our Grand Slam winners and probably throw in the correct year, too. Tennis, so rich in history, people and events, is all the better for it.

Money—Despite declarations by Navratilova that she yearns to be remembered as the greatest champion ever; by Lendl, who insists that he'd trade all his tournament triumphs for a major title; and by Borg, who used to denigrate other big-time tournaments by saying Wimbledon, the U.S. Open, and the French Open were the only tournaments that mattered, the ITF apparently had other ideas about what truly motivated top competitors. It would attach a $1 million bonus to anyone winning its "new" Grand Slam concept. Now, incorrectly assumed some British writers, you could start a new Grand Slam bid after every major title victory with the lure of megabucks as well.

It flunked. Noah captured the 1983 French Open but planned to skip Wimbledon even if he hadn't been suspended for forty-two days. Connors didn't "condescend" to play Australia after taking the U.S. Open in 1982 and 1983.

If the idea is to restore the Australian Open (men's side only with its recently mediocre fields) to its former glory, the growing belief is that a January date can best attract Grand Slam winners and other high-ranking players. Today's superstars may be super-rich, and occasionally greedy, but they know what matters most.

Surface—Baseball players do battle in stadia with different dimensions, and golf courses challenge golfers with imaginative and unique layouts. But court surfaces so widely diverse in composition and playing characteristics have made tennis and especially its ultimate prize, the Grand Slam, so fascinating and rewarding.

FASCINATING FACTS:

- Don Budge lost only one set in four finals when he captured the Grand Slam in 1938, and three of the four finals lasted less than one hour.
- Arthur Ashe recommended that tennis players "Go right out and play" after watching Grand Slam tournaments on TV.
- Just before she died, Maureen Connolly, the first female Grand Slammer in 1953, gave her daughter Cindy a list of the books she wished Cindy would read.
- Margaret Court, who captured the Grand Slam in 1970, started playing tennis as a left-hander but switched to play right-handed as a teenager "to stop the boys teasing me."
- Pete Sampras, who owns a record thirteen Grand Slam singles titles, says breaking Jack Nicklaus's (golf) record of eighteen Grand Slam titles has "always been a kind of a fantasy of mine."
- Steffi Graf achieved the only "Golden Slam" in 1988 when she won the Grand Slam plus a gold medal at the Seoul Olympics.
- In 2001 Andre Agassi called winning the Grand Slam in tennis "as great an achievement as you can have in any sport."

As publisher Gene Scott perceptively explained in *Tennis Week,* "Part of the magic of Budge et al's feat is that they won the French on one surface and made the adjustment to grass in less than a month. A smart player can now train exclusively for the fast surfaces of Wimbledon and the U.S. Open in one year, keep on serving and volleying for the Australian and have nearly five months to prepare for the French on clay. It's not cricket. It's not tennis."

No amount of money, no tortured logic, and no defiance of years of wonderful tradition can change the fact that the Grand Slam remains the highest, most treasured individual honor in tennis. It takes talent, skill, dedication, versatility, stamina, and a bit of luck.

When the current controversy dies down, the true Grand Slam will survive intact because real sports don't ruin their most cherished tradition. And besides, anyone can tell the difference between a Grand Slam and a Grand Sham.

Notes

1. ITF General Secretary David Gray's January 4, 1983, letter to me (see page 223) clearly states: "In spite of all that we have read on this matter, it has never been my Committee of Management's intention to alter the basis of the classic Grand Slam i.e. the capture of all four titles in a year."
2. Allison Danzig's April 28, 1984 letter to me (see page 224) stresses: "I am entirely in accord with you in standing for the concept of a Grand Slam requiring that the four major championships be won in the same calendar year."

THE INTERNATIONAL TENNIS FEDERATION
Church Road, Wimbledon, London SW19 5TF
Telephone: 01-947 9266
Cables: Intennis, London, SW19 Telex: 919253

From the Secretary

Mr. Paul S. Fein,   4th January 1983
23 Beekman Drive,
AGAWAM, MA 01001

Dear Mr. Fein,

Thank you for your letter of 1st December, which Philippe Chatrier has asked me to answer. There seems to be some confusion. The ITF's only initiative in this matter has been the organisation of the offer of a bonus of $1m. to any player who holds all four Grand Slam titles simultaneously. Our present plan is to offer the bonus for three years, from the recent Australian Championships. Thus, Johan Kriek and Chris Evert Lloyd are one quarter of the way towards $1m. Any other player who seeks the bonus must begin a sequence of victory at the French Championships in 1983 and then win the remaining three titles.

In spite of all that we have read on this matter, it has never been my Committee of Management's intention to alter the basis of the classic Grand Slam i.e. the capture of all four titles in a year. I hoped that we had made this clear when we published details of the bonus in our Newsletter.

With best wishes,

                                        Yours sincerely,

                                        David Gray
                                        General Secretary

DG/SS

13 The Birches
Roslyn, N.Y. April 28, 1984

Mr. Paul S. Fein
25 Beekman Drive
Agawam, Ma. 01001

Dear Mr. Fein:

I am sorry to have taken so long to reply to your letter of April 12 in regard to the Grand Slam of tennis. My wife has been in the hospital.

I am entirely in accord with you in standing for the concept of a Grand Slam requiring that the four major championships be won in the same calender year. There is no question that this was the understanding all the way until the International Federation and the Men's International Professional Tennis Council voted in 1982 that winning four major titles consecutively sufficed, whether or not they all fell in the same CALENDAR YEAR.

I could not believe that the British lawn tennis writers supported the I.T.F. and the Council. The English are usually sticklers for convention and tradition.

Had Martina won the French championship and her name been added to those of Budge, Laver, Margaret Court and Maureen Connolly as having ACHIEVED THE GRAND Slam, it would have been a reflection on the integrity of tennis. The game has enough for which to apologize in the court conduct of some its high ranking players.

I congratulate you on your thoroughly workmanlike presentation of this whole business.

Sincerely,

Allison Danzig

I am for letting the let rule on the service stand.

33

Analyze This! How to Think Smart about Tennis Issues
2001

The main dangers in this life are the people who want to change everything—or nothing.

—NANCY ASTOR, THE FIRST WOMAN MEMBER OF
PARLIAMENT IN ENGLAND (1879–1964).

Since tennis was accused of being near death in the mid-1990s, tennis leaders have proposed a never-ending stream of reforms. Some advocates tweaked the rules a bit, while others wanted to revamp the scoring system, court procedures, code of conduct policy, rankings and seedings, and racket regulations. The would-be reformers presented data about the problem as well as various criteria they consider important, and then analyzed both and drew conclusions. When the tennis world doesn't share their convictions, these advocates have been known to shake their heads in disbelief.

That made me think. Are the advocates making untenable assertions and dubious arguments? Are tennis fans smarter than they think and perhaps even smarter than the advocates are? Is the sport simply not in need of much change?

I've concluded that some lines of reasoning the advocates regularly use, while initially plausible, break down under scrutiny.

Argument—"It's hard to imagine another sport where there's been only one major rule change in seventy-five years."

Rebuttal—The advocates nearly always trot out this bromide, which translates to "Change is good—embrace it as other sports do, or else tennis will plummet in popularity." In truth, tennis has adopted *several* important on-court and organizational rule changes during the past seventy-five years besides the tiebreaker. The foot-fault rule was made less stringent, the Davis Cup Challenge Round was abolished, foreign seedings were discontinued, a Code of Conduct with penalties for violations was enacted, the WTA created age-eligibility rules for whiz kids, appearance money (guarantees) was legalized, racket size and stringing pattern requirements were legislated, the "double-hit" and "carry" rules were liberalized, changeovers were lengthened, and bathroom breaks were included in the rules.

Second, like a brilliant constitution that doesn't require frequent amendments, tennis' rules were created by forefathers with wisdom and vision. By contrast, certain pro sports, such as basketball, enacted major rule changes during the past half century because the sports evolved tremendously and much more than tennis. For example, the twenty-four-second clock and goaltending rules became necessary, even inevitable, to accommodate the increasingly athletic style and physical size of NBA players.

Third and most important, it's not the quantity of changes that matters but rather the *quality*. Tennis should support beneficial and fair reforms—as well as traditions—and oppose the contrary. For example, tennis is far *worse off* because of the rule which allows women pros two bathroom breaks per match. Not only do bathroom breaks violate tennis' "play shall be continuous" rule, but they also are exploited as strategic maneuvers when a player is either tiring or losing momentum, as Martina Hingis and others have admitted.

And while we're on the subject of rule changes, let's respect both schools of thought. Just as traditionalists should not be derided as head-in-the-sand, do-nothing reactionaries and dogmatic purists, reformers need not be dismissed as crazy radicals hell-bent on turning the game upside down.

Argument—"On-court coaching should be allowed in pro tennis because it's allowed in every other sport."

Rebuttal—The above assertion is inaccurate. But what's relevant here is the wrongheaded claim that because a given rule is prevalent (or even universal) in other sports, it should be uncritically or automatically accepted as a rule in tennis.

Having said that, I still believe sports analogies often have considerable merit in analyzing tennis issues and proposing constructive solutions. Since analogies tend to erase differences, though, analyzers and analogizers must be careful.

For example, what is best for pro football—which is a city franchise, team, and contact sport with many players and coaches and few contests per season—may not be what is best for an individual, non-contact, and international sport like pro tennis.

Even comparisons with a similar individual, *mano a mano* sport such as boxing can be misleading. Would anyone seriously suggest that boxing should become more like tennis and make its combatants aware of the score? Of course not. This would allow boxers to coast to victory, and that would diminish the warlike, primal appeal of the "sweet science," as fight fans witnessed in Oscar De La Hoya's strategical debacle against Felix Trinidad.

The main point here is that boxing is unique. What suits boxing may or may not suit other sports that have little or nothing in common with it.

Tennis has its unique aspects, too. For example, the service let appears to be a quirky and inconsistent application of tennis rules since play continues on net cords. The most applicable sports analogy here, however, is the foul ball in baseball. The first two foul balls count as strikes, but subsequent foul balls do not, unless the foul ball comes on an attempted bunt. That may seem inconsistent to some, but it's actually a highly intelligent rule because it makes an important distinction based on the hitter's count.

Similarly, for several reasons too lengthy to cover here, important distinctions based on major differences between the service-let and net-cord *situations* make the traditional service-let rule fair and reasonable.

Argument—"It's so simple, really. Let them have only one serve," Neale Fraser, the 1960 Wimbledon and 1959–1960 U.S. champion and Australian Davis Cup captain for twenty-four years, told *The Telegraph* (UK) in 1994. "Why give guys a second chance of winning the point with equipment which is so advanced in a way which those who started the game could never have envisaged?"

Rebuttal—Philippe Chatrier, the late, highly esteemed ITF president, and Bunny Austin, the late 1930s British star, also advocated one serve to curb rocket serving that seems to produce aces and return errors with monotonous regularity. They contend this major rule change would redress the offensive-defensive imbalance on the pro tour.

They're right—although today's serving power crisis is confined to the men's circuit, and even there, mainly on grass and fast indoor courts.

While a one-serve rule would solve one problem, its "overkill" would create three new serious problems. First, virtually every pro would resort to serving safe, high-arcing, kick serves all the time for fear of single faulting. The emasculation of the serve would end first serves and also produce a boring sameness of spin serves.

Second, every "single fault" would result in the outright loss of a point, and single faults would far exceed the number of double faults that players previously committed. That drastic change would frustrate players, create fewer played-out points, and result in even more "dead time."

Third, and most important, is the hitherto undiscussed dilemma our sport would face. Should the one-serve rule extend beyond the pro tour (or tours) to the entire tennis world?

A one-serve rule would prove totally impractical and, in fact, destructive for the millions of recreational players worldwide. Many of them now struggle to get even a modest percent of their first serves in at any speed. They absolutely *need* two serves. Otherwise, they would "single fault" points away almost every game. And that ineptitude—or inconsistency, to put it kindly—would ruin their enjoyment of the game. And yet two *drastically different, coexisting* rules for serving won't work either.

This dilemma provides a clear and valuable lesson that illuminates the "change versus tradition" debate from yet another important angle: *The rules for the pro sport should differ in degree but not in kind from the amateur game, with rare exceptions.*

Analogies with other sports illustrate this crucial axiom. NBA games last longer (forty-eight minutes) than college games (forty minutes), which last longer than high school games (thirty-two minutes). That difference in *degree* (time length) does not materially change basketball at different playing levels and ages and thus poses no problem. However, if the NBA decided to award six points for long-distance shots made—instead of the current three points at all levels—that rule change would drastically distort the way the game is played at the highest level. The same distortion would occur if Major League Baseball decided a strikeout would require five strikes, rather than three.

A certain uniformity for the most basic rules of every sport makes it much more understandable and appealing for players at *all* levels as well as fans. That same rationale holds even more true in tennis because such a high percentage of its fervent fans are participants who continue to play tennis throughout their lives.

Argument—"The best team may not always win.... With this format, the underdog has a better chance to win."

Rebuttal—In the rush to streamline the scoring system and decrease match time in order to attract bigger college tennis crowds, some coaches say the darnedest things. The American college coach who made the above statement favors a reform (radical by any standard) that the NCAA is experimenting with: having a tiebreaker replace and thus decide the entire third set and the match.

While noting he's for *any* format that shortens matches, this coach honestly admitted to *Tennis Week*: "My agenda is to get a format change so I can put together a team that can beat Stanford. We are like so many teams. When we have to go the distance, the best team is pretty much going to win."

What's wrong with the coach's thinking?

For starters, and in fact clinchers, the better team, on a given day, is *supposed to* win. That's what happens in a legitimate sport (which tennis is), a sport that presents opponents with a fair test of skill and will (which tennis does), and a sport with an extremely fair scoring system (which tennis has).

That does not mean luck—an entirely different issue—cannot play a role or even decide a match. Only in rare circumstances, though, can a net cord, horrendous bounce, vicious gust of wind, incorrect line call, etc., change the outcome of a match, and that's typically when it occurs on set or match point. Otherwise, and thankfully, the better singles player, doubles team, and college team *always wins on a given day*. Hooray! I say. That, of course, is what is supposed to happen.

But what about the poor underdog? Before we lament his fate, let's acknowledge that thousands of (so-called and genuine) underdogs win tennis matches every day at every competitive level around the world. Some underdogs have only one chance in a hundred of pulling off an incredible upset, while others have as much as a 40 or 45 percent chance.

Whatever the odds, the underdogs, who possess a never-say-die spirit, view such matches as a wonderful challenge, a chance to prove they really are the better players on that day. They ignore relative rankings, the results of previous matches, and what so-called experts predict. These court warriors aim to win fair and square. They know that playing a mere tiebreaker after splitting two sets would be the absurd equivalent of the NBA playing an overtime period after only three quarters of play. Unlike the aforementioned coach, these underdogs don't want a *better but bogus* chance to win—just an *equal* chance to win. They want a legitimate athletic test of skill and will.

Eager to demonstrate Thomas Carlyle's maxim that "Nothing is more terrible than activity without insight," the ITF is implementing precisely this new scoring format at the 2001 Australian Open. Its mixed doubles matches will comprise two standard sets, with a tiebreaker used to snap a one-set-all deadlock with the aim of speeding up matches.

Of course, the tiebreaker was created to shorten and enliven sets—which thirty years ago had too often become protracted—*not to replace them*. It should be quite obvious that a player must get to 6-all in games in order to *earn the right* to play a tiebreaker, regardless of which set it is. Now mixed doubles victories at the Oz Open will be faster but hollow. How sad!

Argument—"You have times in tennis where the odds are pretty strong that the pattern of a match is not going to change ... if someone is leading 4-0 in a set, for instance, or has two service breaks. This system would bring you closer to the crisis points sooner, especially as many people believe that the highest proportion of real quality points come in tiebreakers," argues Bart McGuire, CEO of the Sanex WTA Tour. McGuire proposes that a) women would play best-of-five-set matches (instead of best-of-three); b) a normal set would be won with five games (instead of six), with tiebreakers going into effect at 4-4 (instead of 6-6); and c) the fifth set would be confined to, or rather be replaced by, a tiebreaker won by the first player to win ten points.

Rebuttal—Just as the mostly discredited no-ad scoring system damages the integrity of the *game* with its "sudden-death" ending on the seventh point, the proposed incredibly shrinking set destroys the integrity of the *set*. Keep in mind that a tennis player can win fewer total points and even fewer total games and still win a match, but she still must win more sets. So winning those sets must always remain a fair test of skill and will, and unduly shortened sets preclude that.

What else is wrong with the above proposals? Since women's tennis is played far more aggressively and skillfully by many more world-class players than ever before, it has become far less formful and more subject to upsets. That also means that thrilling comebacks within matches, sets, and games happen often. Players frequently overcome deficits of 4-0 and two service breaks because holding serve is far from a given.

Furthermore, this well-meaning advocate errs badly by suggesting that "crisis points" are played solely, or even mostly, in the tiebreaker. The *fluctuating crises* of ad-in and ad-out—which surround the temporary sanctuary of deuce—bring out our best and worst and thus add a true excitement and strategical richness to tennis. Those fluctuating crises occur quite often in women's tennis precisely because their superb service returns can negate their serves (more effectively than in men's tennis), and each point and game often produce dramatic mini-wars of their own.

Indeed, many of the greatest matches ever played featured epic battles at deuce. The 1995 Wimbledon final most riveted fans when Steffi Graf dueled tenacious Arantxa Sanchez-Vicario at 5-5 in the third set in a game that lasted twenty minutes and thirty-two thrill-packed points. Graf finally won that crucial game on her sixth break point and took the classic encounter 4-6, 6-1, 7-5.

Finally, while the five-set format is intended to prove women can go the distance, their so-called fifth set is an imposter. Shortening sets damages their integrity and validity, but *replacing* a set—of *any* length—with a tiebreaker further makes a mockery of this fundamental part of the scoring system.

The supreme irony of this proposed three-part reform is that it destroys one of tennis' crowning glories: its brilliant scoring system. Unlike soccer and hockey, which suffer from too little scoring, and basketball, which stockpiles points at an incredible rate, tennis points count more or less depending on the situation and score—hence the exciting, big-point expressions such as "break point," "game point," "set point," and "match point."

We owe a huge debt of gratitude to the game's nineteenth-century pioneers for creating a clever and nuanced scoring system that helps test players athletically, physically, and mentally in ways that also entertain fans. Likewise, Jimmy Van Alen, a revolutionary who invented and tirelessly promoted the tiebreaker, deserves abundant credit for giving sets and matches thrilling climaxes and definitive endings.

Since the tiebreaker arrived, however, advocates have fervently pushed ill-advised reforms, such as allowing only one serve, abolishing the service let, bathroom breaks, on-court coaching, and no-ad scoring.

Let's hope the twenty-first century brings brilliant innovations to the rules of tennis—rather than misguided revolutions born out of a perceived desperation.

FASCINATING FACT:

- Bud Collins' *Tennis Encyclopedia* recounts how Jimmy Van Alen experimented with his "Van Alen Simplified Scoring System" (VASSS)—which formed the basis for sudden-death tiebreakers in 1970—at his pro tournaments at the Newport Casino. The players disliked his radical innovations, such as single-point scoring and twenty-one- or thirty-one-point games, no-ad scoring, and medal play. Pancho Segura summed it up best when he deprecatingly said: "It seems half-VASSS to me."

PART 5

Twentieth-Century Retrospectives

34

Open Tennis Ushers in a Golden Era
1999

If tennis is to realize its full potential, it must find a solution to the professional/amateur problem which has plagued it for so many years," wrote legendary champion Bill Tilden in his 1948 memoirs, *My Story*.

"Only through such a solution can there be free competition among not just a few of the great players of the world—but among all of them," stressed Tilden. "The sporting public wants to see the best. It doesn't give a hoot whether that best is amateur or professional."

Since the first pro tour in 1926, all the premier tournaments had allowed only amateur players, while many of the best players were professional. Imagine if Pete Sampras, Andre Agassi, and Patrick Rafter were banned from the Grand Slams, Super 9 events, and Davis Cup. That's the way big-time tennis was until Open Tennis forever changed the game, mostly for the better, in 1968.

A second compelling reason for dramatic change was the immorality that had come to characterize the traditional amateur game. Nevertheless, many national association leaders—such as Lawrence A. Baker and Martin L. Tressel in the United States, Basil Reay in Great Britain, and "Big Bill" Edwards in Australia—fearing the loss of power (to new pro factions) that Open competition would inevitably cause, clung desperately to the hypocrisy of "shamateurism." This corrupt system entailed under-the-table payments to marquee and even lesser players that typically far exceeded the unenforceable rules for expenses.

Since the 1930s repeated attempts to overthrow the status quo had failed. "The terrible thing is that professional tennis should have taken over in the 1930s," wrote pioneer pro Jack Kramer in his 1979 memoirs, *The Game*. "There was some genuine agitation for an open game amongst the tennis federations as early as 1930—had the USLTA been on the ball and worked for open tennis, it might well have become a reality 50 years ago—but the motion failed by a hair, and so the pros began picking off the best amateur heroes."

The All-India Lawn Tennis Association proposed the abolition of the distinction between professionals and amateurs at the International Lawn Tennis Association's annual meeting in 1947, but the proposition was rejected unanimously. In 1953, Norman Brookes, the revered president of the Australian tennis federation, proclaimed his desire to promote Open Tennis. And in 1960, with all the leading countries backing Open Tennis, a proposal put before the ILTF failed to pass by a mere five votes.

However, the movement toward an open game lost momentum when the United States Lawn Tennis Association passed a resolution on February 2, 1963, opposing the principle of Open Tennis. Gladys Heldman, the authoritative publisher and editor of *World Tennis* magazine, blasted the USLTA vote in an editorial. "It was an astonishing move since there is no question that the majority of tennis players, tennis officials, and sportswriters in this country are in favor of open tournaments. This resolution set the USLTA back 100 years." Across the Atlantic, highly respected editor Philippe Chatrier used *Tennis de France* magazine as a bully pulpit to attack the hypocrisy and inertia of the amateur game.

On December 14, 1967, Derek Penman, the courageous chairman of the British Lawn Tennis Association, eloquently presented the moral case before the LTA Council in the proposal to "go it alone" (if need be) on open tournaments starting April 22, 1968.

"We know the so-called amateur players bargain for payments grossly in excess of what they are entitled to but without which they cannot live," pointed out Penman. "We know that tournament committees connive at this, else there would be no players at their tournaments. We feel we owe it not only to ourselves but to our players to release them from this humiliating and hypocritical situation and that the players should be able to earn openly and honestly the reward their skill entitles them."

Despite periodic exposés in the press—such as Kramer's "I Was a Paid Amateur" in *This Week* magazine in 1955—shamateurism was long tolerated. These "athletic gigolos," as Tilden called them, were variously cajoled, bribed, and punished. In 1954 the United States Lawn Tennis Association finally allowed amateurs to represent sports clothing manufacturers, while Italians Fausto Gardini and Beppe Merlo were suspended by their tennis federation for denouncing the amateur fiction. By the early 1960s, former Italian federation president Giorgio de Stefani, a diehard opponent of Open Tennis, cynically, and rather ironically, paid Italian number one Nicola Pietrangeli to make sure he remained an amateur player.

In Australia, where looser amateur rules prevailed in the 1950s and 1960s, so did a more blatant form of shamateurism. Sporting goods manufacturers, such as Slazenger's and Dunlop, gave Ken Rosewall, Roy Emerson, Rod Laver, and other premier players nominal jobs and a year-round salary that covered their expenses. In exchange for the subsidy, they played exhibitions and used company rackets.

Meanwhile Kramer, considered Public Enemy Number One in Australia for signing many of the country's amateurs to pro contracts during the 1950s, quit his job as pro promoter in 1962 and told *Sports Illustrated*: "We had all the best players, but the public didn't want to see them." The public wanted to see pros play amateurs, to appreciate how good the pros really were. (A late 1963 *World Tennis* magazine poll of the public, players, trainers, and officials found that 87.2 percent favored Open Tennis.)

Laver, who won the Grand Slam in 1962 but then lost nineteen of his first twenty-one matches to Rosewall and Lew Hoad as a pro, admitted: "I didn't find out who were the best [players] until I turned pro and had my brains beaten out for six months at the start of 1963."

FASCINATING FACTS:

- In 1937 English star Fred Perry was asked to resign all his club memberships, even the honorary ones, after he turned professional.
- Pauline Betz Addie, the 1946 Wimbledon and U.S. champion, was suspended by the USLTA in 1947 merely for her public support of a women's professional tennis tour.
- Gordon Forbes, a fun-loving South African, when asked what he did for a living, used to answer: "I'm an amateur by profession."

But amateur tennis, its talent steadily drained by the pros, was hurting, too. By the mid-1960s elite drawing cards Emerson and Manolo Santana, the most appealing of the dwindling amateur stars, were raking in weekly fifteen-hundred-dollar appearance payments from tournament promoters desperate to attract crowds. "There is no such thing as amateur tennis," declared Emerson, who for several years had turned down lucrative pro contracts.

The momentum toward Open Tennis accelerated in 1967. Former U.S. Davis Cup captain George MacCall organized a new pro group featuring Laver, Rosewall, Emerson, and Fred Stolle, while Dave Dixon, a New Orleans promoter (with then-silent partner, Texas oil multimillionaire Lamar Hunt), conscripted younger amateurs such as Wimbledon champ John Newcombe, Tony Roche, and Cliff Drysdale. The latter troupe was dubbed "The Handsome Eight," and their organization, World Championship Tennis (WCT), would play a pivotal role in igniting pro tennis in coming years.

These developments further made up the mind of Herman David, the visionary president of the All England Club, which had staged a highly successful (sell-out attendance every day and high BBC ratings), forty-five-thousand-dollar, eight-man trial professional event at Wimbledon in August 1967. Laver, a Grand

Slammer back in 1962, beat Rosewall in a final that far outclassed the humdrum amateur Wimbledon final two months earlier when Newcombe routed sixteen-to-one underdog, German Wilhelm Bungert, a part-time player who devoted most of his time to his sporting goods business.

David kept the pressure on by publicly denouncing amateurism as "a living lie," and on October 5, 1967, he propelled the LTA to adopt a two-pronged text that abolished the distinction between amateurs and professionals. Equally precedent-setting, the document called for an "open" Wimbledon in 1968—which the LTA ratified by a 295-5 vote at its annual meeting on December 14.

FASCINATING FACTS:

- Whitney Reed, a free-spirited Californian ranked number one in the U.S. in 1961, when asked what he did when he wasn't playing the amateur circuit, would reply, "I have a paper route."
- In 1967, when Billie Jean King ranked number one in the world as an amateur, she made about four thousand dollars in under-the-table payments; John Newcombe, the number one amateur, collected about fifteen thousand dollars.
- At the first U.S. Open in 1968, champion Arthur Ashe, who opted to remain an "amateur" to stay eligible for Davis Cup, received twenty-eight dollars daily for expenses, plus a hotel room, while runner-up Tom Okker, who declared himself a "registered player," pocketed the first prize of fourteen thousand dollars.

(Fans were "voting" for Open Tennis, too, by shunning what would be the last amateur Grand Slam event, the 1968 Australian Championships on grass at Kooyong. A mere seven thousand spectators attended the star-depleted tournament, and about half that number watched unheralded Aussie Bill Bowrey beat Spanish clay-courter Juan Gisbert in the final.)

The British revolt stiffened the resolve of the hitherto conservative USLTA, which voted overwhelmingly (15-1) in favor of Open Tennis on February 3, 1968. "We don't know what we're getting into," admitted Robert Kelleher, the intrepid USLTA president. "Nobody's prepared for open tennis, or even knows what it means. But I believe the time is now, even if I get tarred and feathered for it."

Twenty years later, Kelleher explained in the *Boston Globe* why he plunged into uncharted waters: "Tennis wasn't on TV. Only one tournament in the U.S. drew halfway decent crowds, the Nationals at Forest Hills. The game had fallen way behind. I felt opens were a realistic answer."

The ILTF dealt the deathblow to "shamateurism" at its historic March 30, 1968, special meeting in Paris. Its sixty-six representatives from forty-seven nations voted unanimously to approve twelve open tournaments in eight countries for 1968.

For the first time in history, all the world's best players who chose to do so competed at an open tournament, the British Open Hard-Court Championships in Bournemouth, England, on April 22. Mark Cox, an amateur, initially stole the show by upsetting aging pro Pancho Gonzalez and first-year pro Emerson, before Laver routed him in the semis. Another old pro, Rosewall, then beat Laver to collect the first "open" paycheck, a modest twenty-four hundred dollars. Virginia Wade won the women's title but declined the $720 first prize, worrying about giving up her amateur status at this uncertain time.

Just about everybody else was ecstatic, though, especially the pioneering organizers of the tournament. "We knew Open Tennis was going to be a success, but we didn't know it was going to be a bonanza!" enthused the LTA's Derek Hardwick.

The brave new world of Open Tennis would bring record crowds, strange categories such as "registered players" and "contract professionals" (which were soon abolished), a surge of corporate sponsors, tournament entrepreneurs and opportunistic player agents, undreamed-of prize money, endorsement contracts and television coverage, intense political battles among rival factions for control of the game, the birth of year-round men's and women's pro circuits, and dramatic growth in tennis worldwide.

On the debit side, the Davis Cup declined in prestige as did doubles and mixed doubles events. Defective pro ranking systems failed to count all bona-fide tournament matches, allegations of tanking surfaced too often, and appearance money (guarantees)—both legal and illegal—continued to sully the game.

But no one who lived through both the amateur and Open eras would choose the former, even while waxing nostalgic over bygone wood rackets and sporting gentlemen. In most ways, tennis today is better, bigger, and more entertaining than ever.

FASCINATING FACTS:

- Tennis ranked number one in China in a 2000 survey asking about the sport that people most aspire to learn.
- The 2000 U.S. Open, which sparked $419 million of new spending that otherwise would not have occurred, had the second-largest economic impact—after the Atlanta Olympics—of any sporting event in American history.

35

Teen Queens Fascinate the Sporting Public
1999

Charlotte "Lottie" Dod belonged to another century, but the first teen queen would have endeared herself to today's brash breed—and not just for her awesome victories. "The Little Wonder," as this English girl was nicknamed, still holds the record as the youngest (at fifteen years, 285 days) player to win Wimbledon; indeed, she was unbeaten over five years, from 1887 to 1888 and from 1891 to 1893.

Defying the Victorian conventions of her time, the athletic Dod exhorted her sisters: "Ladies should learn to run, and run their hardest, too, not merely stride." A great many ladies would heed her advice and see the newfound benefits of a vigorous game.

Dod, who relished smashing and volleying, also believed long dresses spoiled a lady's play, and play spoiled long dresses. She sensibly contended: "Ladies' dress, too, is a matter for grave consideration; for how can they ever hope to play a sound game when their dresses impede the free movement of every limb?" In her school uniform, Dod could shun those ground-sweeping dresses with their bustles, corsets, petticoats, and long drawers and instead wear a white dress that ended just below the knee, with black shoes and stockings and a jaunty cricket cap.

The twentieth century's first teen queen, May Godfray Sutton, captured the 1904 U.S. title at seventeen but really made tennis history in 1905 by becoming the first overseas player and first American to win Wimbledon. *The Leicester Chronicle* reported her performance in glowing terms: "Magnificently muscular, she appears to care nothing for the minor graces, nor even the little tricks and dodges in which her male compatriots indulge. She is all for the rigor of the game."

She was also dressed for success. The athletic and boundlessly enthusiastic Californian shocked the staid Brits with her mildly emancipated costumes.

Instead of confining, medieval sports attire, uninhibited Sutton wore shorter skirts and fewer petticoats, eschewed high-collared shirtwaists, and audaciously rolled up her sleeves to bare her elbows. Her fame was such that three years later Wright & Ditson introduced The Sutton Star Racket "with her approval." Could monetary compensation be far away?

Suzanne Lenglen and Bill Tilden, two larger-than-life 1920s champions during the "Golden Age of Sports," would transform tennis from a snobbish, elitist game into a sport popular with the masses. But Lenglen was in her twenties by then, and World War I had limited her practice opportunities and deprived her of tournament competition and titles that would truly qualify her as a teen queen by today's standards.

FASCINATING FACTS:

- Monica Seles was named Yugoslav "Sportswoman of the Year" when she was twelve.
- In 1990 the Women's Tennis Association changed its age-eligibility rules four times to benefit rookie teen phenom Jennifer Capriati.
- Venus Williams was fourteen when she started giving motivational speeches to groups.

Nonetheless, her formative years were noteworthy because she became the first tennis champion who was a prodigy driven by a well-meaning but fanatical father. Charles Lenglen, an unfulfilled bicycle racer, got his vicarious thrills by astutely molding his daughter. To develop her accuracy, he moved a handkerchief to various spots around the court and rewarded her with a five-franc piece every time she hit it. For consistency, he made her practice hours against a wall and even built a concave backboard to produce irregular bounces to improve her anticipation. At fourteen, Suzanne won the ladies' singles and doubles at the World Hardcourt Championships in Paris in 1914.

Unfortunately, nothing short of perfection satisfied Papa Lenglen. If Suzanne practiced poorly, he punished her by denying her jam on her bread. A stern taskmaster, he sometimes scornfully scolded Suzanne on the court in front of others. She became so drained emotionally and physically that she looked older than she actually was. When she turned professional in 1926—after losing only one match of consequence in the previous seven years—she confided to friends, "At last, after fifteen years of torture, I can enjoy my tennis."

Maureen Connolly's meteoric rise to stardom a generation later was masterminded by Eleanor "Teach" Tennant, a domineering but brilliant coach who had driven an earlier prodigy, Alice Marble, to greatness. Nicknamed "Little Mo" because her devastating ground-stroke power was likened to that of the battleship "Big Mo," she captured all nine Slam events she contested from the 1951 U.S. Championships to the 1954 Wimbledon, a record that will never be matched. Connolly became the first woman to win *the* Grand Slam—all four major titles—in 1953. A tragic horseback riding accident prematurely ended her career at nineteen.

Cute and charming off the court but cold and ruthless on it, the 5'4", 130-pound California teenager was taught to hate her opponents by Tennant, from whom she split in 1952. Nell Hopman, wife of the legendary Australian Davis Cup captain Harry Hopman, took over in 1953 and, as Connolly revealed, taught her to "win with love, not with hate."

Like Lenglen, the obsessed Connolly fascinated the sporting public and was not as happy as she looked. In her autobiography, *Forehand Drive,* Connolly confided: "I have always believed greatness on a tennis court was my destiny, a dark destiny, at times, where the tennis court became my secret jungle and I, a lonely, fear-stricken hunter. I was a strange little girl armed with hate, fear, and a Golden Racket."

Margaret Smith, a tall Australian girl, quit school to dedicate herself to tennis at fifteen. In 1957, she wrote in her autobiography, *The Margaret Court Story,* "I had collected a total of sixty tennis trophies and I was looking around for more worlds to conquer. Tennis was now all-absorbing for me, and I practically lived on the court." Her conquests would total a career record sixty-two Grand Slam titles in singles, doubles, and mixed doubles as well as a singles Grand Slam in 1970 and tennis' only mixed doubles Grand Slam (with Ken Fletcher) in 1963.

Court, and not Martina Navratilova a generation later, deserves credit as the original trailblazer for physical fitness in women's tennis. Under the supervision of Olympic trainer Stan Nicholes at Frank Sedgman's Melbourne gymnasium, Court was the first woman tennis player to use weights. Dozens of double knee jumps every day, jumping rope, and two-hundred-yard wind sprints also made her the best-conditioned and strongest player of her era. Soon enough the rigorous circuit training paid off as the seventeen-year-old phenom upset reigning queen Maria Bueno and won her first major crown, the Australian Championships, in 1960.

FASCINATING FACTS:

- Pam Shriver was selected as Women's Tennis Association "Comeback Player of the Year" at age eighteen.
- After playing teenaged Martina Hingis in mixed doubles at the Hopman Cup, Goran Ivanisevic ranked Hingis number one among all opponents who had returned his rocket serve.
- The German edition of *Penthouse* magazine offered eighteen-year-old Steffi Graf four hundred thousand dollars to pose nude. She declined.

Billie Jean Moffit, seventeen, and Karen Hantze, eighteen, a couple of bubbly, serve-and-volleying California teens, shook up the tennis world in 1961 by becoming the youngest and first unseeded team to win the Wimbledon doubles. The next year Karen, then Mrs. Rod Susman, stunned everyone again by winning the singles crown. Instead of defending her title in 1963, Susman gave birth to a daughter. Billie Jean (King), whose passion for playing and changing the game had no bounds, would develop into an all-time great as well as one of the founders of the Virginia Slims women's circuit and an outspoken crusader for women's rights and equal prize money.

Evonne Goolagong, the only aboriginal from Australia to develop into a world-class player, and Chris Evert, a whiz kid from Florida, emerged as immensely popular teen queens in the early 1970s. The serene Goolagong, a graceful natural athlete, stunned the tennis world by capturing both the French Open and Wimbledon in 1971 at age nineteen.

Evert first gained notoriety at age fifteen when she shocked world number one Court at a small North Carolina tournament just after Court completed her Grand Slam. Poker-faced but cute and attractive, Evert stole the show at the 1971 U.S. Open by staving off six match points against Mary Ann Eisel on the stadium court before her first national TV audience. The public loved her fighting spirit, poise, and especially her sportsmanship.

"Crowds also liked Chris because of her all-American looks," wrote Billie Jean King in her book about women's tennis, *We Have Come a Long Way*. "Chris considered herself more feminine than most of the women playing professional tennis when she became a star, and she cultivated her image as America's sweetheart, right down to her mascara, hair ribbons, and brightly polished fingernails."

Evert's parents wisely limited her play as a teenager, insisting that she finish high school, so that she didn't capture her first big titles, the French Open and Wimbledon, until she was nineteen. That cautious approach kept her both injury-free and mentally fresh and undoubtedly enabled her to last an extraordinary twenty years on the tour, where she amassed eighteen Grand Slam singles titles and a record seven French Opens.

Future teen queens would typically have far shorter and/or more checkered careers. Tracy Austin, who matched Evert in baseline consistency and tenacity, became a celebrity at fourteen, won the 1979 U.S. Open at a record-youngest sixteen, and added another U.S. title in 1981. But her slight, 5'4" body broke down from overuse, and, sadly, she was forced to quit the game at only twenty-one.

"Too much, too soon"—a new cautionary slogan—also ruined Andrea Jaeger. Equally naive Jaeger surrendered much of her childhood and teenage life as a devoted follower of her hard-driving, one-dimensional father-coach, Roland, who liked to tell tennis parents, "Your child plays for himself last. First he plays for you, then for his coach, then for himself."

Unfortunately, Mr. Jaeger was right. Although undersized Andrea was a splendid competitor and reached number two in the world, she played and played and played, even when she should have rested and recuperated, until her painful shoulder simply gave out. Seven surgeries couldn't restore it, and like Austin she retired at twenty-one without the major titles she had appeared destined for. "I don't think I really reached my potential at all," she lamented.

By the late 1980s and 1990s, teen queens abounded as tennis became increasingly international and lucrative. Training and competition for prodigies started earlier, and taller, stronger females pounded ground strokes with brutish power. Experience mattered less than ever. Steffi Graf, a super-athletic German, and Monica Seles, a Yugoslav who emigrated to the United States, exemplified the new breed.

Graf, an intense perfectionist with a middle-distance runner's body, first awed us as a fourteen-year-old when she captured a gold medal at the 1984 Olympics, when tennis was a demonstration sport, and she confirmed that surefire potential by winning the 1987 French Open over the legendary Martina Navratilova just days before her eighteenth birthday. Despite enduring frequent injuries and illnesses and her father's highly publicized scandals—an extramarital affair and paternity suit in 1990 and a conviction for tax evasion in 1995—Graf racked up twenty-two career Grand Slam singles titles. As a nineteen-year-old, she won an unprecedented "Golden Slam" in 1988, the four majors plus an Olympic gold medal.

Seles was a giggling girl when she upset Graf to take the 1990 French Open at a then-youngest sixteen years, six months. She loved the limelight as much as the introverted Graf shunned it, and she idolized the glamorous Lenglen. "My dream is to be like Suzanne Lenglen, to fly through the air and hit a volley flying—both my feet off the ground," Seles once said. Her dreams and innocence were dashed when Gunther Parche, a crazed German, stabbed her in the back in 1993, in order to help Graf regain the number-one ranking. Before that tragic crime changed the course of tennis history, Seles had dethroned Graf and grabbed eight Grand Slam titles.

Jennifer Capriati was still playing for fun while making millions in endorsements when she amazingly reached the final of her first pro tournament in 1990. Magazine cover headlines such as *Sports Illustrated's* "And She's Only 13!" and *Newsweek's* "The 8th Grade Wonder" heralded her seemingly certain greatness. With youthful naivete, Capriati said, "I learned that it will be fun if it's all like this."

Although her fairy-tale rookie year ended with a top-ten ranking, and she won an Olympic gold medal in 1992, Capriati confided, "There's a lot of pressure on me from everyone." The destructive pressure came mostly from her domineering father, who usually didn't know best and forced her to practice, compete, and travel far too much. But it also came from unrealistically high expectations, intense media coverage, and the demands of her sponsors and the WTA Tour, eager to exploit its hot commodity.

Capriati, who craved a normal teenage life, rebelled against all of it, burned out prematurely, and finally dropped out of both the pro tour and school. The downward spiral escalated. Capriati moved out of her parents' home, was cited for shoplifting, went into a drug rehabilitation facility, was arrested for possession of marijuana, and entered rehab again. She even contemplated suicide. Now twenty-three, she's rejoined the tour and appears happy as her latest comeback is gradually succeeding.

Martina Hingis. Hans-Jürgen Dittmann

How will today's controversial teen queens **Martina Hingis, Venus and Serena Williams,** and **Anna Kournikova** turn out?

With their brash personalities clashing, sparks will fly from their repartee as much as from their rivalries. "To me, the off-the-court war of words is the most interesting thing," says Evert, now a TV tennis analyst and mother. "They all think they're going to be the greatest ever. They're so confident, it amuses me. That's as entertaining as going out to watch them physically play against each other."

FASCINATING FACTS:

- Tracy Austin was eleven years old when she was drafted by the Los Angeles Strings to play World Team Tennis.
- In 1991, when Monica Seles was eighteen, *Tennis* magazine asked, in a tennis fall poll: "Should Monica Seles be made to wear a bra on court?"

36

Western Forehands and Two-Handed Backhands Change the Way Tennis Is Played
1999

W here have all the artists gone?" became the popular lament starting in the late 1980s.

While powerful, state-of-the-art rackets, towering athletes, and bogus ranking systems (that didn't count many early-round losses and thus rewarded erratic sluggers) accounted for much of the problem, two burgeoning trends in playing styles had also accelerated the evolution of slam-bam tennis: the Western forehand and the two-handed backhand.

Sixty years before Bjorn Borg parlayed his Western forehand into six French and five Wimbledon titles, "Little Bill" Johnston whacked Western forehands, which he developed on slick, high-bouncing California cement and asphalt courts, and won the 1915 and 1919 U.S. Championships and the 1923 Wimbledon. "His forehand drive will always be renowned as one of the greatest shots the game has ever known," praised "Big Bill" Tilden, Johnston's longtime archrival.

But why did the Western style die out for decades until Borg revived it?

"Nailing down this historical coffin, the California Western was defeated by the Eastern American style [Tilden and Co.] and by the Continental style [Frenchmen Cochet and Lacoste and Englishman Fred Perry]," wrote authoritative Paul Metzler in *Australian Tennis Magazine*.

The Continental style, rarely used today, had the important advantages of not requiring a grip change for any stroke and being especially adaptable to taking the ball on the rise. Its major drawbacks were that it required a tremendously powerful wrist, such as Perry and Czechoslovakian star Karel Kozeluh possessed, to produce pace on the forehand, and its underspin tended to make balls fly and result in errors, especially against high-bouncing balls.

Although Johnston, who followed Western stylist and 1912–1913 U.S. champion Maurice McLoughlin ("The California Comet"), was the last great men's singles player to employ the Western game—Helen Wills Moody was the last woman star—formidable Americans Frank Shields, John Doeg, George Lott, Gregory Mangin, and Berkeley Bell hit first-class Western forehands well into the 1930s. The last three so impressed a young Don Budge when he saw them in California that he switched to the Western and used it for four years. Meanwhile, other rising California stars, such as Ellsworth Vines, Lester Stoefen, Bobby Riggs, and Elwood Cooke, were arming themselves with the flat, Eastern drive, or a modified Continental.

"I was an exception in that when I first came East I used the Western grip," recalled Budge in his book *Budge on Tennis*. "However, when I started out in the game, my brother, Lloyd, taught me the Eastern. I changed to the Western, and I lived to regret it as a big mistake."

FASCINATING FACTS:

- In 1949 Jack Kramer wrote: "The use of two hands not only weakens your strokes but robs you of confidence and gives your opponent a psychological advantage."
- In 1989 Bobby Riggs said the most dramatic change in tennis has been "the beautiful development of the two-handed shot."

By 1934, though, Budge realized that the Western forehand was ill-equipped to handle low, skidding balls on grass, then the predominant surface. "There were times when I was ready to give up in disgust," he admitted. But, after he reverted to his original Eastern grip, Budge's game markedly improved. And in 1938 he achieved tennis immortality as the first player to capture the Grand Slam, all four major tournaments.

When Borg first arrived on the tennis scene in the early 1970s, skeptics derided his Western game as unsuitable for grass, on which three of the four Slam events were still contested. He would prove them wrong soon enough by amazingly winning five straight Wimbledon titles from 1976 to 1980.

While Borg boasted many attributes besides his Western forehand—such as incomparable speed, concentration, and stamina, plus a rock-solid two-handed backhand—his phenomenal success inspired a generation of baseline clones, not only in Sweden, but around the world.

Nearly every French Open men's singles champion following Borg, from 1982 to 1999, took advantage of Western or semi-Western grips and strokes and often open stances: Ivan Lendl, Mats Wilander, Michael Chang, Jim Courier, Sergi Bruguera, Gustavo Kuerten, Carlos Moya, and Andre Agassi. With much larger and more dynamic graphite rackets, they could pummel the ball far harder, and with much less chance of error, than Borg ever could with his tiny wooden frame.

Western forehands also produce vicious topspin that proved most effective on hardcourts—which the U.S. and Australian Opens had converted to in 1978 and 1988, respectively. These "killer forehands," as well-known coach Nick Bollettieri called them, were ugly (unlike the elegant, classic Eastern forehand) but devastating weapons.

Two-handed backhands, the second major trend in playing styles, also delivered more power and better topspin and would profoundly change the game, especially for juniors and women.

Like the Western forehand, two-handedness once had a few leading practitioners only to disappear almost completely for years. In the early 1930s, Australian Vivian McGrath attracted worldwide attention and some criticism (supposedly for throwing players off balance!) for his heretical two-handed backhand. "Watching them [McGrath and John Bromwich], I could never help thinking how much better they would have been with an orthodox stroke," wrote Tilden in his 1948 memoirs, *My Story*.

McGrath disproved the naysayers, though, with big wins over American stars Ellsworth Vines, Wilmer Allison, and Johnny Van Ryn and became the youngest Aussie, at sixteen, to be selected for his Davis Cup team. Fellow countrymen Bromwich and Geoff Brown became double-handed champions in the late 1930s and 1940s, as did diminutive Ecuadorian Francisco "Pancho" Segura on the forehand side. Jaroslav Drobney, Wimbledon champion in 1954 and runner-up in 1949, called Brown's two-handed backhand "the fastest shot in the game," while many experts considered Segura's two-handed forehand one of the greatest tennis shots in history.

Since none of these four standouts had ever seen any other play until his style had been formed, renowned Aussie Davis Cup captain Harry Hopman rightly predicted in 1951 in *Sporting Life:* "For that reason I believe that we have not seen the last of the two-handed players."

Even Hopman could not have foreseen the spectacular, two-handed revolution that Borg, Jimmy Connors, and Chris Evert ignited in the 1970s. The then-unorthodox two-handed backhand soon became the rage as coaches everywhere started teaching it to youngsters eager to emulate those charismatic champions.

Girls and women, who traditionally had problems generating and handling pace with one-handed backhands, benefitted most from the two-hander. As 1980s doubles star Pam Shriver noted, "The biggest change I've seen in the twenty years I've played [on the pro tour] is that the backhand side is so tough to attack now. You see so many wonderful two-handers. Chrissie started that trend."

Indeed, in the season-ending 1979 world rankings, only Evert and little Tracy Austin among top-tenners swatted two-handed backhands. In the August 9, 1999, rankings, seven of the top ten women did. Steffi Graf, the greatest all-court player in history, once confided that she wished she had a two-handed backhand.

Critics of two-handed shot-makers, such as conventional-stroking former champs Jack Kramer, Tony Trabert, and Budge, contend that they rarely make good volleyers, lack finesse, and must run farther and harder to reach balls. Other astute observers, such as Bill Bowrey, believe two-handedness militates against developing a complete game and nominate superstar Pete Sampras, who converted from a two-handed backhand to a one-hander at age fourteen, as the complete player.

"Pete has a good style for juniors to model their game on, because he can play both at the net or on the baseline," Bowrey, then Australia's national coach, told *The Age* newspaper in Melbourne in 1996. "I think the volley game will come back in the way he does it."

Like the Western forehand, the two-handed backhand is here to stay. While not ideal for the superior athlete with the complete game, it has proven a godsend for millions of recreational players and even the majority of world-class players.

One question invites an answer in the twenty-first century: Will two-handed forehands also become the norm?

FASCINATING FACTS:

- After Bjorn Borg won the 1974 French Open, reporters frequently asked him when he would start using a one-handed backhand.
- From 1884 to 1996, one woman player with a two-handed backhand, Chris Evert, won Wimbledon singles titles. From 1997 to 2001, three women with two-handed backhands, Martina Hingis, Lindsay Davenport, and Venus Williams, did it.
- When Billy Carter, the late brother of former president Jimmy Carter, was being taught a two-handed backhand, he quipped: "But that won't give me a free hand to hold the beer."

37

The Tiebreaker Shortens and Enlivens Matches
1999

The tiebreaker made an epochal impact on tennis in 1970. Jimmy Van Alen, a New England aristocrat with revolutionary ideas, created the game's first major scoring innovation to replace boring marathon sets and matches with thrilling climaxes.

Five years earlier Van Alen had unveiled his "sudden death" best-five-of-nine-points tiebreaker as an experiment at the pro tournament he sponsored at the Newport (Rhode Island) Casino. In 1967, the longest (147 games) match in history—Dick Dell and Dick Leach outlasted Len Schloss and Tom Mozur 3-6, 49-47, 22-20 at the Newport Casino Invitational—further convinced Van Alen that the time had come for his scoring reform.

The nine-point tiebreaker made its Grand Slam debut at the 1970 U.S. Open, where farsighted director Bill Talbert welcomed the innovation, and tennis was never the same again. Whenever a set reached 6-6 in games, red flags flew while a gigantic crimson banner was unfurled inside the stadium. Fans rushed to the court, and an eerie silence and tension charged the atmosphere.

It was tiebreaker time. Excitement was mounting fast. Not only did the tiebreaker give tennis a definite "finish line," but if and when the score reached four points all, *both players faced simultaneous set point and/or match point.* While spectators, tournament schedule-makers, and television executives loved it, many players, at least initially, didn't.

"I feel like I'm going to have a heart attack playing sudden death," said the great Pancho Gonzalez at the U.S. Open. "It's terribly nerve-wracking." A skeptical John Newcombe said, "It's like rolling dice."

Disgruntled players signed a petition to outlaw the tiebreaker, claiming it was too gimmicky, short, and unfair because it gave one player an extra serve on the decisive ninth point. Although the "sudden death" version lasted five years at Forest Hills and for a while on the Virginia Slims circuit and in American colleges, the other three Slam tournaments would adopt the International Tennis Federation's more conservative best-seven-of-twelve-points tiebreaker. It was devised by Peter John (based on Van Alen's theme) and was consistent with tennis' "win by two" tradition.

In 1971 the All England Club adopted the nine-point tiebreaker, the first scoring change at Wimbledon in ninety-four years. A year later Wimbledon opted to put the twelve-point tiebreaker into effect at 8-games-all, waiting until 1979 to reduce it to 6-games-all. Davis Cup competition did not use tiebreakers until 1989. Today the U.S. Open plays the tiebreaker at 6-all in every set, while the other three Slams revert to traditional scoring in the fifth set of men's matches and third set of women's matches.

While in theory the twelve-point tiebreaker could continue forever, in practice it has often produced scintillating denouements. Tennis fans were treated to the most famous tiebreaker of all time in the unforgettable 1980 Wimbledon final. Bjorn Borg, gunning for his fifth straight Big W title, led John McEnroe two sets to one when the fourth-set tiebreaker sent pulse rates soaring.

No one better captured this "nerve-twanging tension" than Mariana Simionescu, then Borg's wife, in her book *Love Match: My Life with Bjorn:*

> And so to the tiebreaker.... As always at such moments, the crowd stirs with special feeling. It's like the drum-beating that heralds the tumbril carrying the convicts sentenced to death. It's like a dawn in the Middle Ages, when all the balconies in the scaffold square are booked because no one wants to miss the moment of the beheading.
>
> ... The tiebreaker is in fact a tournament, as Ion Tiriac once said. You mount the horse, grab your spear and on you go. Only the helmets, like those used by modern fencers, are lacking. The one who falls is recognized rather by the colour of his horse.

This racket jousting lasted twenty-two minutes in a fluctuating tiebreaker that brought point-by-point agony and ecstasy, depending on whom you rooted for. There were winners off seeming winners, furious attacking, and scrambling for each precious point.

At 4-3 for Borg, Mariana, sensing the precariousness of any tiebreaker lead, recalls: "Tennis was already a knife with a very sharp edge, but the tiebreaker made it cut both ways, because it won't admit a single mistake." After McEnroe staved off a second match point for 7-all, the crowd was at its wits' end as much as the players. "I have the feeling that the whole stadium is a boat at the mercy of giant waves, bobbing on the crest only to be sucked into the abyss the very next moment," she remembers.

When Borg edged ahead 11-10 with an easy volley, the crowd exploded. "The sixth match point! The crowd just doesn't stop clapping," relates Mariana. "They all realize, perhaps, that no director can stage such a performance."

Amidst the excruciating excitement, Borg had lost five championship points, while Mac prevailed on his seventh set point to take the historic 18-16 tiebreaker. The stoical Swede, renowned for his stellar play under pressure, somehow shook off the disappointment and quickly regrouped. He ultimately won the fifth set, 8-6, for the title.

But tennis was the biggest winner, thanks in large part to the tiebreaker.

FASCINATING FACTS:

- The longest tiebreaker in professional tennis men's singles history, 24-22, was played at the 1992 Copenhagen Open when Finland's Aki Rahunen defeated Denmark's Peter Nyborg 7-6, 2-6, 6-3 in the first qualifying round.
- The longest tiebreaker in professional tennis men's doubles history took place at Wimbledon in 1985. Sweden's Jan Gunnarsson and Denmark's Michael Mortensen needed a 26-24 tiebreaker to close out their 6-4, 6-4, 3-6, 7-6 first-round victory over Australia's John Frawley and Paraguay's Victor Pecci.
- The longest tiebreaker, in terms of points, in professional women's tennis history was played at the WITA Championships at Amelia Island, Florida, in 1984. Rosie Casals and Kathleen Horvath took a 20-18 tiebreaker to wrap up a 5-7, 6-1, 7-6 first-round victory over Sandy Collins and Beth Herr.
- The longest tiebreaker, in terms of time, in professional women's tennis history took place at the 1984 Ginny of Richmond, Virginia, tournament. Vicki Nelson-Dunbar edged Jean Hepner 6-4, 7-6. Their 13-11 tiebreaker lasted an astounding one hour and forty-seven minutes.

38

Althea Gibson Breaks the Color Barrier
1999

G iven the same chance as others have had, blacks would dominate our sport as they have done in other sports," asserted Arthur Ashe, tennis' first black men's champion, in 1988.

For the first half of the twentieth century, blacks had no chance to compete at, let alone dominate, world-class tournaments. A major reason for this racial discrimination was that white athletes in tennis and other sports were afraid of competing on an equal basis with blacks.

"For 120 years, white America has gone to extraordinary lengths to discredit and discourage black participation in sports because black athletes have been so successful," Ashe wrote in a *New York Times* column.

In the not-so-good old days, the "Whites Only" signs on tennis courts didn't refer only to clothes. To end that separate but unequal segregation and to promote the grassroots game among black Americans, the American Tennis Association was organized in 1916. Before the ATA, black players, chiefly from the Northeast, participated in invitational interstate tournaments, the first being staged in Philadelphia in 1898. But since blacks were barred from playing in United States Lawn Tennis Association–sanctioned tournaments prior to 1940, the ATA struggled for years to overcome that towering barrier to equality.

Despite a shortage of rackets, balls, courts, topflight coaching, and funds for travel, outstanding black players such as Ora Washington, Jimmie McDaniel, and Oscar Johnson Jr. emerged. Washington, a superb all-around athlete, captured seven straight ATA national women's singles titles from 1929 to 1935.

McDaniel was "the greatest black tennis player of them all," according to Sydney Llewellyn, a self-described archivist of black tennis from New York's Harlem neighborhood. "McDaniel was better than Ashe. He was bigger, stronger," Llewellyn told *Tennis USTA*. "He was a tall lefty, maybe 6'5". He'd take two steps and be all over the net. He had it all. He would have won a bunch of Grand Slams somewhere along the line, if he had had the chance."

He didn't because his heyday, albeit an obscure one, ended in the 1940s. Johnson, dubbed "the Jackie Robinson of tennis," came closer. As a skinny seventeen-year-old from Los Angeles, he broke ground as the first black to play in and win a USLTA national tournament, the 1948 National Junior Public Parks. Five years later promoter Jack Kramer offered Johnson a pro contract, but a snapped elbow tendon prematurely finished his career.

Althea Gibson, born in 1927 as the daughter of sharecroppers, was an athletically talented tomboy who would often play hooky from school in Harlem to play street paddleball (she was New York City's women's champion at age twelve!), pool, and basketball. A mischievous kid, whose abusive father taught her to box, Gibson got into fistfights with both girls and boys.

Being both street-smart and street-tough, Gibson learned early in life how to take care of herself. However, she would still need the financial and moral support of others, especially two black physicians, Hubert A. Eaton and R. Walter Johnson, as well as the sponsorship of 1930s champion Alice Marble, to make it in the lily-white tennis world.

By 1949 Gibson, a perennial ATA women's champion, had developed into a formidable, if somewhat raw, player. After reaching the quarterfinals of the Eastern Indoors and National Indoors events, she was primed to compete at Forest Hills in the USLTA Nationals in 1950. But would she be allowed to play in the USLTA's summer grass-court tourneys in order to qualify for the Nationals and to give her best performance there?

Marble, who had heroically fought Nazi racism as an American spy (getting shot in the back by a double agent) during World War II, challenged the wavering USLTA to allow Gibson to participate. In a rousing, courageous letter published in the July 1950 *American Lawn Tennis* magazine, Marble wrote:

"I think it's time we faced a few facts. If tennis is a game for ladies and gentlemen, it's also time we acted a little more like gentle people and less like sanctimonious hypocrites. If there is anything left of sportsmanship, it's more than time to display what it means to us. If Althea Gibson represents a challenge to the present crop of women players, it's only fair that they should meet that challenge on the courts, where tennis is played.

"But if she is refused a chance to succeed or to fail, then there is an uneradical (sic) mark against a game to which I have devoted most of my life, and I would be bitterly ashamed.

"The entrance of Negroes into national tennis is as inevitable as it has proven to be in baseball, in football, or in boxing; there is no denying so much talent.

"I've never met Miss Gibson but, to me, she is a fellow human being to whom equal privileges ought to be extended."

Althea Gibson.
International Tennis
Hall of Fame

Marble's eloquent rebuttal of the USLTA's discriminatory policies resulted in Gibson's being accepted at the Orange Lawn Tennis Club in South Orange, New Jersey, the USLTA National Clay Courts in Chicago, and the USLTA Nationals, but only after they required her to be tested to confirm she was a woman. New Jersey's Maplewood Country Club, however, rejected her entry. The ATA deplored the New Jersey association's "snobbishness, prejudice, and bad judgment," and also objected to the implied quota of black players (somewhere from two to five) that henceforth would be allowed to enter the Nationals.

At Forest Hills, Gibson, a graceful serve-and-volleyer who described her game as "aggressive, dynamic, and mean," finally, at age twenty-three, demonstrated her unmistakable prowess to the whole world. She nearly beat three-time Wimbledon champion Louise Brough in a thrilling 6-1, 3-6, 9-7 second-round battle.

Gibson then faced several disappointing years on the amateur tour, where her cold and unapproachable personality made her a solitary, forlorn figure. Nearly all the white girls shunned her. Hostile crowds heckled her—sometimes calling her "nigger"—or ignored her spectacular shots. Prying newspapermen pestered her, and to make matters worse, the Negro press beat her brains out because she was "not militant enough" as a civil rights crusader. Rather than admit her, some bigoted tournaments simply went out of business.

An extended tour of Southeast Asia for the U.S. State Department in 1955 with Ham Richardson, Karol Fageros, and Bob Perry gave Gibson a chance to work on her game without tournament pressures and did wonders for her. Rejuvenated, she took the 1956 French singles and doubles titles to become the first black in tennis to win a Grand Slam event.

Gibson reigned as the undisputed queen of tennis in 1957 and 1958 by capturing both the Wimbledon and U.S. championships. After winning her first Wimbledon, she received heaps of telegrams from fans and luminaries, such as President Dwight D. Eisenhower, Averell Harriman, and boxing champion Sugar Ray Robinson. And upon her return to New York, she was honored with a rare ticker-tape parade up Broadway to City Hall, where Mayor Robert Wagner gave her the medallion to the city.

Gibson recalled the culture shock of her incredible 1957 Wimbledon adventure in her 1958 autobiography, *I Always Wanted to Be Somebody*:

"It seemed like a long way from 143rd Street.

"Shaking hands with the Queen of England was a long way from being forced to sit in the colored section of the bus going into downtown Wilmington, North Carolina.

"Dancing with the Duke of Devonshire was a long way from not being allowed to bowl in Jefferson City, Missouri, because the white customers complained about it."

Like Jackie Robinson and other black pioneers, Gibson paid a considerable price on her long, hard road to glory. "If I've made it, it's half because I was game to take a wicked amount of punishment along the way and half because there were an awful lot of people who cared enough to help me," she wrote. "It has been a bewildering, challenging, exhausting experience, often more painful than pleasurable, more sad than happy. But I wouldn't have missed it for the world."

Ashe secured his own niche in tennis history as the first black man to win a Grand Slam crown at the inaugural U.S. Open in 1968 and again as champion at the 1970 Australian Open and 1975 Wimbledon. Despite being a paragon of dignity and humanitarianism, Ashe lacked the personal charisma to inspire a new generation of black youngsters to take up tennis. "What we need is an American Yannick Noah. In many respects, I wasn't a very good role model," Ashe acknowledged in 1987. "We need someone who's got flair and can play in-your-face tennis. And he should comport himself like Julius Erving."

For nominees, how about those marvelous Williams sisters? Venus and Serena got game, sass, and class. And together, they could dominate tennis just as Ashe predicted.

FASCINATING FACTS:

- The Chicago Prairie Tennis Club, founded in 1912, was the first black tennis club in the United States.
- On December 24, 1929, the secretary of the National Association for the Advancement of Colored People (NAACP) sent a letter to the USLTA protesting the barring of two black players from a tournament.
- On March 26, 1947, Dartmouth College refused to drop a black player from its squad for a match at College of William and Mary in Williamsburg, Virginia. The meeting was cancelled.
- The Republic of South Africa was banned from Davis Cup competition for its racial policies on March 23, 1970.
- The South African Open allowed nonwhites to participate for the first time on March 27, 1972.
- After Althea Gibson retired from tennis, she was a sports administrator, boxing official, singer, and movie actress performing alongside John Wayne.
- In 1964 Althea Gibson made history as a professional golfer when she became the first black woman to earn her LPGA player's card.
- At one time Althea Gibson boasted a 195 bowling average and said, "I could have been a professional bowler."
- Althea Gibson used to train with boxing great Sugar Ray Robinson to improve her footwork.

39

The Racket Revolution Changes Tennis Forever
1999

The first shots in the racket revolution were fired at the 1967 U.S. Championships. Billie Jean King, Clark Graebner, and Gene Scott wielded the new Wilson T2000, a strange-looking steel racket invented by 1920s champion Rene Lacoste. Observers wondered if the trio were prescient pioneers or merely foolish gamblers.

"Billie Jean won the tournament that year, and she could have played with a pogo stick and won," recalls Scott, then a young lawyer. "She was the best. So it really didn't say anything about the racket. But Clark got to the final. I was a part-time player, and all of a sudden I reached the semis. So people said it can't be him, it must be the racket."

Other players experimented with the small-headed (sixty-three square inch) but explosive Wilson T2000, including Englishwoman Ann Haydon Jones, the Wimbledon titlist in 1969. The weapon gained its greatest notoriety when Jimmy Connors used it to win three-fourths of a Grand Slam in 1974. Most players though, including King, disliked the split-shaft steel racket's hard-to-control "trampoline effect" and reverted to traditional wood rackets.

Endorsements would play a role, too, in those uncertain times. Rod Laver, who had captured the Grand Slam in 1962 and 1969 with wood, simultaneously signed contracts to play with three different kinds of rackets in different parts of the world—a wooden Dunlop, a wooden Donnay, and an aluminum Chemold.

Surprising as it may seem, several of the so-called breakthroughs in racket technology and design of the last third of the twentieth century had been tried decades before. For example, William Larned, winner of seven U.S. singles titles, invented the steel-framed racket in 1921. A year later the Dayton Steel Company introduced metal rackets with metal strings (piano wire), which were especially popular with schools and institutions because of their durability, despite being very head heavy. At about the same time the Birmal, another metal racket with metal strings, was made in Birmingham, England. Gerald Patterson, a thunder-serving Australian who captured the 1919 and 1922 Wimbledon titles, tried a steel racket with wire strings in 1925 but suffered one of his worst seasons. Patterson switched back to reliable wood, and thus the newfangled weapon didn't catch on.

Today's prevalent open-throat design was actually patented in the late 1920s for wood rackets. The legendary Bill Tilden both used and advertised the color-ful, open-throat Top-Flite, one of the most popular rackets of all time.

Englishman Frank W. Donisthorpe built the first extra-long rackets in 1915. Twenty years later Donisthorpe invented the unique triple-branch wood racket, the most bizarre-looking instrument since lopsided rackets were in vogue in the 1880s. It would take a true pioneer to brandish a frame that looked like a snow-shoe, and Henry Wilfred "Bunny" Austin was surely that in the mid-1930s. The British Davis Cup star had already made tennis history as the first male interna-tionalist to wear shorts on Wimbledon's Centre Court in 1933, and for that, sensi-ble trendsetting Austin will be more remembered and appreciated.

None of these innovations, intended to strengthen wood rackets (which easi-ly warped and cracked) and strings, survived very long. And various other designs, such as flat-top and triangular racket heads, models with a slot in the middle of the handle, concave wedges at the throat, and diagonal stringing, all disappeared by 1940. However, laminations, along with the use of several pieces of wood rather than one, did gradually strengthen frames, while synthetic glue, introduced in 1934, became standard for every racket by the late 1930s. Rackets, made of wood and oval in shape, then remained remarkably similar for the next thirty years.

Arthur Ashe, winner of the 1968 U.S. Open with a wood racket, helped pio-neer the new generation of rackets in 1969 by playing with the intriguing Head Competition, an aluminum-fiberglass open-throat model. Dubbed the "snow-shoe," it weighed 12.25 ounces and its racket head covered sixty-eight square inches, which made it an ounce lighter and three square inches larger than tradi-tional wood frames.

Howard Head, whose metal skis revolutionized the ski industry in the 1950s and 1960s, changed tennis forever with the first oversized racket, the Prince Classic, in 1976. "The Prince is the shape the tennis racket should've been in the first place," Head triumphantly told *Sports Illustrated*. "I have no doubt that in three or four years it will be the conventional frame and the others will be thought of as small, funny-looking, and old-fashioned. This is no boomlet. It's an absolute explosion."

Providing four times the effective hitting area of conventional wood rackets, Prince's new line did prove a godsend for the less competent recreational player as well as talented tournament players. Don Budge, the 1938 Grand Slammer, called the Prince "by far the best racket I've ever played with." Pam Shriver, a gawky sixteen-year-old, used the Prince Classic and shocked everyone by reaching the 1978 U.S. Open final. More and more, people concluded: It must be the racket.

Bjorn Borg and John McEnroe bucked the trend by winning major titles in 1981 with wood, as did Chris Evert in taking the 1982 U.S. Open. But, significantly, Martina Navratilova became the first player to capture a Grand Slam title with a big-headed racket at the 1982 French Open, just three weeks after switching to the elliptically headed Yonex R-7. The following day, seventeen-year-old Mats Wilander became the first man to win a Grand Slam crown with a large-headed racket.

By the mid-1980s nearly every big-time tournament competitor had abandoned wood and was capitalizing on the technological advances. But not everyone liked this trend. The bigger, stiffer graphite rackets produced far more power than wood rackets, and John McEnroe, among others, claimed that was ruining the pro game.

"There is no doubt in my mind that part of the reason for Boris Becker being number five in the world right now is the fact that he is not playing with wood," argued McEnroe in 1985. "I know he is a strong boy, but he would never have come on as fast as he has if we had all been playing with wood rackets. Occasionally when I see one of those old wood Dunlop Maxplys we used to play with laying around, I get an urge to pick it up and play with it again. For me, that was real tennis. You couldn't get away with no-brain hitting with those rackets."

FASCINATING FACTS:

- John McEnroe still owns seventy-five wood rackets.
- Pete Sampras advises kids that the only way to master strokes is "to play with wood rackets until [age] fourteen or so."

The ruling bodies of tennis didn't agree with McEnroe. Although the International Tennis Federation had acted swiftly to ban the devilishly unfair double-strung or "spaghetti" racket (which produced wildly spinning, unpredictable shots) in 1978, it failed to promptly limit the size of racket heads, which had increased to a whopping 130 square inches by 1982. At that time, more than half of all rackets sold were oversized.

The pros loved them, too. Oversized weapons served as "equalizers" for undersized whiz kids Michael Chang and Arantxa Sanchez, who grabbed singles crowns at the 1989 French Open, and for precocious Monica Seles, the youngest (until Martina Hingis in 1997) Grand Slam champion this century, at Roland Garros in 1990.

Siegfried Kuebler, a German engineer and inventor, created the revolutionary wide-body concept in 1984 and sold it to Wilson, which introduced its first wide-body racket in 1987. Like the oversized head, which expanded the "sweet spot" and thus aided off-center hits, the extremely stiff wide-body helped amateur players, especially juniors and seniors (over forty-five), generate the power they needed. It was also the racket of choice for some women pros such as Seles, Sanchez-Vicario, Jennifer Capriati, and Navratilova.

Few leading men pros, however, switched to the wide-body. For all or most of their pro careers, number-one ranked players Pete Sampras, Stefan Edberg, and Jim Courier used a mid-sized (eighty-five-square-inch) Wilson Original Pro Staff graphite that first hit the market in 1984. They found it potent enough. "I'd rip holes through windscreens with a wide-body," once quipped Courier.

The next development in the never-ending quest for the perfect racket was the extra-long racket, or long-bodies, which were mostly one and two inches longer than the standard twenty-seven-inch adult frames. Chang played with a twenty-eight-inch version of the Prince Graphite Original, the Chang Precision 730, and reached the finals of the 1995 French Open and 1996 Australian and U.S. Opens. Amanda Coetzer and Mariaan de Swardt, neither a top-tenner, raised eyebrows as the only two players to beat superstar Steffi Graf in 1995, and they did it with twenty-eight-inch rackets. Soon after, Hingis, Seles, Marcelo Rios, and Mark Philippoussis hopped on the long-body bandwagon.

Long-bodies boasted several advantages for both pros and amateurs. Frames one inch longer produced an estimated 10 percent more power, and rackets two inches longer generated about 17 percent more power. A longer racket enabled players to reach more balls and to hit serves from a higher point for more consistency. A disadvantage was that its length made it a bit unwieldy and thus harder to maneuver at the net.

Responding to the blitz of longer rackets marketed in 1996 and 1997, the ITF decided to limit racket length to twenty-nine inches in the pro ranks starting January 1, 1999, and everywhere else in the year 2000. The ITF contended that super-long rackets could give players at all levels an unfair advantage in serving, which "constitutes a threat to the nature of tennis."

With changes in size, shape, width, and length going about as far as they can, and graphite the best material from a cost and performance basis, how else could racket technology "push the envelope"?

Fear not. With invention the mother of necessity, racket manufacturers informed us that space-age materials could enhance graphite and make rackets lighter, stiffer, and more shock-absorbent and powerful than ever. Since 1997, titanium, a super-strong material that largely composes NASA's space shuttle, and hyper carbon, a fiber which is four times stiffer and stronger than titanium and 65 percent lighter, have resulted in seven-ounce rackets that can hit devastating bombs.

But aren't rackets that allow Greg Rusedski to serve 149 miles per hour and Richard Krajicek to whack forty-nine aces in a match *already* potent enough?

Have these rackets *already* upset the crucial balance between offense and defense, reduced finesse and strategy, and made the sport less fair, at least for men pros, and less charming and entertaining? Should the ITF put a "speed limit" on the power that high-tech rackets can produce?

And what next? A computerized, uranium racket that makes you glow every time you hit a winner?

FASCINATING FACTS:

- In 1988, for the first time, no player at the Wimbledon Championships used a wooden racket.
- The highly innovative Arthur Ashe Competition HEAD tennis racket was selected as a piece of sports memorabilia by The Smithsonian National Museum of American History.
- In 1982, Arthur Ashe said, "Any weekend player who doesn't use a mid-sized, or moreover an oversized racket, is just plain nuts."

PART 6

The Ten Greatest Matches in Tennis History

Introduction

What makes a classic match? What makes an event so momentous that the world almost stands still and watches, an episode so fascinating that we remember and savor it for years?

Here are the criteria I used to choose my ten greatest matches:

The Event—Was the match staged at a premier event such as Wimbledon, the U.S., French, and Australian Opens or the Davis and Fed Cups where reputations hang in the balance and legends are made?

Historical Significance—Did the political, national, psychological, and cultural implications of the match equal, or even transcend, the importance of the match itself?

Brilliance—Quite simply, was the caliber of play high, sometimes brilliant, and occasionally sublime?

Competitive Balance—Were the combatants evenly matched, and did they provide a taut, unpredictable *denouement?*

Career Impact—Did the match have a lasting impact on the career of either player or perhaps even both players?

Contrasts—Could the sporting public and perhaps even the world's masses identify with and passionately favor one player more than the other, because of their contrasting characters, personalities, and court styles?

Star Appeal—Did the duel involve the greatest champions or tennis giants? Did it come at the zenith of their careers and during a famous rivalry?

The most-storied encounters have contained many of these dynamic elements. But, before plunging ahead with my ten greatest matches, I acknowledge that, inevitably, I have omitted some spectacular duels that others would have selected.

40

Bjorn Borg Defeats John McEnroe 1-6, 7-5, 6-3, 6-7, 8-6 in the 1980 Wimbledon Final

O ne of the most extraordinary contests in the annals of sport—or any endeavor in which two men test their wills against one another," testified Frank Deford, the distinguished American sportswriter. "The character of Bjorn Borg's performance surpassed the achievement itself."

The achievement was staggering enough. Barely twenty-four, Borg had won his thirty-fifth straight match at Wimbledon and his fifth consecutive title, a feat unequaled by any modern men's champion from Tilden to Laver. With five French Open titles also in hand, the imperturbable Swede confessed, "It is my ambition to be remembered as the greatest champion of all time."

No matter where tennis historians ultimately place Borg, many rate his 1-6, 7-5, 6-3, 6-7, 8-6 epic over archrival John McEnroe as the greatest Wimbledon final and the most thrilling, mind-boggling, excruciatingly tense match ever.

The enormously gifted New Yorker, lambasted by the British press and a villain to Wimbledon fans for his childish tantrums and rages, started fast and permitted Borg only thirteen points in his first nine service games, through 5-all in the second set. But, suddenly, with Borg ahead 6-5 and McEnroe serving at 15-30, Borg turned the match upside down by ripping two backhand service return winners to take the second set. An early break then gave Borg the third set 6-3.

Two superb crosscourt backhands gave the popular Borg a vital service break for 5-4 in the fourth set. He had held serve for fifteen straight times and had only to serve out for the championship. He quickly reached 40-15, double match point. Surprisingly, the bearded wonder with the low pulse rate and the concentration of a yogi, succumbed to nerves. He was human after all.

He volleyed tentatively, and Mac stayed alive with a service return winner to even it at 5-all. Then, on to 6-all for a tiebreaker—a scoring innovation Wimbledon's traditionalists had only reluctantly and never completely accepted. (Final sets must still be played out conventionally.)

No firsthand witness or any of the hundreds of millions of worldwide television viewers would ever forget this tiebreaker. There were winners off seeming winners, furious attacking and scrambling for each precious point. Match points alternated with set points as the score mounted—and neither athlete would yield an inch. Finally, at 16-17, Borg buckled under the tremendous pressure and netted a volley, his old weakness. The thirty-four-point ordeal lasted twenty-two minutes, as long as some sets. The champ had five championship points, the challenger seven set points.

The fluctuating, electrifying, incredibly tense drama had already exhausted most fans. Many wondered if Borg could compose himself and come back after he lost the opening two points of the fifth and deciding set. "I am saying to myself," he recalled, "Don't get tight now, don't give up." He didn't, for sure.

Serving powerfully and accurately, the lithe, broad-shouldered, 5'11" Swede won nineteen straight points on his serve and twenty-eight of the last twenty-nine. McEnroe kept pace, though with more trouble, trailing love-40 on service in the second and eighth games before holding. Finally at 6-7, 15-40, Mac could tempt fate no longer. On the eighth match point, Mac attacked off a second serve, volleyed into the corner, and fell in a futile lunge for Borg's backhand crosscourt passing shot. Borg fell to his knees and thrust his arms skyward—his annual Wimbledon victory gesture.

McEnroe, who had walked onto Centre Court to a chorus of boos, walked off it to reverberating cheers of appreciation for his mature behavior as much as his marvelous play.

Lance Tingay, the esteemed journalist at London's *Daily Telegraph,* called the heroic duel the best he had seen in his forty-three Wimbledon finals. "For sure, it is the best match I have ever played at Wimbledon," said the champion.

FASCINATING FACTS:

- Bjorn Borg used to wear a T-shirt on which was emblazoned the message: "Never love a tennis player; to him love means nothing."
- A British expression for doing something quite unspeakable is "Doing a McEnroe."

41

Suzanne Lenglen Defeats Helen Wills 6-3, 8-6 in the 1926 Cannes, France, Final

"This girl must be mad," Suzanne Lenglen remarked when she learned Helen Wills was playing the Riviera circuit and forcing a long-awaited showdown. "Does she think she can come and beat me on my home courts?"

Destiny would allow only one meeting between the two greatest women players of the game's first seventy-five years. From 1919 on, "La Grande Suzanne" was invincible. She had captured six Wimbledons, six French titles, and had lost only twice in tournaments, defaults caused by illness.

If Lenglen's reign was at its peak, Wills's talent was just beginning to crest. She had won the American championships in 1923, 1924, and 1925. As unbeatable as Suzanne, Helen would not lose a set in singles from 1927 to 1932 and would eventually wind up with eight Wimbledon and seven U.S. crowns.

Al Laney, one of America's best sports journalists, described the much-heralded clash of immortals:

"This was the meeting of two girls, one French, the other American, in an otherwise unimportant tournament on the French Riviera. Only a girls' tennis match, but it was blown up into a titanic struggle such as the world has never seen before. By the time it came off, it was of worldwide interest and never again in the history of sport was such an event allowed to be played in such ridiculous and fantastic circumstances. It could have filled Yankee Stadium as it turned out."

Picture the scene. After the Great War, Lenglen had become a truly national figure, the symbol of resurgent French pride. She would defend that against the challenger from the New World. One could hardly find two more contrasting personalities either: Lenglen with her fiery, operatic Gallic temperament and

Wills with the unemotional, reserved demeanor that earned her the nickname of "Little Miss Poker Face."

Their dress and games followed suit. Symbolizing the new postwar freedoms, Suzanne wore a skirt that scandalously exposed her thighs, a low-cut blouse, and her famous brightly colored bandeau. Helen appeared in a schoolgirlish, white middy blouse, pleated skirt, and her trademark white eyeshade. On the court the Frenchwoman showed a stunning all-court audacity spiced with balletic movement and acrobatic leaps; the stolid, unimaginative Californian blasted unerring ground strokes into the corners.

Hundreds of reporters and cameramen had flocked to the little Carlton Club in Cannes. The stands were filled with distinguished guests—kings, barons, counts, rajahs, authors, capitalists, and financiers. A mob seethed and struggled to get in or at least get a glance at the match somehow. Some climbed eucalyptus trees, others stood on top of motor cars, and many watched from nearby rooftops. The fortunate or well-connected who bought seats paid a then-astonishing twelve dollars (four times as much as the highest-priced ticket for a Forest Hills final) to see the super-spectacle. The atmosphere was positively electric.

The match lived up to its larger-than-life billing. Suzanne, the heavy (three-to-one) favorite, played near-perfect tennis to win the first set 6-3 against the somewhat nervous Helen. High-strung Suzanne, who was said to have been kept up until 2:30 the previous night by her parents reminding her of the honor at stake the next day, felt the pressure, too, and frequently sipped brandy during the changeovers.

The intensity of the fray was relieved by comedy emanating from a eucalyptus tree where small boys hid in the leafy branches. "At intervals they fell out, or were dragged down by red-faced gendarmes who disturbed the peace more than the boys," recalled Wills in a *Saturday Evening Post* piece seven years later.

In the second set, Helen sped up her powerful ground strokes and jumped ahead 3-1. The crowd grew noisier as they witnessed the tide turning. Had the grand diva finally met her match?

Here the twenty-year-old American made the fatal mistake of changing her attacking strategy. While Helen eventually resumed her hard hitting, Suzanne, who was tiring and having coughing spasms, pulled in front and finally reached 6-5, 40-15, double match point.

Then came the most contentious and dramatic moment of all. After a long rally, Wills smacked a forehand into the corner that caught the Frenchwoman flat-footed. "Out!" was heard—the match was over. Suzanne ran to the net to shake hands. But, no, the linesman, Lord Charles Hope, pushed through the frenzied mob of people to tell the umpire, Commander George Hillyard, that a spectator had made the call and that the ball had clearly been good.

The umpire reversed the call. Without a murmur or protest, a tense Lenglen returned to her task, like a true champion. She lost that game for 6-all but took command with a variety of teasing shots, and on her third match point, put away a smash off a deep lob. She had won 6-3, 8-6.

The exhausted champion collapsed on a bench and burst into tears. Her tyrannical mother cruelly chided her, "Good God, how badly you played."

Meanwhile, Helen stood alone and ignored amidst the tumult. Suddenly a young man vaulted over the balustrade and congratulated her. "You played awfully well," he said. It was Fred Moody, whom she married four years later.

FASCINATING FACTS:

- In the 1920s Suzanne Lenglen was the first woman player to wear lipstick on the court at Wimbledon.
- Suzanne Lenglen was the first world-class woman tennis player to train regularly with men.
- Helen Wills Moody wrote five mystery novels, and as a syndicated writer, she interviewed famous aviator Amelia Earhart on the same day she won the final at the 1932 French Championships.
- Suzanne Lenglen was so outstanding in the early 1920s that the French Davis Cup Committee asked permission to include her on their nation's team.
- Bill Tilden admitted that Suzanne Lenglen was the only player who was a bigger draw than he was.

42

Don Budge Defeats Gottfried von Cramm 6-8, 5-7, 6-4, 6-2, 8-6 in the 1937 Davis Cup Interzone Final

When old-timers rekindle tales of glory, the 1937 Budge–Von Cramm classic produces an intriguing array of plots and characters: a miracle shot, Hitler, a heroic comeback, Tilden, Davis Cup stakes, and matchless sportmanship.

Baron Gottfried von Cramm cut a tall, elegant figure and possessed immaculate, copybook strokes. Easily the finest player ever to come out of Germany until Boris Becker fifty years later, he had the misfortune of being eclipsed by Fred Perry and then Don Budge so that he never won Wimbledon, although he was thrice a finalist. He was also a baron who dropped both the aristocratic title of "Baron" and the "von" because they didn't suit his sports-man personality.

"The most charming, interesting and intriguing personality that tennis has known for many a long day is my good friend Baron Gottfried von Cramm of Germany," declared tennis legend Bill Tilden in his 1938 memoirs, *Aces, Places and Faults*. "Here is a player of transcendent skill, a player who can produce tennis that for periods will sweep any player in the world from his path."

As a boy Budge didn't even like tennis; baseball and football were his first loves. During the early and mid-1930s, the tall, lean Californian with red hair and freckles developed an awesome backhand and improved his forecourt game. By the spring of 1937, with Perry having turned pro, Budge was ready to rule the amateurs and bring back the coveted Davis Cup to America after an eleven-year

Don Budge. International Tennis Hall of Fame

absence. The years 1937 and 1938 saw him win not only every tournament match he played but also the first Grand Slam of tennis.

In the 1937 Germany-U.S. Interzone Final, with the survivor heavily favored to defeat England in the Challenge Round, the score stood at 2-2 after world number three Henner Henkel's victory over 5'4" Bryan "Bitsy" Grant. The climactic final match was staged on the Centre Court at Wimbledon before a packed stadium that included Queen Mary.

Hitler,[1] whose Nazi pride was reportedly wounded by the Olympic triumphs the year before of a non-Aryan named Jesse Owens, was intensely interested in having Germany win its first Davis Cup. "War talk was everywhere," Budge recalled. "Hitler was doing everything he could to stir up Germany." With the swastiska fluttering over the lawns of the All England Club, the atmosphere was filled with tension even though Von Cramm was a known anti-Nazi and remained one of the finest gentlemen and most popular players on the circuit.

The stylish German took the first two sets, playing the match of his life, then yielded the next two. The shot-making throughout was nothing less than scintillating as winners and earned points far exceeded unforced errors.

When Budge fell behind 4-1 in the fifth set after losing a love game, his situation appeared desperate, almost hopeless. "[Von Cramm] was playing the tennis of his life, and it seemed that no player that ever lived could have stood up to him," wrote Allison Danzig, the *New York Times'* renowned tennis journalist. "The gallery's delight knew no bounds, for it was unmistakably devoted to Von Cramm's cause." The mostly British crowd felt that their team, the holder of the Cup, would have a better chance of beating Germany in the Challenge Round the following week than it would have of defeating the United States.

Bill Tilden, who led the United States to its last Davis Cup victory in 1926, was, curiously enough, coaching the German team, according to some reports.[2] With a smug grin on his face, Tilden, applauding loudly for Von Cramm throughout and sitting near American show business celebrities Ed Sullivan, Jack Benny, and Paul Lukas, gestured to Henkel that the match was "in the bag." Sullivan, who with the others was furious at Tilden's unpatriotism and bad taste, leapt to his feet and hissed at Tilden, "Why, you dirty son of a bitch!"

Budge, as legend has it, calmly reassured his team captain, Walter Pate, "Don't worry, Cap, I won't let you down. I'll win this one if it kills me."

But how?

The courageous American then made the "illogical decision" to attack Von Cramm's second serve and come to the net. The tactic worked. Von Cramm's serve began to fail, and Budge broke back for 3-4 and held for 4-all.

"The brilliance of the tennis was almost unbelievable," wrote Danzig. "The gallery, enraptured by the scintillating display to a degree that it forgot its allegiance to the Baron, looked on spellbound as two great players, taking their inspiration from each other, worked miracles of redemption and riposte in rallies of breakneck pace that ranged all over the court."

The score went to 5-5 and then 6-6 when Budge gained another service break for 7-6. With the suspense unbearable, Budge served for the victory. Four times he had match points and four times Von Cramm gallantly fought back to deuce. On the fifth match point (the eighteenth point of the game), the two traded deep ground strokes before Von Cramm blasted a crosscourt forehand and moved into the net. Budge raced after the ball, took a desperate swipe, and crashed onto the grass.

The ball skimmed the net just past Von Cramm's outstretched racket and landed six inches inside both lines. "It was the greatest shot I ever made," Budge recalled—and many have called it the most famous shot in tennis history.

The disappointed but noble loser shook Budge's hand and said: "This was absolutely the finest match I have ever played in my life. I'm very happy that I could have played it against you, whom I like so much. Congratulations." And they threw their arms around each other.

FASCINATING FACTS:

- President George Herbert Walker Bush's all-time sports heroes are "Lou Gehrig, Babe Ruth, Don Budge and Gene Mako, the doubles team."
- Baron Gottfried von Cramm disdained the Nazi government and was once quoted in a British newspaper as calling the führer, Adolf Hitler, "a house-painter."
- Don Budge had tea with famous Spanish cellist Pablo Casals nearly every day during the 1938 French Championships, and after Budge won the tournament, Casals gave a two-hour concert in Budge's honor.
- It took twenty-three minutes and forty-five seconds to sell ten thousand Davis Cup tickets—at $260 Australian ($135 U.S.) each—for the three-day semifinal between host Australia and Sweden at the Olympic Park tennis center in September 2001.

Notes

1. This legendary Davis Cup duel produced one of tennis' most fascinating but, it turns out, apocryphal stories. According to Budge, "I remember just before we took the court, Von Cramm was called to the telephone. It was a long-distance call from Hitler himself exhorting Von Cramm to win for the Fatherland. Gottfried came out pale and serious and played as if his life depended on every point."

   Dr. Heiner Gillmeister, a distinguished sports historian from Germany, setting the record straight, says: "The alleged phone call is a myth, although the story has been repeated over and over again, not least by Donald Budge himself—I heard him say this on a videotape. I have discussed the question with Rolf Goepfert, [who was] on the German team which played the Interzone Final against Australia in 1938. He attended the Germany versus United States match in 1937, knew Von Cramm well, and told me that the story was altogether invented. Also, Egon Steinkamp, Von Cramm's biographer, would have nothing of it. And Wolfgang Hofer, the former president of LTTC 'Rot-Weiss' Berlin (the capital's leading lawn tennis club) and a very good player in his youth during the 1930s, confirmed that the Hitler story is a myth. [Furthermore] Hitler most certainly was not at all interested in tennis, and that is why perhaps the German tennis-playing public was intensely interested. Also, that Hitler was peeved about the non-Aryan triumphs in the 1936 Olympics cannot be said with any certainty."

2. The veracity of these journalistic reports may never be ascertained. In Tilden's *Aces, Places and Faults*, Tilden, who described himself as "the most

ardent admirer of the German people," wrote on page ninety-one: "[I]n November 1935 the German Association brought me to Germany to coach the German Davis Cup team...."

On page 150 of Ted Tinling's 1979 memoirs, *Love and Faults,* he wrote: "Tilden, who had brought a lot of criticism on himself by accepting the appointment as coach to the German team, was sitting in the stands."

However, a skeptical Dr. Gillmeister says: "That Tilden coached the German team is very, very unlikely. I have consulted *Der Tennissport,* the relevant and official German tennis journal at that time. In all the 1937 issues preceding the Davis Cup Interzone final, there is only a reference to Tilden's competing at a professional tournament in Cologne a few weeks before the Budge–Von Cramm match and beating his old German rival Hans Nusslein in the process. There is no reference whatsoever to other activities of Tilden in that year, let alone to his coaching the German team. The German team was captained by Dr. Heinrich Kleinschroth, as truly a German as any!"

43

Arthur Ashe Defeats Jimmy Connors 6-1, 6-1, 5-7, 6-4 in the 1975 Wimbledon Final

"When I walked on court I thought I was going to win. I felt it was my destiny."

Arthur Ashe's confidence was hardly shared by the rest of the tennis and betting world. William Hill bookmakers had made Jimmy Connors an overwhelming twenty-to-three favorite to win. The brash basher from Belleville, Illinois, with the Prince Valiant hairdo had set an Open Era record in 1974 by winning 96 percent of his singles matches—99 of 103—and fifteen tournaments, including Wimbledon, U.S. Open, and Australian Open titles. (He had been barred from entering the French Open because he played World Team Tennis). What's more, young Jimbo was rolling again at the 1975 Wimbledon Championships with straight-sets victories over John Lloyd, Vijay Amritraj, Mark Cox, Phil Dent, Raul Ramirez, and Roscoe Tanner, putting him into the final. Connors had also beaten Ashe in their three previous encounters.

On the other hand, Ashe, at thirty-one, seemingly had his best years behind him. He had come of age by upsetting defending champion Roy Emerson at Forest Hills in 1965. He then reached the 1966 Australian Championships final, peaked by winning the 1968 U.S. Open, gained the Wimbledon semifinals in 1968 and 1969, captured the 1970 Australian Open, and came very close at the 1972 U.S. Open when he lost a five-set final to Ilie Nastase. Episodic brilliance, yes, but it was overshadowed by a "bridesmaid" reputation for losing fourteen of his previous nineteen finals coming into 1975. Acknowledged Ashe: "I was conscious of people saying I couldn't win the big matches."

Ashe theorized that his sharp intellect, and particularly his penchant for over-analyzing and worrying about losses, had gotten in his way and partly prevented him from fulfilling his high potential. "It bothers me, especially as I get older and realize that my chances are running out," he wrote in his book *Portrait in Motion* in early 1975. "It's nice to win a Bologna; hell, it's nice to win anything. But I want a Wimbledon. I want another Forest Hills. Those are the victories people measure you by." Some observers also believed he was distracted by outside commitments, such as his business ventures and his heavy involvement in tennis politics as ATP president. (A fascinating subplot was that two weeks before their Big W showdown, Connors filed a $5-million libel suit against Ashe for calling Connors "unpatriotic" for his refusal to join the U.S. Davis Cup team. Ashe accentuated their split by walking on Centre Court wearing his Davis Cup jacket.)

So what made this huge underdog so sure he was destined to win? It was a shrewd strategy conceived with the help of friends Dennis Ralston, Erik van Dillen, Donald Dell, Marty Riessen, Charlie Pasarell, and Freddie McNair on the eve of the final. The objective was to bring out the worst in Jimmy's game by concentrating on his assorted weaknesses even if that meant abandoning Ashe's formidable, if not always reliable, power game.

Since Connors was awesome against hard-hitting Tanner in his 6-4, 6-1, 6-4 semifinal rout, Arthur would adopt a totally different strategy. Rather than typically slugging it out—just what Jimmy craves—he would serve wide on both sides and often at three-quarter pace (for added swerve), feed him low balls down the center to exploit his shaky forehand approach shot, softly slice forehands and backhands during rallies, and throw up plenty of lobs to the backhand side.

How the game plan worked! Ashe adroitly executed his new stratagem to the letter. The flustered Connors had only his old plan of blasting back pace with even greater power. But there was little pace coming at him, and his inflexible game plan and stubborn character only hastened his disintegration.

In two of the worst sets the twenty-two-year-old Connors was ever to play in a Grand Slam event, he erred and erred as the cagey Ashe served effectively and volleyed consistently (even on his suspect forehand side) and lobbed artfully. Amazingly, the score stood at 6-1, 6-1 for Ashe. Even Connors's explosive, intimidating return of serve—the best tennis had ever seen at that time—had broken down.

Not only was sixth-seeded Ashe playing intelligently, but he appeared totally nerveless. During the changeovers he sat motionless with his eyes shut, almost in a Buddha-like trance that apparently relaxed his body and mind and enabled him to focus narrowly on his next move.

When Ashe broke serve to lead 3-2 in the third set, there even seemed a chance his remote forty-to-one odds to win in straight sets might pay off. But Connors, ever the game battler, abruptly recovered when Ashe blew an overhead to lose serve for the first time. Pumped up—he kept slapping his thigh—and finally displaying his normal form, Connors escaped two break points at 5-all, held serve for 6-5, and then cracked two mighty service returns to take the set 7-5.

Connors's momentum continued into the pivotal fourth set. He held serve in the first and third games and broke serve in the second game with two more beautiful service returns for a 3-0 advantage.

But Ashe neither changed his well-conceived plan nor cracked under pressure. Instead, the pressure adversely affected Connors, who lost his serve for 3-2 and became more tentative. Jimmy's spurt had fizzled out. In the ninth game, Ashe broke his serve again, blasting two backhand winners, with the loss of just one point. It was 5-4 now, and Ashe literally served for the championship, as he started and finished the clinching game with sharply swerving, dominating serves. The new king punched the air with his fist in a victory gesture of satisfaction and joy.

Ashe, the ninth-generation descendant of West African slaves who, as a boy in segregated Richmond, Virginia, in the early 1950s, wasn't permitted to play in Byrd Park, even for tournaments, had won the biggest tournament of all and achieved a life's ambition. As he revealed in his 1981 book, *Off the Court,* this shocking upset may have carried greater significance than anyone then imagined.

"Looking back, I believe my victory over Connors that day was the most significant singles match of the seventies," wrote Ashe. "I fully believe that if Connors had beaten me, he would also have won the U.S. Open that fall (he lost in straight sets to Manuel Orantes of Spain) and that Bjorn Borg would not have won five straight Wimbledons. If Jimmy had won our match, he might have found a way to beat Borg, and Borg's ascendancy would have been delayed, or maybe it wouldn't have happened at all."

FASCINATING FACTS:

- Among the famous people who wrote or phoned Arthur Ashe in April 1992 after he publicly revealed he had AIDS were Nelson Mandela, president George Bush, former presidents Richard Nixon and Gerald Ford, Supreme Court Justice Clarence Thomas, Elizabeth Taylor, Sugar Ray Leonard, and Pele.

- Jimmy Connors once said that his biggest disappointment in tennis was that "my grandmother (who taught him and died in 1972) never saw me reach the top."

- In 1973 Arthur Ashe said that he considered his ability to speak only English "the greatest failing of my life."

- The only question thirty-eight-year-old Jimmy Connors had about playing World Team Tennis in 1991 was, "Are there any fines?"

44

Chris Evert Defeats Martina Navratilova 6-3, 6-7, 7-5 in the 1985 French Open Final

The ultimate rivalry in all of sports was Chris Evert and Martina Navratilova," averred Arthur Ashe. Indeed, no two champions have ever faced each other so often, for so long, and so memorably as America's sweetheart and the supremely athletic Czech who defected to the United States in 1975.

From 1973 to 1989, when Evert retired, these all-time greats collided eighty thrilling times (Navratilova won forty-three) and in fourteen Grand Slam tournament finals (Navratilova led 10-4). "Not only did we bring out the best in each other, but we brought it out for years longer than if either of us had been alone at the top," Navratilova said in 1989.

The best match in the enduring "Chris and Martina Show," many believe, came June 8, 1985, on Stade Roland Garros's salmon-hued clay courts in Paris. Although Evert Lloyd (recently separated from Englishman John Lloyd) flourished on the slow clay and owned five French titles, Navratilova was clearly favored after humiliating Evert Lloyd 6-3, 6-1 in the 1984 final and winning fifteen of their previous sixteen contests. What's more, Evert Lloyd hadn't prevailed in a Grand Slam final between them since 1982.

Navratilova had taken over the rivalry and the number-one ranking by training rigorously and scientifically. Her regimen included tennis kinetics, exercise machines, weightlifting, running, basketball, and nutritionist Robert Haas's low-fat, high-carbohydrate diet. It transformed her hefty, 167-pound body into a muscular, dynamic, 144-pound physique. "With my new silhouette, I felt like a new person," she wrote in her autobiography.

During 1983 and 1984 Navratilova's high-powered serve-and-volley game steamrolled to six straight Slam singles crowns and seven more in doubles. "It is

Chris Evert. Hans-Jürgen Dittmann

the challenge of making history and the titles which motivate me all the time," she said.

But Evert Lloyd was highly motivated, too. "Once you've been number one, you can never be satisfied with less," she once confided. So she copied Navratilova's training methods—especially lifting weights under the supervision of Australian expert Stan Nicholes—and became leaner, stronger, faster, and fitter. Needing more versatility and power, Evert Lloyd also added a reliable volley with Dennis Ralston's coaching and switched to a more powerful graphite racket.

Evert Lloyd, an unerring baseliner with steely concentration, was helped strategically and psychologically that gusty final day by John, who was back at her side. He suggested that she hit more looping balls to the forehand to stymie Navratilova's chip-and-charge offense.

The tactic worked in the first set, which saw Evert Lloyd go ahead 3-0, Navratilova tie it 3-all, and Evert Lloyd consistently hit backhand winners to take it 6-3. The Parisian spectators, known for looking down on women's tennis—hitherto whistling derisively during interminable rallies and even sneaking off for refreshments—didn't budge from their seats as they rooted ecstatically for the stylish Floridian.

Evert Lloyd, seemingly playing the best tennis of her life at the age of thirty, led 4-2 in the second set and had two break points at 15-40. But Navratilova escaped that crisis with two terrific serves and saved the crucial game with a lunging backhand volley.

The fluctuations continued when Navratilova broke serve for 4-4 and had a set point at 5-4, but she had to break serve again at 6-5 to force a tiebreaker. Aided by an Evert Lloyd double fault, she grabbed the cautiously played tiebreaker 7-4 to square their sixty-fifth match at a set apiece.

In the deciding set of what Navratilova later called "the closest, most suspenseful final we've played," both warriors would courageously fight back from behind. Evert Lloyd, who told herself to hit out confidently as she had in the opening set, broke serve for 3-1 and had two points for a 4-1 lead but failed to convert them. Navratilova took the game with a backhand winner and held serve at love for 3-all.

But Navratilova lost a break point and her vital momentum when she missed a passing shot in the seventh game and disgustedly dropped her racket. Ahead 4-3 now, Evert Lloyd cracked a spectacular running forehand passing shot to break serve for 5-3.

Suddenly, Evert Lloyd lost ten of twelve points and trailed for the first time in the match at 5-5, love-40. Down triple break point, the situation looked desperate. But Navratilova failed to attack, and Evert Lloyd saved her second break point on a beautiful backhand winner and her third break point when, surprisingly, she out-reflexed Navratilova in an exciting volley duel. Evert Lloyd then captured the game for a 6-5 edge.

To seize her seventeenth major singles title, the thirty-year-old underdog would have to break Navratilova's wicked lefty serve one more time. With the capacity crowd of sixteen thousand screaming on every shot, Evert Lloyd reached championship point. In an unforgettable ending to the two-hour, fifty-two-minute classic, Navratilova attacked with a deep approach, and Evert Lloyd nervelessly defended with a pinpoint down-the-line backhand passing shot that eluded her lunging rival and landed inches in.

Evert Lloyd jumped for joy. She had reclaimed Paris, and the rivalry, while not quite equal, was competitive and compelling again. Navratilova, dejected but gracious, walked around the net, and the two Open Era giants warmly embraced.

"It was one of the most incredible matches you can ever imagine," Navratilova said. "It had about everything."

What was nearly as incredible as the extraordinary rivalry was the strong friendship that the two proud, determined women maintained.

Seven years later in an interview, Evert explained their special, symbiotic relationship: "We were just so different in every way that I think the contrasts just made our matches so appealing. Towards the middle of the rivalry we disliked each other. But there never was anyone like Martina for me, and there was never anyone like me for her."

"And we had both achieved so much and learned so much at the same time from each other, so why be enemies? We should just be friends."

FASCINATING FACTS:

- After marrying Chris Evert, former British number one John Lloyd lost nineteen consecutive matches.
- Chris Evert and Martina Navratilova once had a double date with Dino Martin and Desi Arnez, Jr.

45

Ken Rosewall Defeats Rod Laver 4-6, 6-0, 6-3, 6-7, 7-6 in the 1972 WCT Finals Final

With all the tennis matches flooding television these days, it's difficult for younger buffs to imagine that it wasn't always this felicitous way. A masterpiece of breathtaking shot-making between two aging superstars in 1972 helped turn Americans on to tennis and convinced television moguls that the one-time sport of the wealthy few was now perfect for the viewing masses.

Because their careers spanned the amateur, pro, and open eras, it was quite fitting that Australian legends Ken Rosewall and Rod Laver should usher in the television age. Rosewall, a thirty-eight-year-old marvel of consistency and durability, had won his first Australian Championship way back in 1953, his second in 1955, and then not again until the Open Era in 1971 and 1972. His French titles were likewise spread amazingly from 1953 to 1968 and his United States titles from 1956 to 1970.

Laver has called his good Aussie friend "the least appreciated great player in the history of tennis." Rosewall never received the credit he deserved because he spent his prime years with the vagabond pros, from 1956 after signing his first contract with promoter Jack Kramer all the way to 1968 when Open Tennis finally allowed him to enter the prestigious tournaments again. (One can only guess at how many more major titles he might have amassed during those twelve years.) Even when Rosewall dethroned the mighty Pancho Gonzalez as pro king in the early 1960s, the public knew little about it.

Over the years the two welterweight-sized champions had fought each other frequently and evenly. Laver praised his rival in his memoirs, *The Education of a Tennis Player:* "Kenny and I have brought the very best out of each other. He knows what's coming and so do I. The only way I'm going to beat him is to have a very good day. He anticipates my shots so uncannily that I simply have to hit them bloody well enough that his anticipation and his legs are no use."

Laver, a wristy, super-talented shot-maker with topspin off both sides (a rarity then), deft volleys, and terrific hand and foot speed, captured the Grand Slam in 1962 just before turning pro. He, too, lost all chance of piling up "Big Four" titles until the long-awaited Open Era arrived. When it did in 1968, Laver conclusively proved his supremacy again. He became tennis' only *double* Grand Slammer in 1969 and its first millionaire in 1971, the year Rosewall beat him for the title at the inaugural World Championship Tennis Finals in Dallas, Texas.

Most observers predicted Laver would take the WCT Finals rematch in 1972 and grab the only prestigious title that had eluded him. Laver, belting powerful, topspin shots, raced to a 5-1 lead but barely hung on for the first set 6-4 when Rosewall countered with pinpoint backhand passing shots and telling volleys. Rosewall, ironically nicknamed "Muscles" for his small 5'7", 140-pound stature, breezed through the second and third sets aided by Laver's periodic double faults. The roller-coaster fluctuations continued in the fourth set when Laver, down 1-3, fought back to 6-all. He then won the tense tiebreaker 7-3.

When Rosewall, who had pulled ahead 4-2 in the final set, lost his serve to make it 4-all, he had his "hangdog" look—stooped shoulders, dragging feet, and tired expression—that was so misleading to opponents. The hot glare of television lights in the airless Moody Coliseum made the muggy ninety-degree heat even more unbearable. Both players were on the verge of exhaustion, although the exciting, high-caliber exchanges belied it. "Down the stretch it was hack and grub time," Laver would say later.

By the time the climactic tiebreaker arrived, after three hours of live national TV coverage, NBC network had preempted three regularly scheduled programs and the tennis had spilled into "prime time." A record tennis audience of 23 million watched spellbound, riveted by the sight of two terrific athletes displaying their superb skills in a thrilling finish. For many first-time tennis viewers, the other programs could wait.

"Rocket" led the tiebreaker 5-4, only two points from the championship and the record fifty-thousand-dollar prize, with two serves coming up. But victory was not to be. Rosewall ripped both serves back with his legendary backhand, one forcing an error and the other an outright winner. The stunned Laver then returned Rosewall's serve into the net and the torrid duel was over.

The 1972 WCT Finals showdown was a spectacular advertisement for the game. Television was to prove a crucial ingredient in America's 1970s tennis boom that would eventually spread to other nations such as Sweden, France, Germany, Argentina, and Japan.

"Television is an incredible vehicle," explained Mike Davies, then executive director of WCT. "Nothing in the history of communications can compare with it. It is quite possible for a player to play one match on national television before more people than he would ever play live to in his whole career."

During the WCT's twentieth anniversary celebration in 1989, Laver recalled, "It's incredible how much impact one match can have. No matter where I would go, people would say, 'Hey, that was a great match.' That is the match that everyone remembers."

FASCINATING FACTS:

- In 1999 the United Arab Emirates ranked first among nations in total hours (301) of Wimbledon television coverage, while Britain ranked number sixty-four in total hours (173).
- Ken Rosewall didn't lose a set when he won the 1971 Australian Open at age thirty-six.

46

Boris Becker Defeats Kevin Curren 6-3, 6-7, 7-6, 6-4 in the 1985 Wimbledon Final

Who could have foreseen that an unknown German boy too young to drive, legally buy a beer, or vote would fearlessly conquer Wimbledon and captivate the stunned sports world with his scrambling, gambling style?

Boris Becker, or *Herr Wunderbar* to millions of joyous and proud Germans, shredded the record books. King Boris became the youngest player (seventeen years and 228 days old), the first unseeded one, and the first German to win the Gentlemen's Singles Championships in its 108-year history.

If Becker were destined for greatness, it wasn't obvious, at least to the West German Tennis Federation. At age ten he was suspended from its youth program for being "too crazy," according to Ion Tiriac, his manager. The federation withdrew its free training when it concluded that Becker, at thirteen, showed no special promise other than his extreme determination. A mere year later though, he proved his critics wrong by becoming national junior singles and doubles champion.

A month before his spectacular Wimbledon, ever-confident Becker portentously remarked about the veteran stars he was about to eclipse: "Great players, but how long have they been at the top? Connors ten years, for McEnroe six. Perhaps their edge is going? Perhaps it is time for the young men to take over?"

Two weeks later, when Becker displayed awesome power against a strong field to capture the Stella Artois Grass Court Championships for his first Grand Prix title, it prompted runner-up Johan Kriek to predict, "If the guy plays like this, he can win Wimbledon." Unconvinced, the Ladbrokes bookmakers made this freckled-faced, strawberry-blond kid who didn't even shave yet a hundred-to-one long shot.

The arrival of the swashbuckling superstar provided plenty of roller-coaster thrills to start the Becker legend. Although Becker was fortunate to avoid playing the top three seeded players—John McEnroe, Ivan Lendl, and Jimmy Connors—he overcame score deficits and injury to beat the players who beat them, four seeded players overall, and the unseeded but formidable Henri Leconte.

"Boom Boom" lived up to his new nickname (which he disliked because of its warlike connotations) from the first round when he disposed of veteran Hank Pfister in four sets. Afterwards Pfister commented: "At seventeen his power and poise are incredible. The guy is going to win this tournament sometime." Certainly far sooner than Pfister would have guessed! Becker next surrendered just four games in annihilating Matt Anger, best known for being Tracy Austin's ex-boyfriend.

In the third round, seventh-seeded Joakim Nystrom, a clever, counterpunching Swede, served for the match at 5-4 and 6-5 in the fifth set. Each time Becker, undeterred by adversity, fought back with service breaks and eventually prevailed 9-7.

"He has so many shots, so much natural ability. But more than anything else, he has courage," Tiriac had said before Wimbledon. Courage, the trait of champions, enabled Becker to escape from near-defeat against sixteenth-seeded Tim Mayotte, a grass court specialist and perennial contender. Behind two sets to one, 5-all and 30-40, Becker slipped on the grass and twisted his ankle. He was in severe pain, but his coach, Gunther Bosch, exhorted him to go on. After being taped up during a crucial five-minute break (for some reason—maybe destiny?—he wasn't defaulted for exceeding the three-minute limit, to the consternation of many members of the media as well as players), Becker valiantly limped through and survived a fourth-set tiebreaker to ultimately triumph 6-2 in the fifth.

With momentum now and the support of English fans who loved his never-say-die spirit and bold shot-making, Becker stopped the dangerous Leconte, who earlier ousted Lendl in a close, four-set quarterfinal. Afterwards Frenchman Leconte colorfully analyzed: "Boris never thinks about it; he just plays. I see his plan. He just hit ball, make winner, win, say thank you, and go bye-bye." Fifth-seeded Anders Jarryd fell next, again in four sets. A premier service returner, the Swede simply could not handle the thunderous, 130-mile-per-hour serves from the broad-shouldered "Boom Boom."

That set up an intriguing final between the dashing, exuberant prodigy and quiet, serious twenty-seven-year-old veteran Kevin Curren, the number-eight seed. Curren, a South African–born, newly naturalized American, had sensationally overwhelmed defending champ McEnroe 6-2, 6-2, 6-4 and Connors 6-2, 6-2, 6-1 and was slightly favored.

But what the still-growing 6'2", 175-pound man-child lacked in Centre Court experience, he more than made up for in maturity, composure, and self-confidence. "I think maybe I do all right with the pressure," Becker understated before the biggest match of his life.

Conversely, Curren wasn't quite up to the challenge. He had held his explosive serve forty-four straight times entering the final, yet the unawed Becker easily broke him in the second game when Curren nervously netted an easy volley, flubbed an overhead, and then double-faulted on break point. Becker would serve out the 6-3 set with four service winners, two of them aces.

While Curren never seemed to find the groove on his serve, his ground strokes became smoother and more consistent. And he fought tenaciously. He escaped a love-40 hole at 3-all in the second set and kept holding serve to take it to a tiebreaker.

Curren fell behind 3-0 but then played a marvelous tiebreaker. Two big serves made it 3-2; Becker countered with a service winner for 4-2. Curren won the last five points, the last two with a beautiful backhand service return and a precise backhand down-the-line passing shot.

Curren went in front 4-3 in the pivotal third set with another backhand passing shot for his first and only service break of the three-hour and eighteen-minute match. But with deadly firepower, Becker roared back, put Curren down love-40 in the next game, and at 30-40 broke him with a bullet-like crosscourt backhand passing shot. At that point, "I thought I would win," Becker confided afterwards.

Becker quickly held serve for 5-4. On the first of his eight set points, he angered Curren by blatantly stalling when Curren was about to serve. Curren survived two more set points with Becker ahead 6-5, but the steamrolling teenager took the first six points of the tiebreaker and seized it for the third set.

Instead of choking in the biggest set of his young career, Becker was having fun. With boyish enthusiasm he was acrobatically diving for volleys and falling and rolling safely, the way Boris Breskvar had coached him years ago in Leimen. Becker joyfully punched the air with his fists after terrific shots. He energetically imitated a man cycling without a bicycle. And between points, like the soccer player he used to be, he bounced balls on his feet and head and chest.

The wunderkind broke the veteran in the first game of the fourth set, which was all he needed. Becker's only mini-crisis came on a break point in the second game. But, after taking a deep breath, he pounded his nineteenth ace. He routinely served out the final game; at 40-30, championship point, he whacked another mighty serve that caromed wildly off Curren's racket frame.

As the crowd stood and loudly cheered tennis' newest prodigy, Tiriac was so flabbergasted that he sat staring in the VIP's box at his extraordinary protégé. He remarked: "Crazy, crazy! He doesn't know what he's done. And, honest to God, I don't know what he's done."

Besides turning the tennis world upside down with his records-smashing triumph, the wunderkind was fervently celebrated throughout Germany as a national hero. *Die Zeit,* the influential weekly, best summed up Becker's symbolic impact on its front page.

"For a few days the Germans let their hearts be warmed by an underaged tennis professional, because he embodied in the game what they in reality have lost: joy in achievement, determination, and sheer unlimited self-confidence. It was as if we had all won at Wimbledon."

FASCINATING FACTS:

- Puma believed Boris Becker's Wimbledon victories generated $50 million in sales for the company.
- In 1985 Israel honored Boris Becker as its Athlete of the Year.
- In 2000, then-retired Boris Becker ranked number two, behind only Chancellor Gerhard Schroeder, among Germans for the total number of articles written about him in his country.
- Barbara Becker received about six times more money ($14.4 million) in an out-of-court settlement of her divorce case with Boris Becker than what she was entitled to by a prenuptial contract.
- Boris Becker described his three winning Wimbledon fortnights that culminated with a Sunday final, championship point, and the celebrations, saying: "It's like a long foreplay that ends with a huge orgasm."
- In 1990 soccer legend Franz Beckenbauer described Boris Becker as "by far the greatest sportsman Germany has ever had—bigger even than Max Schmeling."

47

Henri Cochet Defeats Bill Tilden 2-6, 4-6, 7-5, 6-4, 6-3 in the 1927 Wimbledon Semifinals

In 1927 Bill Tilden was no longer the supreme tennis player in the world. But his mystique had grown throughout the 1920s to legendary proportions. "Big Bill" conjured up an abundance of adjectives: egotistical, opinionated, temperamental, controversial, witty, scrupulous, arrogant, willful, and enigmatic.

Most of all, though, he was a magnetic figure of sport's "Golden Age" in the larger-than-life mold of Babe Ruth, Jack Dempsey, and Red Grange. "When he came into the room, it was like a bolt of electricity hit the place," recalled his Davis Cup colleague George Lott. "Immediately, there was a feeling of awe, as though you were in the presence of royalty. You knew you were in contact with greatness, even if remotely."

When mediocre ability frustrated his serious acting ambitions, Tilden had the court become his stage. "The player owes the gallery as much as an actor owes the audience," he wrote once. His theatrics included the five-ball stunt where he grabbed five balls in his huge left hand, cracked four aces in a row, and then casually tossed the fifth ball into the stands. Though he was generally a renowned sportsman, he could also produce a withering stare after a bad call. On hot days he would douse himself with pitchers of ice water.

Tilden's ultimate attention-getter was intended not only to rally the crowds to his side—they were usually against him—but also to confirm his aura of invincibility once more. "Big Bill" would fall far behind in the score, then launch a spectacular comeback as cries of "Tilden's in trouble!" spread excitedly through the stands. Then, of course, the great master would heroically prevail.

It was Henri Cochet, though, who authored one of the most astounding turn-arounds in tennis history, and, ironically, it came against Tilden in the 1927

Wimbledon semifinals. Tilden considered Cochet his nemesis because he was the only player with a winning record against Tilden during their amateur years. Cochet, one of the immortal "Four Musketeers" who led France to a six-year (1927–1932) Davis Cup reign, was greatly respected by Tilden as "one of the great tennis geniuses of all time."

In his 1948 memoirs, *My Story,* Tilden wrote: "I know of no man who was a harder fighter; yet he always remained the sportsman.... At his peak as World Champion, he had an unshakable belief in his star. It was inconceivable to him that he could lose, no matter how far in the hole he might find himself, and it was remarkable how many times he was right in that belief."

Cochet had to summon all his resiliency and tactical cleverness—he abandoned his baseline game and charged the net—to rally from two sets down against unseeded but talented American Frank Hunter in the Wimbledon quarterfinals, prevailing 3-6, 3-6, 6-2, 6-2, 6-3. Tilden reinforced his status as the favorite to win The Championships by sweeping through five opponents with the loss of only one set en route to the semis.

With his cannonball serve, crushing ground strokes, and subtle spins, Tilden overwhelmed the much smaller Cochet to seize a seemingly insurmountable 6-2, 6-4, 5-1, 15-all lead. "Cochet searched in vain for an effective weapon to stem the tide as Tilden went steadily on, literally hitting through his man, dominant, domineering, and arrogant," wrote prominent American journalist Al Laney in *Covering the Court: A Fifty-Year Love Affair with the Game of Tennis.* "It was the Tilden of 1921–25 back on top, piling up the games."

Suddenly and incredibly, the thirty-four-year-old Tilden became impotent as he erred wildly and lost *seventeen* straight points.

Cochet soon took the third set 7-5 and began calling the tune with artful rallying, especially softballing to defuse Tilden's power game, hitting the ball on the rise, and frequent volleying coups. No gimmickry or gamesmanship could save the tiring Tilden after that. (Wimbledon had no ten-minute rest period after the third set, as did Forest Hills.) Still, Tilden gamely fought on. He reached 4-all in the fourth set before bowing 6-4 and even led 3-2 in the decisive set with his serve to follow only to lose the last four games to his much younger and fresher twenty-six-year-old foe.

How could such a tennis giant so thoroughly in command of an important match totally collapse?

Tilden tried to explain "the most mysterious match of tennis history" in his 1938 book, *Aces, Places and Faults.* "For nearly three sets I played the greatest tennis of my life, when suddenly with victory almost in my grasp, my entire game collapsed and I could do nothing right to the end.

"I have heard many interesting, curious, quite inaccurate accounts of what happened," wrote Tilden. "One ingenious explanation was that King Alphonso of Spain arrived at 5-1 in the third set, and I decided to let him see some of the match. Ridiculous! I didn't even know he was there! Another was that a group of Hindus hypnotized me. If they did I didn't know it, but they certainly did a swell job.

Bill Tilden. International Tennis Hall of Fame

"Personally, I have no satisfactory explanation. All I know is my co-ordination cracked wide open and I couldn't put a ball in court. I think if an explanation must be found, it was the heat. It was the first hot day of the tournament and I may have had too much sun."

The dramatic reversals weren't over for the two valiant champions at that historic Wimbledon. Cochet again surged back from a two-set deficit to overcome fellow "Musketeer" Jean Borotra 4-6, 4-6, 6-3, 6-4, 7-5 in the final. And, ironically, Tilden and Hunter, down 6-1, 6-4, 5-3, 40-15 on Cochet's serve in the doubles final, turned the tables and somehow survived to vanquish Cochet and Jacques Brugnon, the defending champions, for the doubles crown.

FASCINATING FACTS:

- Henri Cochet believed that a beginner should hit a ball against a wall for six months before playing on a tennis court.
- Bill Tilden was cut from the University of Pennsylvania varsity tennis team because he wasn't good enough.
- Bill Tilden authored ten books, including three autobiographies, and at his peak earned twenty-five thousand dollars a year writing special newspaper columns about tennis.
- During his prime in 1922, Bill Tilden had half of his middle finger on his right hand removed because of a staph infection. Yet his domination continued unabated as he lost only one match in 1923.
- When an Associated Press poll named Bill Tilden as the greatest tennis player of the half century in 1950, Tilden received ten times more votes than the runner-up.

48

Jack Crawford Defeats Ellsworth Vines 4-6, 11-9, 6-2, 2-6, 6-4 in the 1933 Wimbledon Final

I have seen and played Vines when he showed the most amazing tennis I have ever seen," 1920s superstar Bill Tilden once wrote. "It was stupefying; there was absolutely nothing I could do to stop him that day. It was hard even to *see* the ball, let alone hit it."

Ellsworth Vines's brilliant career flashed by as fast as his blinding power. He triumphed at the U.S. Nationals in 1931 when he was only nineteen and added Wimbledon and another U.S. title in 1932. At the 1933 Wimbledon the precocious Californian demolished all opposition until his classic encounter with Australian Jack Crawford. Later that year, still a tender twenty-one, Vines turned professional, and in the late 1930s, he embarked on a successful career as a pro golfer.

Vines hit nearly every ball with frightening power. But he also hit so flat and with so little margin for error over the net and near the lines that on a given day he could be awesome or wildly erratic. His biggest gun was a thundering serve clocked at 128 miles an hour—faster than Pancho Gonzalez's 118, Arthur Ashe's 112, and Lew Hoad's 110. He served a then-record thirty aces in a Wimbledon match. And he ended that 1932 Wimbledon final with a memorable ace so bullet-like that Bunny Austin couldn't tell whether the ball whistled by him on his forehand or backhand side.

Crawford, a husky six-foot, 185-pound Australian, gave the impression of having stepped out of the past with his long-sleeve cricket shirt, immaculate white flannels, hair parted in the middle, and old-fashioned square-headed racket. His game has been acclaimed by experts as the most stylish ever. With textbook perfection he stroked—better yet, caressed—the ball with a graceful and effortless grandeur. "He played all his strokes immaculately and with apparent ease, and any one of them could be taken to be his favorite shot," wrote Australian authority Paul Metzler in his acclaimed book *Tennis Styles and Stylists*.

While Vines suffered a letdown in 1933 after his terrific 1932 campaign, Crawford won his third straight Australian title and knocked off French star Henri Cochet in straights set for the French crown.

After again whipping third-seeded Cochet in a tough, four-set semifinal, Crawford faced Vines in what many cognoscenti have considered the greatest-ever Wimbledon final. In the first set a vintage Vines blasted service aces and forehand winners for a 6-4 lead. "Gentleman Jack," as this immensely popular sportsman was known, smiled and bowed toward his opponent in acknowledgement. But with a resourcefulness that complemented his artistry, Crawford began moving in to take Vines's deadly serve on the rise and boldly rush net. The masterly strategy paid off as Crawford, the underdog, captured the vital second set 11-9.

Then, attacking Vines's relatively weaker backhand, Crawford took the third set more easily at 6-2. After falling behind early, Crawford decided to conserve his energy and conceded the fourth set 6-2 when a revitalized Vines returned to his first-set form. After two hours of high-standard play, the match stood dead even, each having won twenty-three games. The best was yet to come.

Both competitors held their serves in the tense, deciding set up to 4-all, although Vines barely missed by inches on break point chances at 2-all and 3-all. Crawford held serve behind some beautiful running ground strokes against Vines's vulnerable backhand to go ahead 5-4.

Then, instead of standing far behind the baseline, Crawford boldly moved four feet inside of it, blocked back Vines's blistering cannonball, and took the opening point on a well-placed lob. Vines volleyed a sharp service return into the net for love-30. An exquisite backhand passing shot made it love-40 and triple championship point. The discouraged Vines netted another volley. Crawford had surprisingly broken the legendary serve of Vines at love and pulled out the 4-6, 11-9, 6-2, 2-6, 6-4 marathon.

The utterly sporting and nonpartisan crowd went wild. It was the first Wimbledon victory by a British Empire citizen since another Australian, Gerald Patterson, prevailed a decade earlier.

A. Wallis Myers, the esteemed correspondent for the *Daily Telegraph,* watching his thirty-fourth Wimbledon final, wrote: "There have only been ten five-set finals in the history of the meeting. Today's, for superlative play, refined coordination of strokes and tactics, continuous speed in service and the fighting vigour of both men at the finish, must rank first."

FASCINATING FACTS:

- Before a tournament, renowned California coach Mercer Beasley used to train flat-hitting Ellsworth Vines by raising the height of the net about six inches and pulling it as tight as he could.
- During his careers as a pro tennis player and later as a pro golfer, Ellsworth Vines beat the world's best player in both sports—Bill Tilden and Ben Hogan.

49

Monica Seles Defeats Steffi Graf 6-2, 3-6, 10-8 in the 1992 French Open Final

If one could order a classic match, like a sumptuous meal, the ingredients would surely include two great champions dueling in the final of a premier event, shot-making of the highest caliber, a crowd passionately favoring one player more than the other, and a thrilling, unpredictable *denouement*.

The 1992 French Open final between Monica Seles and Steffi Graf contained all these compelling and memorable elements. When the flamboyant Seles arrived at Paris, she had racked up an astounding 52-5 record at Grand Slam tournaments, winning her last four. The equally intense but reserved Graf had captured a rare Grand Slam sweep plus an Olympic gold medal in 1988 and reigned as number one for three and a half years before Seles deposed her in March 1991.

Seles, who had taken the previous two French titles, pulverized double-handed ground strokes on both sides and crushed foes with a killer instinct that elicited admiration if not endearment. "I've never seen anyone hit that hard from both sides," said seven-time French champion Chris Evert, who lost to Seles in the rookie's second (!) pro tournament in 1989.

Still only twenty-two after nine years on the tour, Graf had recovered from the trauma of her father's highly publicized marital indiscretions and was playing superlative tennis again. Her forehand, probably the most devastating shot in women's tennis history, powerful (hundred-mile-per-hour-plus) serve, and tremendous foot speed bedazzled opponents, while Seles marvelled at Graf's perfect physique and overall athleticism. "I think Steffi is the ideal, what any athlete in tennis would want to reach," said Seles.

Monica Seles. Hans-Jürgen Dittmann

Although Seles, a native of Yugoslavia based in the United States since 1986, had beaten Graf in the 1990 French final, Graf had won their last two matches and enjoyed a 5-2 edge overall. Most experts believed Graf needed more variety in her repertoire—such as drop shots, net rushes, topspin backhands, and changes of pace. Otherwise, Seles would almost certainly beat her at her own baseline game on the slow, salmon-colored clay.

As always, Seles came out slugging, or as she aptly described her style, "I go for every shot and give it everything I've got." That proved more than sufficient because she reeled off eleven of the opening twelve points, broke Graf's serve at love in the second game, and grabbed the opening set 6-2 in twenty-six minutes.

Graf's game came to life in the second set just as the gray, sixty-six-degree Parisian afternoon began to brighten. A big forehand produced her first service break and a 3-2 lead. After trading breaks in the next two games, Graf escaped from three break points—two with her explosive forehand and the other with a rare topspin backhand winner—to hold serve and go ahead 5-3. Her confidence was growing, and she walloped her seventeenth forehand winner to break Seles at love to finish off the 6-3 set and even the match.

Since Graf abandoned an all-court game, her forehand would have to be the deciding factor in the climactic third set. Graf pounded a crosscourt forehand winner to start the final set and went on to hold serve. She led for the first time in the match.

With the pressure rising and the stakes increasing, Seles hit even harder and screeched her trademark "ee-AHHH" even louder. She smacked a backhand

Steffi Graf. Hans-Jürgen Dittmann

winner to hold serve for 1-all and then belted another winner down the line on her fourth break point to go in front 2-1.

With the drama building, many of the seventeen thousand Court Central spectators were screaming for Graf between every point. The courageous German needed every bit of support as Seles's booming shots were dictating the baseline exchanges.

Both women held serve over the next three games which left Graf trailing 4-2. The players slugged it out like two heavyweights in a brutal title fight, trying to seize the pivotal seventh game. Graf saved a sensational, eighteen-stroke break point with an inside-out forehand winner and finally held the eighteen-point marathon game to make the score 4-3.

Mentally worn by the ordeal, Graf lost the next game with loose, unforced errors at love. She now found herself one game away from defeat.

Chants of "Steff-ee, Steff-ee" reverberated throughout Stade Roland Garros. In the most exciting game of the fortnight, Graf fought off four championship points—the first one saved by a mighty forehand, the second by a nifty backhand volley–overhead combination, the third by another forehand, and the fourth, surprisingly, by a backhand slice placement. Graf trailed 5-4, but she was still alive.

Seles, frustrated and drained by the previous game, was easily broken at 15 to tie the match at 5-all. Graf then barely escaped a service break when a Seles forehand—which Seles was so sure hit the line that she headed for the changeover—was called out. Both tenacious combatants managed to hold their serves to 7-all.

Ironically, Graf missed a routine forehand put-away to give Seles a crucial service break and an 8-7 advantage. Seles now served for the championship. At 15-love, mercurial Graf made several terrific gets and powered a backhand past a confused Seles, backtracking in mid-court. The crowd roared and Graf pumped her fist. Fired up, she broke back to even the score at 8-all.

But Graf, who played better when she was behind, couldn't sustain the momentum. On the twenty-fourth stroke of a fierce rally, with Graf hammering forehand after forehand before Seles finally pinned her in the backhand corner, Seles broke her with an excellent backhand placement. That made it 9-8 for Seles.

Seles, serving, surged ahead 40-15. When a nerveless Graf staved off a fifth championship point with a forehand winner, the fans went wild. On championship point number six, Seles zeroed in on her foe's vulnerable slice backhand. Graf desperately ran around it, hitting an off-balance forehand into the net. Game, set, and title, Seles!

Ecstatic but exhausted, the eighteen-year-old phenom pumped her fist and raised her racket in victory before spinning toward her proud, happy father-coach, Karolj, and mother, Esther. Seles had become the first woman to win three straight French singles crowns since German Hilde Sperling did it from 1935 to 1937.

Near tears, Graf thanked the French crowd for their wonderful support. "I've been to a lot of places, but I've never had a crowd like this—never, ever before."

Equally gracious Seles told the thoroughly entertained onlookers, "It is the most emotional match I ever played. It is just too bad whoever lost. Both deserved to win."

She couldn't have said it better.

FASCINATING FACTS:

- As a little girl Monica Seles practiced with her older brother, Zoltan, and father, Karolj, in a parking lot where they tied a string to the bumpers of two cars for a net when the only eight tennis courts in Novi Sad, Yugoslavia, were occupied.
- Steffi Graf's lowest singles ranking from March 1987 to June 1997 was number two.
- Monica Seles had 120 sessions with a psychotherapist for treatment of post-traumatic stress after her 1993 stabbing.
- Eighteen illegal trespassers climbed over the wall of the Graf home in Bruhl, Germany, during the 1993 Wimbledon fortnight, according to Peter Graf.
- Steffi Graf revealed it took her seven years to overcome her shyness enough to appear on *The David Letterman Show*.
- In 1992, at age eighteen, Monica Seles became the highest-paid female athlete in the world.
- When Steffi Graf was told that Monica Seles had been stabbed, she reacted: "Oh god, I hope it wasn't one of my crazy fans."

INDEX

About the Author

Paul Fein is an award-winning tennis journalist. His articles have appeared in tennis, sports, and general interest publications in the United States and twenty-five foreign countries.

Fein's diverse tennis background includes being a high-ranking sectional tournament player, a satellite tournament founder and director, a certified teaching pro, a New England tournament consultant, a cable television commentator, and a local tennis club and council president. He lives in Agawam, Massachusetts.